# FROM THE REVIEWERS

"*Super Health* is the single most comprehensive health book I've ever read by a *huge* margin. K.C. has ingeniously transformed the concept behind his perfect food, The Living Fuel, into the ideal health book. Indeed, the many pearls of wisdom in this book are *living* words that actually *speak to you!* K.C. is literally years ahead of his time, and we are the fortunate beneficiaries of his hard work. Read this book and prosper!"
  **DR. MICHAEL A. COREY**, author of *The God Hypothesis*

"My life has been changed dramatically through K.C.'s insight and wisdom in nutrition. This book should be made required reading for medical and nursing school curriculums, because it will reduce sickness and disease and increase life spans. K.C. is part of God's master plan to touch people so they can extend their quality of life through nutrition."
  **PHILLIP GOLDFEDDER, M.D.**, Neurosurgeon,
  Author of *Healing Is Yours*

"Since following the Seven Golden Keys of K.C.'s *Super Health* and taking his Living Fuel at the age of 54, I have slept better and optimized my weight. It has been a catalyst for me to return to fighting and to defend my world championship title. K.C. has changed my life."
  **JAMES SISCO**, Eight-Time World Kickboxing Champion

"I am living proof that good nutrition, exercise, and the other principles laid out by K.C. Craichy will turn your life around. You don't have to feel sick and tired all the time. As you apply this knowledge, you will learn that K.C. can help you go to the next level of health and fitness."
  **ROD MOORE**, Retired U.S. Army Colonel

"K.C. is one of the most respectable authorities on organic nutrition in the world today. The nutritional products he has helped to create I recommend to the very best professional and Olympic athletes in the world as well as to anyone desiring upgrades in their choices of food."
  **BOB COOLEY**, Author of *The Genius of Flexibility*,
  Founder of The Meridian Flexibility System™

"At the age of twenty-five, I was diagnosed with Crohn's disease. Eating high fiber, healthy food was very difficult for me to digest, so my diet was very limited. The Seven Golden Keys program helped me not only digest all types of food, but it has also given me back the energy that was robbed through a depleted immune system. I thank the Lord for K.C. and this program!"

**CHERI HENLEY**, Musician and Mother

"K.C. is a champion for the health of the whole family. As a former healthcare professional and now homeschooling mother, I am constantly faced with how to balance the demands of a busy family with the needs for a healthy lifestyle. He not only tells you how to achieve a healthier lifestyle, but he formulated the products to complete the job. We are continually inspired by his passion for God-honoring nutrition and wellness for all people. Unlike other diet programs, the Seven Golden Keys touch my life both physically and spiritually. Thanks to its simplicity, I can enjoy great health for a lifetime."

**TRACEY RUSSELL, M.S., OTR/L**

"After my sixth abdominal cancer surgery, I experienced problems swallowing vitamin pills and was having trouble with my digestive system. After only a few days on Living Fuel, my digestive system normalized, enabling me to eliminate ten different vitamins. Now I rely on the Seven Golden Keys and Living Fuel for my health and increased energy."

**JOYCE GOMPF**

# SUPER HEALTH

**7 Golden Keys** to Unlock Lifelong Vitality

# SUPER HEALTH

## 7 Golden Keys to Unlock Lifelong Vitality

## KC CRAICHY

BRONZE BOW  PUBLISHING

## Super Health

Copyright © 2005 K.C. Craichy

ISBN 1-932458-32-8

Published by Bronze Bow Publishing, Inc.,
2600 E. 26th Street, Minneapolis, MN 55406

You can reach us on the Internet at www.bronzebowpublishing.com

Literary development and cover/interior design by Koechel Peterson & Associates, Inc., Minneapolis, Minnesota.

Manufactured in the United States of America

IIIIIIIIIIIIIII

I DEDICATE THIS BOOK

*to my Heavenly Father,*

*His Son, Jesus Christ,*

*and the Holy Spirit,*

*through whom all things*

*are possible.*

To sign up for the Super Health Newsletter or an overview of each of the Seven Golden Keys as well as resources and products related to this program, go to:

www.superhealth7.com

# ACKNOWLEDGMENTS

MY ACKNOWLEDGMENTS START with special thanks to *Pastors Randy and Paula White*, for encouraging, supporting, and praying for me. Last summer the two of you motivated me to write this book. Monica and I have never been the same since our lives have been under your covering.

To my precious *Monica*, my dream girl and bride of thirteen years—without you I would be nothing. You are the most shining example of grace in my life. I thank you for all you are, for all you do, and for our beautiful children.

To my precious children, *Kyle, Austin, Sarah*, and *Grace*, for always putting a smile on my face and for all your incredibly insightful questions about this book. Your contributions were wonderful.

To my *mother and father*, for always believing in me and never allowing me to limit myself.

To my sister, *Julie*, and brother, *John*, for your love, support, and prayers.

To *Col. Rod and Karen Moore*—Monica and I thank you for being such true friends and for your wise counsel, support, and powerful prayers.

To *Rev. Phillip Goldfedder*, M.D., *Jess and Seena Scarborough, Tommy Combs, Marc Miller, Joan Hunter*, and *David and Esther Crownborn*, for your powerful prayers and friendship.

To *Sheronne Burke*, for being so supportive and for introducing me to Bronze Bow Publishing.

To *Jordan Rubin*, for your commitment to changing lives, for your endorsement, and for showing me how to be competitors and friends.

To *Leonard Smith*, M.D., for reviewing the nutrition chapter. I value your knowledge, experience, and friendship.

To *Don Colbert*, M.D., for your endorsement and for caring so much about your readers and patients.

To *Scott Eibel*, for your herculean effort in supporting me in this book project while skillfully managing the operations of Living Fuel, Inc.

To *John Peterson*, for partnering with me on this book project and for your tremendous contribution to the exercise chapter. Together we are going to change the way people exercise.

To *Lance Wubbels*—you are a tremendous writer with an awesome attitude and work ethic. You have had an incredible impact on the quality and excellence of this book.

To *Wendie Pett*, for your contribution of excellence to the exercise chapter and for conducting such a quality interview. You are very professional and highly skilled and always have a smile on your face.

To *David Koechel*, for the superior skill in the entire graphic design of this book. And thanks to the rest of your crew at Bronze Bow Publishing. Yours is a first-class publishing operation!

To *Tamara Mariea*, C.C.N. and C.H.M.M.—Monica and I thank God for bringing you into our lives. You are brilliant and incredibly humble. Your knowledge of environmental hazards and detoxification is second to none. Thanks for all your input in the Environmental Hazards and Hydration chapters. I also thank you for your faithfulness to your calling to help children with autism.

To *Michael Corey*, Ph.D., what can I say? Your ability to read and understand complex scientific topics and distill the mountains of information down to nuggets virtually overnight is almost inhuman. Thank you for your contribution to refining the Four Corners' revelation that God gave me in nutrition and for doing a detailed final review of this entire book in three days.

To *Lyndi Schrecengost*—you help us on so many important writings, and I thank you for your research and writing assistance in several areas of this book.

To *Ben Barger*, for all your efforts in summarizing tons of research that I threw on you for this book and for the quality and excellence of your work at Living Fuel, Inc.

To *Brian Suarez*, for your review of the book, for your character, and for the amazing job you do at Living Fuel, Inc.

To *Sensai Mark McGee*, for skillfully reviewing this book, but more importantly for introducing and teaching Christian martial arts to me and my family. Your passion and knowledge of martial arts is unparalleled, and your commitment to building Christian character makes you a tremendous role model. Thank you for your friendship.

To *Marc Fratello*, for your review of this book and your friendship.

To *Margaret Beam*, for your review of this book and your dedication to the Super Health principles.

# TABLE OF CONTENTS

# K.C. CRAICHY

||||||||||||||||||||||||||||||||||||||||||||||||||||||||||||||||||||||||||||||||||||||||||||||||||||||||||||

## SHARING A VISION FOR OPTIMAL HEALTH

A leading health advocate, author, speaker, and entrepreneur, K.C. Craichy is an authority in natural health, nutrition, and fitness. His mission is to change lives through a truly "whole person" approach to health that includes nutrition, lifestyle changes, fitness, spirituality, and much more.

K.C.'s wife's struggles with depression and panic attacks and his first child's struggles with chronic ear infections gave him the passion to embark on 10 years of research, trial, and error. The result was the groundbreaking nutritional approach called "The Four Corners of Optimal Nutrition," and eventually to "The Seven Golden Keys to Unlock Lifelong Vitality," which form the basis for this highly acclaimed book, *Super Health*.

K.C.'s personal evolution from an overweight teenager to a health-conscious, athletic adult forged a vision within him to develop a new approach to healthy living—a simple, no-nonsense health strategy that would help people of any age and any stage of health look, feel, and live better. This became the genesis of Living Fuel, Inc., the preeminent nutrition company in the U.S. Founded in 2001, Living Fuel builds upon K.C.'s past experience of owning and operating conventional and alternative healthcare and fitness companies, as well as his passion for understanding health and his collaborative work with many of the top medical and nutritional practitioners and researchers in the United States.

K.C., his wife, Monica, and their four children live in Tampa, Florida, where his company is based. As the Founder and CEO of Living Fuel, Inc., he also shares his vision as a health consultant and speaker on the topic of Optimal Health. K.C. serves on the Clinical Nutrition Review Board (CNCB), which is the testing and certification body for the Certified Clinical Nutritionist (CCN) designation. For more information about K.C. and Living Fuel, go to www.living-fuel.com or call 1-866-580-FUEL.

# FOREWORD

K.C. CRAICHY IS A SPIRIT-FILLED CHRISTIAN
with a passion to see members of the Body of Christ made whole in
body, mind, and spirit. I have come to know K.C. as a sharp busi-
nessman, a diehard health enthusiast, and the leader of a godly family.
But what draws me to K.C. is his undying love for Jesus and dedication to the Great Commission.

In *Super Health: The Seven Golden Keys to Unlock Lifelong Vitality*,
you'll learn foundational, life-giving principles that will equip you to live
the long and vibrant life your Creator intended you to live. Common-
sense advice, such as the importance of daily hydration, stress reduction,
and prayer, is combined with a vast amount of research that flies in the
face of much conventional thinking. K.C. crushes widely held dangerous
myths about health, such as the "all fat is bad" recommendation that has
led to today's widespread obesity and disease.

You'll learn how to incorporate super foods, such as green juices,
coconut products, chia seeds, and berries, into your daily life. You'll
gain an understanding of The Four Corners of Optimal Nutrition
(Calorie Restriction with Optimal Nutrition, Low Glycemic Foods,
Healthy Fats, and High Antioxidants), and how applying them to your
daily regimen can transform your health. Most importantly, you and
your family will enjoy a level of health that honors God the Creator,
Healer, and Sustainer.

If you just want to drop a few pounds to look better in a bathing
suit, there are plenty of diets out there to try. But if you want to
empower your body, mind, and spirit for an abundant purpose-filled
life, I encourage you to read *Super Health*.

And remember to make today the first day of the rest of your health.

**Jordan S. Rubin**
Founder of Garden of Life and *New York Times*
Best-selling Author of *The Maker's Diet*

# PREFACE

SUPER HEALTH IS A FAMILIAR TOPIC TO ME, and one close to my heart. The standard American diet is deplorable! Too busy to eat sensibly, most Americans eat "on the go," consuming "dead foods" that actually shorten their life span.

The average American consumes "junk food," drinks too much coffee and soda, gets an inadequate amount of sleep, rarely exercises, and is literally stressing themselves out! *Live hard; play harder!* But at what cost? Eventually our chosen lifestyle will have us seeking a physician to prescribe medications to treat various diseases that were acquired through an unhealthy diet and poor lifestyle choices.

K.C. Craichy's *Super Health* was born out of years of research and a passion to help set people on a personal journey to good health by supplying the necessary tools for optimal health. It began when serious health issues impacted his own family that could not be resolved through traditional medicine, but rather through K.C.'s own research, which resulted in changes in diet and lifestyle, strategic supplementation, and the power of prayer. He became determined to provide everyone he could reach with simple healthy alternatives for diet and exercise as well as practical advice on lifestyle changes that will help to prevent diseases and promote optimal health.

**Don Colbert, M.D.**
Author of *Deadly Emotions; Toxic Relief; What Would Jesus Eat?* and the best-selling *Bible Cure Series* and more!

# Introduction

*Do you not know that you*
*are the temple of God*
*and that the Spirit of God dwells in you?*
*If anyone defiles the temple of God,*
*God will destroy him.*
*For the temple of God is holy,*
*which temple you are.*

1 CORINTHIANS 3:16

In the 2004 film *Super Size Me*, Morgan Spurlock embarks upon a month-long descent into fast-food Armageddon. Spurlock, a 30-something, 6'2", 185-pound man, decided to begin a one-month, three-meal-a-day "Mac Diet" (McDonalds food only). Prior to the experiment, Spurlock was healthy, physically active, and consumed a reasonable 2,500 calories a day. Thirty days later, he was eating more than 5,000 calories a day and suffering from depression, rapid mood swings, high blood pressure, low sex drive, and symptoms of addiction. He had gained 24.5 pounds, his cholesterol shot up 65 points, and his body fat average jumped from 11 to 18 percent.

After just two weeks on the diet, all three of the physicians with whom Spurlock consulted encouraged him to abandon the diet, as he was showing signs of having seriously compromised his liver. These physicians were astonished to discover that a fast-food diet could wreak so much havoc in the body. Although his was an extreme experiment, Spurlock had set out to answer his own question, "Why are Americans so fat?" It didn't take long to figure it out. I highly recommend that you rent this documentary from your local video store—it will change the way you think...and (hopefully) the way you eat!

Spurlock's culinary adventure illustrates well the dangers of a diet that is high in trans fats, calories, and oxidative stress, and exacerbated by processed dead foods and lack of exercise—the classic sedentary American lifestyle. With two out of every three adults and 37 percent of American children suffering from obesity, it's abundantly clear that we cannot fool the human body. We reap what we sow. It has gotten so bad that a recent analysis of the effect of obesity on longevity in *The New England Journal of Medicine* concluded that the steady rise in life expectancy during the past two centuries may soon come to an end.[1]

I know a thing or two about America's obesity problem. The root of my passion for super health comes from being overweight as a youth in the late '70s. I had no idea why I was heavy, but went through all the struggles associated with being tormented and joked about in school. At the time, nutrition was not a big issue. In high school, however, I discovered the value of nutrition—conquering my battle with weight and sparking a lifetime commitment to healthy eating, exercise, and positive life habits.

I studied and tested every major diet since the late 1970s, including the Pritiken Diet, Eat to Win Diet, Fit for Life Diet, Atkins Diet, The Zone Diet, Sugar Busters Diet, and the Reversing Heart Disease Diet. What I discovered was that all these diets had their benefits but were nevertheless flawed, as they were not sustainable over long periods of time. The more I experimented with different dietary approaches, the more I realized their limitations and often harmful nutritional advice. Many of these diets were difficult to implement and advocated food and lifestyle choices that are known to compromise health and undermine performance.

I have been an entrepreneur for a long time and was involved in multiple business ventures early in life. In the mid '80s, I bought a health club, which propelled me into the fitness side of health. Later, I invested in and became President and CEO of a medical device company. I also got involved in various conventional and alternative medicine businesses that broadened my overall vision of health and preventative medicine. What I was learning about health, fitness and nutrition, along with what I was experiencing on the business side of these fields, gave me a unique perspective. I saw how often the goals and products being promoted in the fitness industry were out of sync with the medical and nutritional ideals and principles of good health. To me, the objectives of optimum health and maximum athletic performance should be one in the same. I became determined to find a nutrition and fitness strategy that would result in maximum performance and optimal weight.

Health challenges started to consume my own family, first with my wife, who suffered with depression, panic attacks, and other health issues after the birth of our first child. This was followed by my two-year-old son, whose ear infections could not be remedied with antibiotics. Both challenges were solved largely through changes in diet, strategic supplementation, and the power of prayer. This grounded me in the need for clinical nutrition. At that point I made a vow that I was going to discover a dynamic, no-nonsense approach to health that would make people of any age and any stage of health look, feel, and live better, and that I would get this information out to the world.

I thought my mission could be accomplished through a unique natural health company that I founded during the height of the dot-com era. The company exclusively broadcasted 40 of the top natural health radio shows live on the Internet and recommended and sold the highest quality natural products. As was the fate of many Internet ventures at that time, my company crashed—a financial disaster for me and my family. It was truly a low point in my life, as I no longer had the security of my nest egg to fall back on. I truly had to trust God, and God alone. It was a time of seeking the Lord's will for my life. One day, while mixing my family's morning nutrition shake, which was a combination of numerous natural ingredients, including greens and protein, I told my wife, Monica, that I was tired of mixing all those ingredients and was going to develop the perfect food. She, being the princess that she is, didn't bat an eye and simply said, "Do it."

For the next year I pursued that passion along with a nuclear physicist turned nutrition scientist, Hank Liers, Ph.D., whom I had met at my previous company. On the day that my youngest daughter, Grace, was born, the "perfect food" (Living Fuel) was packaged and ready to be sold. Within nine months, Living Fuel products were in every state in the United States and are now sold worldwide, primarily through doctors, health practitioners, and top fitness trainers. It is really awesome to see God's hand on this business as we focus on quality and excellence and continue to build the very best nutrition products on the market.

Through years of research and working with some of the top minds in nutrition and medicine, I developed a safe, simple, and complete lifestyle program that enhances performance, promotes energy, nurtures overall health, and can be sustained over a lifetime. I call this "whole person" lifestyle program *The Seven Golden Keys to Unlock Lifelong Vitality*, which includes the groundbreaking nutritional approach, *The Four Corners of Optimal Nutrition*.

The book in your hands is the culmination of many years of research and trial and error. I wrote it because I care deeply about health and wellness, and because I believe we have a responsibility as Christians to be living examples of the abundant life. We can't live abundantly if it is a challenge to drag ourselves out of bed in the morning . . . if we don't have the energy to play with our children . . . if the stresses of life are preventing us from reaching our highest God-given potential. I believe we must proactively take our lives and our health into our own hands. Modifying our lifestyles and food choices doesn't just affect us alone. It impacts the health of our families, our communities, and ultimately the planet.

*Super Health* is a complete manual for physical, mental, emotional, and spiritual renewal. In these pages you will find a simple, practical, step-by-step guide for unleashing the energy, health, and fitness that your body and spirit have been waiting for. I suggest that you start out slowly and in moderation. As with many of my health recommendations, I want you to approach your nutrition and lifestyle modifications with balance and good sense. Start with a few changes, and I think you'll be excited by the immediate improvements in your physical and emotional well-being.

Some of the chapters, such as "Hydration," "Environmental Toxins," and "Nutrition," are jam-packed with information, which may overwhelm you if you try to process and implement it all at once. Take your time! Read a section, or even just a few pages a day, and reflect on what you are learning. Think about the short-term changes you're able to make now, and the long-term goals you'd like to set for the future. I don't want you to be intimidated and frustrated, but inspired and excited about what you are learning. So just do a little at a time.

The seven-week journal *Living the Seven Golden Keys to Lifelong Vitality*, which can be purchased separately, will provide a framework for your success. Not only is it an easy tracking tool that will help you to plan and organize your health strategy, it also is a "record of accountability," a great way to measure and chart your daily and weekly progress. You might partner with a friend, another family, or even a support group—for encouragement, edification, and sharing of ideas. (Remember, this book is simply a catalyst to begin the journey. It's your responsibility to keep on the path.)

The Seven Golden Keys that comprise this book are based on solid scientific principles, and thousands of people have transformed their health through implementing these teachings into their lives. I am thrilled that you are about to embark on a discovery that can unlock the secrets of living healthier and longer . . . and enjoying it all the more.

You'll find yourself increasingly able to *reclaim your God-given body and to enjoy its fullest potential.*

# Hydration

**Of all the body's needs for health,
water is by far the most important.**

*Our body is comprised of 75 percent water, and water is
responsible for, and involved in, nearly every bodily process,
including digestion, absorption, circulation, and excretion.
Water is our main source of energy, just as it is also the primary
transporter of nutrients throughout the body. This is
why it is so necessary for all anabolic (or building) functions in
the body. Water adjusts the body's temperature and rids the
body of toxic wastes. And yet most of us fall short of our daily
hydration requirements. We also fail to drink pure water that
has the proper concentration of essential trace minerals. Not
drinking enough pure water disrupts the body's natural state
of healthy biochemistry, which leads to sickness and disease.*

*"He who has mercy on them will lead them,
even by the springs of water He will guide them."*
ISAIAH 49:10

SUPER
HEALTH

7 Golden
Keys to
Unlock
Lifelong
Vitality

# Hydration, Health, and the Miracle of Water

*"Be praised, My Lord,*
*through Sister Water;*
*she is very useful, and humble,*
*and precious, and pure."*

ST. FRANCIS OF ASSISI

Water is our life-support system, the blood that runs through our veins, the blue arteries of the earth. In some ways, it is the prerequisite of all other human rights, because it is the ultimate substance that enables us to lead a healthy life . . . not to mention one of dignity and balance. Water is also the most beautiful of all molecular compounds and the most useful as well. In the biblical account of creation, we learn that "the Spirit of God was hovering over the face of the waters" (Genesis 1:2).

The foundation of the entire living world is built on the many unique properties of water—the ultimate biological solvent. Indeed, scientists have shown that "ordinary water" is the *only* conceivable solution in which life as we know it could possibly exist. This makes water the most miraculous of all molecular compounds, as Dr. Michael A. Corey points out at length in *The God Hypothesis: Discovering Design in Our "Just Right" Goldilocks Universe.*[1] Indeed, not only is water the only conceivable solvent in which life as we know it could possibly exist, it is also the only liquid that would enable the survival of sea creatures during winter months, because it is the only liquid whose solid phase is less dense than its liquid phase. This is the miraculous property that enables ice to float on the surface of major bodies of water, thus leaving

the liquid water below to remain a suitable environment for the survival of all sea creatures.[2] This unprecedented property of water also
enables ice to form from the top of the sea, not from the bottom, and
enables ice to melt away during the summer.

But despite the many miraculous, life-giving properties of water,
no other essential natural resource has been more abused, overused,
poisoned, and wasted. According to Marq de Villiers, "Only one-third
of the water that annually runs to the sea is accessible to humans. Of
this, more than half is already being appropriated and used. This proportion might not seem so much, but the demand for water will double
in 30 years. And much of what is available is degraded
by eroded silt, sewage, industrial pollution, chemicals,
excess nutrients, and plagues of algae. Per capita avail-
ability of good, potable water is diminishing in all
developed and developing countries."[3]

The World Water Council reports that in the next
two decades the use of water by humans will increase by
about 40 percent, and 17 percent more water will be
needed to grow the world's food.[4] Some 1.2 billion people
lack a safe water supply; 2.4 billion live without secure
sanitation, and at least five million people die yearly from
water-related diseases, including 2.2 million children
under the age of five.[5] By 2015, according to estimates
from the United Nations and the U.S. government, at
least 40 percent of the world's population, or about 3 bil-
lion people, will live in countries where it is difficult or impossible to get
enough water to satisfy basic needs.[6] There are strong indications that future
international conflicts won't be over oil or territory but over *water*.

On a more local level, average citizens face numerous threats from
the water that flows from their taps. "The U.S. water supply is laced
with residues of hundreds of medicinal and household chemicals, compounds that do not originate at a Dow Chemical drainage pipe but
originate in our own personal plumbing. The contaminants come from
our bladders and bowels, our bathtub drains and kitchen sinks. As

> An old American
> Indian proverb
> says: "The frog
> does not drink
> up the pond in
> which he lives."
> Unfortunately,
> this is precisely
> the opposite
> of what we
> are doing.

much as 90 percent of anything the doctor orders you to swallow passes out of your body and into your toilet. Wastes from farm animals are never treated and are loaded with antibiotics and fertility hormones. As chemists make new concoctions, the water supply takes the hit."[7] (See Golden Key #6—Environmental Hazards/PPCPs.)

Water is an element essential to our survival and shared in common by everyone everywhere, yet we do very little to preserve and replenish it. In the same way, we neglect our bodies, which are often in a chronic state of dehydration and crying out for water to fortify thirsty cells and organ systems. By ignoring the signs, we may be doing ourselves irreparable damage.

## Why Hydrate?

Our body is comprised of 75 percent water, and water is involved in virtually all internal bodily reactions. It adjusts the body's temperature and rids the body of toxins. Although we can go for a month or more without food, we won't last a week without water. Yet the vast majority of us *do not get nearly enough water* to obtain optimal health and freedom from disease.

Part of the reason for this is that thirst is often tied to a sensation, such as dry mouth, or camouflaged behind a number of other bodily perceptions, such as hunger or fatigue. Consequently, by the time we actually experience the sensation of thirst, it's often too late. We're *already* acutely dehydrated, and it is this state of dehydration that can lead to all sorts of negative physical and mental symptoms, and even death itself. A tiny deficiency of water in the body is more than enough to cause our cells to begin to malfunction, catalyzing the downward spiral of most degenerative diseases.

Active hydration is particularly important for us as we age, as dehydration is especially prevalent among men and women over the age of forty. Studies have shown that the elderly are far less likely to recognize bodily thirst than younger people. Our sensory responsiveness dulls somewhat as we age, and so we must be more vigilant about taking water into our bodies, especially at times when we may not "feel" overtly thirsty.

## The Benefits of Hydration

Unfortunately, most of us take water and the essential process of drinking it for granted. According to a survey conducted at Rockefeller University, most people fall short of the well-known recommendation to drink eight to 12 eight-ounce servings a day. Although nearly 75 percent of Americans are aware of the recommendation, only 34 percent consume this amount. Incredibly, 10 percent do not drink water at all. By contrast, Americans drink an average of nearly six servings a day of caffeinated beverages, such as coffee and soda that actually cause the body to lose water.[8]

> **If you are able to make only one immediate health modification, make it your water and hydration habits—the single most critical factor to health and well-being.**

A recent report from the Institute of Medicine found that women who appeared to be adequately hydrated consumed the equivalent of about 91 ounces of fluids each day, and men about 125 ounces. Eighty percent of these ounces came from drinking water (73 ounces for women and 100 ounces for men); the rest came from other beverages and foods. That is actually more than eight glasses (64 ounces). Although this would seem to suggest that we are able to get adequately hydrated through means other than water alone, we need to distinguish between *healthy hydration* and *safe fluid levels*. Your fluid levels may be in the safe range by consuming soft drinks and coffee, but that does not mean you are properly hydrated and receiving the many health benefits that naturally come from drinking the right water. The dangers associated with soft drink and caffeine consumption have been well documented (see Healthy Hydration Tips).[9]

*Healthy hydration depends upon water.* Our goals should be to re-create the mountain stream water that our ancestors once thrived on. The only way to do this is to drink water that contains healthful amounts of essential minerals. Minerals are the ticket to *life* itself, because they provide the essential cofactors for the life-supporting enzymes of the human body. In the natural world, these minerals automatically come mixed in with the spring water. As our bodies cannot operate capably without the proper concentration of these trace minerals, there is bound to be sickness and disease, due to either a lack of the right type of water or a lack of any water at all.

F. Batmanghelidj, M.D., the famous water pioneer and advocate, has described the prolific and profound ways we benefit from water. Here are just a few[10]:

- Water is our main source of energy; it generates electrical and magnetic energy inside every cell of the body.
- Water is the bonding adhesive in the architectural design of the cell structure. It prevents DNA damage and makes its repair mechanisms more efficient.
- Water increases the efficiency of the immune system.
- Water is the main solvent for foods, vitamins, and minerals; it also energizes food and food substances and increases the body's rate of absorption of the essential substances these foods provide.
- Water increases the efficiency of red blood cells in collecting oxygen from the lungs, and it normalizes the blood manufacturing systems in the bone marrow, which helps to prevent leukemia and lymphoma.
- Water clears toxic waste from the body and transports it to the liver and kidneys for disposal.
- Water is the main lubricant in the joint spaces and helps prevent arthritis and back pain.
- Water prevents clogging of arteries in the heart and brain and thus helps reduce the risk of heart attack and stroke.
- Water is directly connected to brain function—it is needed for the efficient manufacture of neurotransmitters, including serotonin; it is needed for the production of hormones made by the brain, such as melatonin; it can prevent attention deficit disorder, and it improves our attention span.
- Water helps prevent the loss of memory as we age, reducing the

risk of Alzheimer's disease, multiple sclerosis, Parkinson's disease, and Lou Gehrig's disease.

▪ Water can help reduce stress, anxiety, and depression, restore normal sleep rhythms, and can integrate mind and body functions, so that we can have a greater capacity to realize our goals.

▪ Water can help to reverse addictive urges, including those for caffeine, alcohol, and some drugs.

▪ Water affects one's appearance, making our skin smoother and giving it sparkling luster; it also reduces the effects of aging.

▪ Water can relieve premenstrual symptoms and reduces the incidence of morning sickness in pregnancy.

## Dying of Thirst—Dehydration and Disease

The human body is the single most sophisticated and complicated machine in existence—by a very wide margin. Indeed, it is so complicated that it actually crosses the invisible line from inanimate matter to "living" matter. It logically follows that any machine that is so complex *must* by its very nature have very specific requirements as to what it needs from the outside world in order to be able to operate at peak efficiency. Of all these needs, *water is by far the most important.*

**Our body will reward us many times over if we hydrate it properly. But this will only happen if we use the correct type of water.**

Without a sufficient amount of water in the body, each of the body's major organ and cellular systems begin to malfunction, because they don't have enough of this vital nutrient to operate properly. The biochemistry behind this amazing fact is masterfully described in Batmanghelidj's book, *Your Body's Many Cries for Water.*

When one's daily water consumption begins to drop off from its minimum bodily requirement, even a "little" bit, the natural state of healthy biochemistry within the cell begins to suffer rapidly damaging consequences. Over time, this persistent state of dehydration can cause many structural changes, even to the genetic blueprints of the body, and can quickly lead to a wide variety of serious diseases.

According to Dr. Batmanghelidj, "Our most painful degenerative diseases are states of local or regional drought."[11] One of his most significant findings is the link between dehydration and increases in histamine production. These increased histamines released in the lungs cause spasms of the bronchioles, making them constrict, which lead to conditions such as allergies and asthma, and can also suppress the body's immune system. Indeed, by providing the body with adequate amounts of water, one can actually cause the disappearance of allergy-causing histamine from areas where it should not be found.

Water shortages have also been tied to gradual rises in blood pressure (hypertension). In addition, when there is chronic dehydration, our brain begins to depend more on glucose for energy, hence our need for sweet food. This in turn is directly linked to diabetes.

But that's just the beginning. Batmanghelidj sees dehydration as being connected to many of our "mystery" medical conditions, from obesity to Alzheimer's to AIDS. He has devoted an entire web site to the therapeutic use of water and the treatment of a wide assortment of degenerative diseases and other important health conditions related to water.[12]

## Water and pH—Managing Acid and Alkaline Levels

Cells produce acidic wastes as they metabolize energy, mainly in the form of lactic acid. Water forms the principal component of the surrounding environment where the cells exist and communicate within. Therefore the pH of the fluids of our body becomes inherently important to intercellular (i.e., cell-to-cell) communication. Cell signaling is involved in literally every system within the body. The biofeedback mechanisms of cellular tissues and organ systems (i.e., the immune system and the endocrine system) greatly depend on the fluid environment between cells and organs to be slightly alkaline, as opposed to acidic. Where there is not enough water and fluids of the proper pH in circulation to wash out local acidity and toxic substances, the following conditions can result: heartburn and indigestion (dyspepsia), inflammation of the colon (colitis), migraines and headaches, joint pains, and lower back pain. Cancer thrives in an acid environment, primarily because it thrives and proliferates when the cellular communication of the immune system is off-line. Acidity also accelerates the aging process. More precisely, *we age because we accumulate acidic wastes*, because cells cannot communicate. This is a profound health-related insight that unfortunately modern medicine seems to ignore.

Diet and lifestyle play a significant role in acid waste accumulation. Stress, whether mental or physical, can lead to acid deposits within the body, just as junk foods can also cause the body to become more acidic. These acidifying foods include meat, sugar, alcohol, fried foods, soft drinks, processed foods, white flour products, and dairy products. We need to strive to maintain an alkaline state in our bodies.

Hydration becomes a very important factor in fighting this acid waste accumulation, as it neutralizes and flushes toxins and acidic waste from our bodies. As an acid-clearing mechanism, water makes the interior of our cells alkaline. Ideally, the water we drink should have an alkaline pH of 7.0 or higher. (Anything with a pH of 7.0 or higher is alkaline, whereas anything with a pH of less than 7.0 is acidic by definition.) Much of the water available on the market today (including tap water) is lower than 7.0, sometimes much lower, which means that it is acidic. The best way to achieve a proper level of alkalinity (or non-acidity) is either through drinking mineral water or filtered water that either results in alkaline pH or ionizes and electrically charges the water to ensure alkaline pH. Ionization improves the water's absorption and movement through the aquaporin (a family of related proteins that reside in cell walls) channels of the cells, ultimately resulting in proper intracellular hydration.

Among other things, ionized alkaline water is a buffer against lactic acid buildup, so that recovery time after exercising is decreased. This, in turn, naturally enables us to experience an improved capacity for aerobic activities. It also provides a greater supply of life-giving oxygen, by providing more hydroxide (or OH-) ions to our body than ordinary tap water, and because it contains structurally smaller molecules, which helps the body to assimilate more water via the aquaporin channels of the cells. This, in turn, enables the body to hydrate much more quickly.

As a natural antioxidant, ionized water scavenges free radicals before they have a chance to oxidize cell tissues.

I highly recommend that you test your water source before and after connecting a filtration system. You can test your water's pH by purchasing a test meter at www.extech-direct.com/pH-Meters/pH-Meter-Index.htm, or you can purchase litmus paper pH test strips at your local pharmacy.

## Water's Role in Bacterial Fermentation

Most of us get irrationally nervous about bacteria. We've been told that all bacteria are harmful and must be destroyed. So we run to the doctor to get a prescription that will kill the bacteria. Unfortunately, antibiotics not only kill the bacteria that have become unstable and pathogenic, they also kill the healthy bacteria that are necessary for digestion, including the elimination of waste products and the natural processing of foods.

Yoshitaka Ohno, M.D., and Howard Reminick, Ph.D., have researched the nature of bacteria and the role of water in stabilizing bacteria. Their findings reveal that bacteria are not the evil scavengers we believe them to be. The real cause of disease is *the way bacteria undergo alterations in the fermentation process* when they become unstable. This is due to oxidation, which alters the structure of bacteria, making them aggressive and dangerous. When this happens, it is called *putrefaction* (which is actually the technical term for "decayed" or "rotten").

The healthy bacteria that result from fermentation perform vital functions in the body. Under normal conditions, fermentation allows bacteria to perform an essential role in maintaining the homeostasis (balance) of the body. From this, we enjoy regular bowel movements to remove waste materials from the intestines before putrefaction overcomes fermentation. With putrefaction, bacteria attack cells. The end result of putrefaction is constipation, when the body is unable to eliminate waste materials, which changes the structure of bacteria to the point that they actually promote the formation of disease in the small intestine and colon. Your body is a complex matrix of many systems that are designed to flow—i.e., blood flow, lymphatic flow, energy flow, digestive flow. When any of these systems become stagnant, the result is symptoms and disease. A river flows, but a pond is stagnant.

Some of the causes of putrefaction include the overuse of drugs and various toxins in our food and water supply. There is a direct correlation between the increase in food and water toxicity, the overuse of prescribed medications, and the subsequent increase in chronic, age-related diseases.

> **The quality, content, and activity of the water in our body, coupled with its stabilization of bacteria and all our other cells, will inevitably affect how well we age and how well our body can control disease.**

What role does water play in all of this? A critical one, to be sure, because water is the great stabilizer of bacteria. In fact, water performs two vital functions to keep the body in a state of harmony and balance. Ohno and Reminick write: "First, the water in our body must be able to prevent toxins and chemical substances from accumulating and creating destructive influences in cells. Water must bring all minerals and nutrients required for metabolism into the cells and remove any substances that can damage the cell. It must be able to protect the cell membrane from damage and invasion. Second, since water is involved in every function of the body, it must act as a conductor of electrochemical activity, such as neurotransmission, by transferring information from one nerve cell to another smoothly and efficiently. When water with a weak electromagnetic signal enters nerve cells, the synapses cannot generate strong impulses between cells."[13]

For water to be most effective in the human body, it is necessary that it contain ionized minerals, which are required to nourish and protect both our cells and bacteria. It should also have a slightly higher pH, which is necessary to assure that the body fluids do not become and remain overly acidic, which then results in putrefaction. However, because of contamination in our environment (such as toxic wastes and chemical additives to our food and drinking water), minerals in our water supply have been depleted, resulting in metabolic disturbances and creating a far more rapid aging process, which in turn tends to lead to all manner of degenerative diseases.

## Hydration and Weight Loss

Every good weight-loss program recommends drinking water as a means of distinguishing true hunger from false "hunger pangs." It also aids and improves digestion. Our volume of food intake then decreases dramatically, and so do our cravings. In addition, with sufficient water intake, we tend to hunger after proteins rather than fattening carbohydrates.

Water also stimulates the sympathetic nervous system (automatic nervous function like control of major organs) for 1.5 to 2 hours. The end result of adrenaline secretion is a gradual loss of stored fat and a reduction of excess weight. Using water as a weight-reduction strategy is often found to be more stable and permanent than other kinds of calorie reduction and dieting techniques.[14] When we drink a glass of water before and during each meal, along with two glasses of water two hours after each meal, we are filled up and are hence encouraged to eat only when food is actually needed by the body.

## Signs of Dehydration

One of the most pervasive health problems in our society today is dehydration. The most common signs are:

- Dry skin
- Muscle cramps
- Constipation
- Fatigue
- Headaches

However, Dr. Batmanghelidj identifies three different kinds of symptoms that we might not typically associate with dehydration[15]:

### GENERAL PERCEPTIVE FEELINGS

- Feeling flushed
- Feeling anxious

- Feeling dejected
- Feeling depressed
- Feeling heavy-headed
- Having irresistible cravings
- Not sleeping well

## THE BODY'S DROUGHT MANAGEMENT PROGRAMS

- Asthma
- Allergies
- Hypertension
- Constipation
- Type II Diabetes
- Autoimmune diseases

## EMERGENCY INDICATORS

- Heartburn
- Dyspeptic pain
- Anginal pain
- Lower back pain
- Migraine headaches
- Colitis pain
- Fibromyalgic pains
- Bulimia
- Morning sickness during pregnancy
- Rheumatoid joint pains

So…the next time you have a headache, feel anxious, or experience bewildering joint pain, instead of reaching for an aspirin or a sedative, try pouring yourself a glass of water! It's exciting that we have such a simple means of fostering optimal health. All we have to do is find the *right* water (i.e., one that offers the greatest health benefits and the least number of toxins), so that we can then begin an active program of serious and long-term rehydration.

## Healthy Hydration Tips

- *Sip water all day long.* Most of us can't process more than about a glass or two of water an hour. Drink more than this, and it will probably just be excreted into the toilet.
- *Drink water when you first get up in the morning* to correct dehydration produced while you slept.
- *Add a little lemon or lime juice to your water.* It helps to normalize your body's pH level because it is alkaline-forming when consumed.
- *Drink water at room temperature,* as ice-cold water can compromise digestion.
- *Limit caffeine intake.* There are many negative issues associated with drinking caffeinated beverages, including adrenal exhaustion, elevated insulin levels, and disruption of sleep patterns. Also, when we consume caffeinated drinks, our bodies get rid of more water than is contained in the drink, resulting in dehydration and depletion of important minerals and nutrients.
- *Never reuse plastic bottles.* Try to avoid drinking out of plastic containers altogether, as all plastic leaches into the beverages they contain and are dangerous to your health (see Golden Key #6— Environmental Hazards/Plastics). When you open a bottle and expose it to oxygen and heat, the plastic becomes more toxic. Even if you think you are washing the bottles well enough to kill bacteria, frequent washing might accelerate the breakdown of the plastic, possibly causing harmful chemicals to leach into the water or other beverages in the bottles. You will find recommended glass bottled waters later in this chapter. You should always have a bottle at the office, at the gym, or on those long car commutes.

> **The health benefits that we will reap from drinking the right water are enormous, because we will finally be restoring the proper balance of water in our body—the balance upon which the enzymatic reactions and other biochemical activities within the body operate most efficiently.**

- *Limit fruit juices, sports drinks, and alcohol.* Fruit juice and sports drinks can increase insulin levels, histamine production, and cause asthma in children, while alcohol dehydrates the body. When you urinate after drinking an alcoholic beverage, you can expel more water than what was initially contained in the alcoholic beverage. This means that on its way out, a beer is taking additional fluids and nutrients along with it.

- *Avoid soft drinks and coffee.* Toxic commercial beverages, such as soft drinks, are made from distilled water and phosphoric acid. Heavy consumers of soft drinks (with or without sugar) spill huge amounts of calcium, magnesium, and other trace minerals into their urine. In addition, all soft drinks are high in dangerous artificial sweeteners or high fructose corn syrups, which is simply sugar that's been burnt. High fructose corn syrup affects the integrity of white blood cells and can decrease your immunity fourfold. These drinks, with a pH of 2.5, have an even bigger impact on fluid pH, lowering them to approximately 4.6. When this happens, your system becomes acidic, and your stomach literally corrodes. This causes a dramatic strain on the body's buffering mechanisms, along with a net loss in calcium, and therefore in bone density. *It takes approximately 32 glasses of high pH water to neutralize one soft drink.*

- *Hydrate before exercise.* The American College of Sports Medicine suggests that you ensure proper hydration by drinking about 16 ounces of water two hours before exercising. This gives your body plenty of time to regulate its fluid levels prior to exercising and helps to delay or avoid the effects of dehydration during exercise. Second, during exercise they recommend that you drink *before* becoming thirsty as well as to drink at regular intervals to replace fluids that are lost through sweating. It takes approximately eight fluid ounces of fluid to replace each pound of body weight lost.

- *Exercise regularly and eat a nutrient-dense diet.* (See Golden Key #3—Exercise.)

## Recommended Beverage Alternatives to Water

Although there are various fluids that can raise our "hydration status," we still need to be aware of the purity, structure, and function of the liquids we put in our bodies. Here are three good alternatives:

### DISCOVER TEAS—ORGANIC GREEN, WHITE, BLACK, AND HERBAL TEAS

- *Mighty Leaf Teas* in silk bags. Many of these teas are organic and caffeine-free. See www.mightyleaf.com.
- *Long Life Teas* in unbleached bags. Many of these teas are organic and caffeine-free. See www.long-life.com.
- *Yogi Tea.* Many of these teas are organic and caffeine free. See www.yogitea.com.
- *Flora Health USA* (www.florahealth.com) produces two healing brands of tea: (1) BIJA Teas From Around the World use organic ingredients wherever possible, and tea bags made of a blend of hemp and tree fibers whitened with non-toxic, non-chlorine, environmentally friendly hydrogen peroxide. (2) Flora Therapeutic Teas are made from herbs selected from pristine environments and are certified organic whenever possible; they are also packaged in unbleached paper tea bags (which means they are dioxin-free). The herbs are dried at low temperatures to protect the quality of the essential oils and tested for heavy metals, pesticides, and microbial content.
- *Mountain Rose Herbs: Handcrafted Teas* (www.mountainrose-herbs.com) are exceptionally fresh and long-lasting loose leaf teas. They are made with certified organic ingredients, and when organic materials are not available, from wildcrafted herbs. They can be purchased in bulk as well.

> **Herbal teas make great tasting, healthy iced tea. Brewed or leftover herbal teas, especially those with a lemon flavor, make great ice cubes.**

*Lemonade or limeade* can be made from fresh organic lemons and limes, spring water, and raw honey, Stevia, or Therasweet™, a therapeutic sweetener.

*Natural sparkling/carbonated waters* such as San Pellegrino (see the recommendations that follow later in this chapter).

## The Problem With Tap Water

Municipalities have a difficult job in trying to balance the dangers of water contaminants with the dangers of processing the water. One thing we can say for sure is that ordinary tap water can be dangerous to your health because of the toxins that are in it, such as the many chlorinated hydrocarbons that naturally form when organic particles are mixed with chlorine. Even tap water that has been filtered and treated with chlorine may still cause gastrointestinal distress in children (10 percent of the serious gastrointestinal illness cases in children are attributed to their drinking water). Adults with weakened immune systems, such as the elderly or AIDS and cancer patients, are also at high risk.[16]

Nearly all municipal water supplies have chlorine or chloramine and fluoride added, and the EPA regulates a number of metals that can come through corroded and leaching pipes, including lead, arsenic, aluminum, antimony, barium, beryllium, cadmium, chromium, copper, iron, manganese, mercury, nickel, selenium, thallium, uranium, and zinc. We are finding out more and more how detrimental these chemicals are to our health. Here are some special concerns worth noting:

### CHLORINE

Lifetime consumption of chlorinated tap water can more than double the risk of bladder and rectal cancers. Chlorine reacts with naturally-found organic compounds in water to form what is called "chlorinated byproducts." Because surface water (found in lakes and reservoirs) usually contains higher concentrations of organic compounds, it also is more likely to contain higher levels of potentially carcinogenic chlorination byproducts as well.[17]

## CHLORAMINE

Chloramine is another "treatment" substance that is used now in many large municipalities, such as Los Angeles and my beloved Tampa. In systems where the concentration of chlorine in the public water supply is already at the highest acceptable level, but where the water still needs more disinfection to protect against microbes, such as those that cause dysentery and cholera, the utility will then add a chlorine/ammonia compound called "chloramines."

Chloramine is represented as a totally safe substance, but it is easy to understand why there is a growing public outcry about its use. When public water utilities increase chloramine levels, their customers are given the following precautions: people with home dialysis machines are warned that their system may not remove chloramines; commercial/industrial water users are advised to review potential operational impacts associated with higher chloramine levels; and people with aquariums and ponds are told that their filters may not be sufficient to remove the chloramines, which may cause their fish to die.

Marc Edward, a professor of Civil Engineering at Virginia Tech, gave this warning to a committee in the U.S. House of Representatives about the hazards of chloramine in our water systems on March 5, 2004: "If nothing is done, there is a likelihood of a major plumbing . . . catastrophe . . . that could cost homeowners [their health] as well as tens of billions of dollars each year. It could be a serious miscalculation to assume [that] a day of reckoning is not approaching. We have proven that not only does chloramine worsen galvanic corrosion between brass/copper or lead/copper [pipes], but it also increases the amount of lead leached to the water when the metals are coupled."[18]

There are many unknowns about chloramines and possible chloramine byproducts. It is ironic and disturbing that there is so much concern about machinery and fish, but chloramines are supposed to be "safe" for the public to drink. We call that a clue!

To learn more about chloramine, go to:
www.itcilo.it/english/actrav/telearn/osh/ic/127651.htm.

## FLUORIDE

Half of all ingested fluoride remains in the skeletal system and accumulates with age. Conditions related to fluoridation of the water include the following:

- *Hip and bone fractures.* Residents of cities that fluoridate their water have double the fluoride in their hip bones compared to the rest of the population. Hip fractures are found to be nearly twice as frequent among people drinking 2.6 to 3.4 parts per million (ppm) of fluoride, as compared to people drinking 1 ppm fluoride in the water. Evidence suggests that fluoridation alters the basic architecture of the bones.[19]

- *Teeth decay and teeth discoloration.* Studies are showing that tooth decay is declining in both fluoridated and non-fluoridated areas, while dental fluorosis, a condition in children characterized by white spotted, yellow, brown-stained, or sometimes crumbly teeth, is on the rise, and more so in fluoridated areas. Intake of excess fluoride (through toothpaste, fluoridated water, and fluoride supplements) can cause dental fluorosis.[20]

- *Lead levels in children.* The chemical most commonly used to fluoridate America's drinking water is associated with an increase in children's blood lead levels. Children can get this fluoride from a variety of sources: food and beverages made in fluoridated cities, fluoridated dental products, fluoride containing pesticide residues in food, industrial fluoride air emissions, and fluoride containing medicines, anesthetics, and other products.[21]

- For more information on fluoride, see www.fluoridealert.org.

## ARSENIC

Ninety percent of the fluoride we use to fluoridate U.S. water systems comes directly from pollution-scrubbing systems of the phosphate fertilizer industry. This hydrofluorosilic acid is an industrial grade product that contains trace amounts of lead, mercury, and arsenic. The National Sanitation Foundation International reported that the most common contaminate is arsenic, which occurs five times more frequently than any other contaminant. Arsenic can cause types of cancers, including prostate, kidney, skin, liver, bladder, and lung. Non-cancerous effects include skin pigmentation, damage to reproductive functions, and a wide range of gastrointestinal, cardiovascular, hormonal, hematological, pulmonary, neurological, and immunological problems.[22]

Cells exposed to arsenic produce about three times as many damaging free radicals as other cells. Fortunately, the use of antioxidants such as Vitamin E and Vitamin C can cut the level of free radicals in arsenic-exposed cells in half. See the shopping list at the end of Golden Key #2—Nutrition for product recommendations.

## ALUMINUM

A report from France indicates that drinking water with high aluminum concentrations may increase the risk of developing Alzheimer's disease and other forms of dementia. Researchers determined that a concentration of aluminum in drinking water above 0.1 milligrams per liter may be a risk factor for dementia and Alzheimer's disease. Nearly 2,700 individuals were followed for an eight-year period to identify new cases of probable Alzheimer's or other dementia illnesses. The sample was divided into 77 drinking water areas, with surveys conducted to determine concentrations of aluminum, calcium, and fluorine in each water supply. The authors point out that their findings support those of several other studies linking aluminum to Alzheimer's, but add that "this result needs to be confirmed using a higher number of exposed subjects."[23]

## Our Top Priority—Correcting the Tap

During one year, a family of four can spend thousands of dollars on water. It is my belief that the most important thing, both from a health and economic perspective, is to correct our tap water. Below is a list of recommended water filtration systems that include both short- and long-term solutions, depending on your budget and feasibility.

Most home filtering units remove organic and inorganic compounds, including lead and other metals, chlorine, chloramine, trihalomethanes, and radon gas. I am suggesting several different filtration options. The two that make the top of my list are the Wellness Filter® and Ionizer Plus®. These systems can be a bit of an investment initially, but the long-term payoffs are enormous. It can save potentially thousands of dollars a year on bottled water costs, and you have the comfort and confidence of knowing the water that you and your family drink is safe. If you are on a budget, you can begin by getting one sink system that filters your drinking water and as many shower head filters as you can afford. Your skin drinks water too.

▪ *The Wellness Filter®.* Developed over 25 years ago in Japan by Haru Naito, a famous physiologist, this filter combines purification and enhancement technologies to produce a purified and enriched water. The system uses multiple layers of purification media to reduce a broad range of contaminants, including VOCs, bacteria, cysts, giardia, cryptosporidium, heavy metals, radioactive compounds, and some pharmaceuticals. The system is believed to be one of the few that offers the reduction of chloramine, a new disinfection alternative to chlorine, in all of its systems—kitchen, shower, sports, and whole house—and restores the balance of acid/alkaline levels. I am excited that the company will soon be offering a new accessory cartridge to removed fluoride from drinking water. I know of no other filter that removes fluoride. The Wellness Filter also includes a patented enhancement stage in its filters that is permanent and that does not require changing or replacement. This stage has been shown to add minerals and reduced ions that help restore the natural acid/alkaline levels in the blood. The super hydrating quality of its water also maximizes detoxification of the body's waste byproducts. The company has scheduled a series of independent clinical studies to establish the efficacy of its filter for improved hydration, detoxification, endurance, and accelerated muscle recovery. This system is highly effective at providing safe drinking water at your tap. See www.wellnessfilter.com.

- *The Ionizer Plus® Water Micro-Filtration, Ultraviolet Disinfection, Ionization* from High Tech Health is a unique combination of an advanced water ionization system *and* a state-of-the-art water filtration system. Although no system can guarantee 100 percent removal of fluoride, it has been well documented through laboratory analysis that it does reduce fluoride to acceptable levels, and in some communities it has reduced fluoride by as much as 95 percent. The ionized water restores proper acid/alkaline balance to your system, detoxifies and hydrates the body, improves digestion and elimination, fights against accelerated aging, and is used and recommended for therapeutic use by many health practitioners. Its superior water filter removes contaminants, chlorine, chemicals, and bacteria, including E. coli, giardia, and cryptosporidium. The ultraviolet rays remove viruses as well. See www.hightechhealth.com.

> **Pitcher filtration systems are not as effective as in-line faucet filtration systems. Compare different water filtration systems at: waterfilter-comparisons.com.**

- *Carbon filters* such as Brita or PUR. Brita filters purport to filter out impurities such as chlorine, lead, copper, mercury, giardia, and more. PUR Pitchers and Watermakers provide dual filtration using a two-step process. The first step reduces lead, copper, chlorine, sediment, chemicals linked to cancer, bad taste, and odor. The second step uses a Pleated Microfilter that removes 99.99 percent of microbiological cysts, cryptosporidium, and giardia. Carbon-based filters are a good baseline option that protect you from many impurities, but they do nothing to guard against pharmacological/biological contaminants or reduce chloramines and fluoride and to restore the balance of acid/alkaline levels.

## Plastic Versus Glass Bottles

The vast majority of bottled waters come in plastic bottles, in spite of the fact that there is a known tendency for small amounts of the plastic in these bottles to leach out into the water itself. Even small amounts of plastic can be damaging, as we do not possess a sufficient means for detoxifying it once it gets into the body. Worse yet, once any plastic molecules enter the body, they begin to cause all sorts of bio-chemical havoc, by hormonal mimicry and other toxic and dangerous processes that can ultimately lead to cancer.

It follows from this that the safest type of bottle to drink water from is *glass*. In the section that follows, I recommend several spring waters and sparkling mineral waters that come in glass bottles. However, glass bottles are sometimes heavy, cumbersome, and haz-ardous if broken, and are hence not as convenient as plastic.

Avoid plastic whenever possible. However, if you must use plastic bottles, here are some things to consider:

- Do not purchase one-gallon cloudy plastic polyvinyl chloride (PVC) containers, since they transfer far too many chemicals into your water. Glass-like clear bottles are a much better form of plastic to use.
- Choose a bottled water that is high in pH, such as Trinity, Penta, or Fiji, as this significantly reduces the likeliness of leaching plastic into the water.
- PET or PETE bottles are generally considered the safest *single-use* plastic bottle choice. PET (polyethylene terephthalate) is brighter than PVC plastic, very transparent, and almost looks like glass. Easy to recycle and remanufacture, this type of plastic is accepted by most curbside recycling programs. There has been some research to suggest, however, that long-term storage of beverages in PET containers may increase the levels of DEHP, an endocrine disrupting phthalate and a probable human carcinogen. Therefore, I recommend this water not be stored for long periods of time, and that the containers *never* be reused.
- A new generation of polyactide (PLA) plastics made from corn rather than petroleum may ultimately be the safest option, but

these plastics are not yet widely available. Two beverage companies in the U.S., Naturally Iowa and BIOTA Spring Water, are using Cargill Dow's NaturalWorks PLA, the first commercially viable polymer derived from corn. Cargill claims that the product performs equal to or better than traditional resins, and PLA is also biodegradable.[24] The NaturalWorks concept shows not only how the beverage industry is responding to growing consumer concern for the environment, but also how important packaging is in differentiating products.

> Remember, all plastics break down under extreme conditions. It is a good idea never to subject plastic containers to high temperatures (as found in storage, microwave, or dishwasher situations). If you can smell or taste the plastic in a bottle, toss it in the recycling bin!

## Bottled Spring Water

Bottled water is a $4 billion-a-year business in the U.S., with about one-third of consumers drinking it regularly. It has also become an increasingly serious health and environmental issue. 1.5 million tons of plastic are used to bottle water, and some bottled water contains bacterial contaminants. Several brands contain synthetic organic chemicals, such as industrial solvents, chemicals from plastic, or trihalomethanes, the byproducts of the chemical reaction between chlorine and organic matter in water, or inorganic contaminants, such as arsenic, a known carcinogen.[25]

Many people are increasingly concerned about the environmental and economic implications of bottled water. We are now paying between 240 and 10,000 times more per gallon for bottled water than we do for tap water. A major shift to bottled water as a means of combating tap water contaminants raises serious equity issues for lower income individuals and families. In addition, the manufacturing and shipping of billions of bottles cause unnecessary energy and petroleum consumption, leading to landfilling or incineration of bottles, which can release environmental toxins.[26]

As more and more of our rivers and streams are being polluted, concerned citizens believe the focus of our efforts should be on cleaning and protecting our water supplies at their source—as well as at water treatment facilities—so that we can begin to feel better and safer about drinking from the tap.

Furthermore, the National Resources Defense Council (NRDC) conducted a four-year study of the bottled water industry, including its bacterial and chemical contamination problems. The petition and report found major gaps in bottled water regulation and concluded that bottled water is not necessarily safer than tap water. The report also found that much of the marketing related to bottled water implies that it comes from pristine sources, when it does not. According to industry and government estimates, about 25 percent of bottled water is actually bottled tap water. And even when bottled waters are covered by FDA's specific bottled water standards, those rules are weaker in many ways than EPA rules that apply to big-city tap water. For example, bottled water plants must test for coliform bacteria just once a week, while big-city tap water must be tested 100 or more times a month.[27]

Not all bottled waters are created equal . . . far from it. Among the hundreds of different brands of bottled water, there is a vast range in quality. Below is a list of products I've researched and now recommend as healthy and relatively safe bottled water choices:

- *Mountain Valley Spring Water*® (glass bottle)—water originates at a protected natural spring in Hot Springs, Arkansas. The natural unique mineral content of this water has remained constant over the last 60 years. It contains calcium, magnesium, sodium, potassium, fluoride, iron, zinc, and a pH of 7.7. This is available in five-gallon glass bottles for water dispensers. www.mountainvalleyspring.com
- *VOSS Artesian Water*® (glass bottle)—derived from a virgin aquifer in central Norway, VOSS is one of the purest waters you can find. www.vosswater.com
- *hiOsilver Oxygen Water*® (glass bottle)—bottled in glass to retain oxygen, this water is high in magnesium, contains sodium, and

a naturally alkaline pH of 8.4. www.hiosilver.com
- *Evian® Water* (glass bottle)—www.evian.com
- *Penta® Water* (glass bottle)—www.pentawater.com
- *Fiji Natural Artesian Water®* (plastic bottle)—naturally alkaline with a pH of 7.5. www.fijiwater.com
- *Volvic®* (plastic bottle)—www.volvic-na.com
- *Essentia®* (plastic bottle)—www.essentiawater.com. This water has an extremely high pH (9.6) and should not be your exclusive source of water because it can neutralize acid and compromise digestion.
- *Trinity Spring Water®* (plastic bottle)—www.trinitysprings.com. This water also has an extremely high pH (9.6) and should not be your exclusive source of water.

The last four waters, because they are bottled in plastic, are not as good as the first three glass bottle recommendations, but they do have higher pH levels, which mean less breakdown of the plastic and less chemical leaching.

*Bottled Water Tip!* Many popular brands such as Aquafina® and Dasani® are highly treated through chemical processing. Because of massive demand, these waters often sit in bottles for as long as two years before they are sold. Generally treated with reverse osmosis and chemicals, this makes them more

**Never drink any beverage that has a plastic taste!**

neutral to slightly acidic, and therefore potentially dangerous to your health because an acidic pH causes the plastic to leach into the water.

## Carbonated/Sparkling Mineral Waters

It's perfectly all right to drink carbonated or sparkling water, but as with other kinds of water, you need to be a judicious shopper. Look for naturally carbonated mineral water with a pH of at least 7.0. The minerals in carbonated drinks trigger those happy endorphins, and the carbon dioxide can help to push toxins out of our system. Drink sparkling water as a treat not a primary beverage. Balance it with spring water and properly filtered tap water. The following waters are some recommendations:

- Highland Spring Sparkling Natural Mineral Water (pH 7.8)
- San Pellegrino Sparkling Natural Mineral Water (pH 7.7)
- Apollinaris Sparkling Natural Mineral Water (pH 7.0)
- Perrier (pH 5.4)—avoid

## Distilled Water

Distillation is a process in which water is boiled, evaporated, and the vapor condensed. This essentially makes the water "dead," in that it is sterile and without life forms and has an acid pH. For very short periods of time (weeks), distilled water has therapeutic uses and can be a good detoxifier. According to famous juicing guru Steve Meyerowitz, distilled water is actually the only water that gives our kidneys a rest. Because distilled water is free of dissolved minerals, instead of the kidneys working to purify the water, the water purifies the kidneys. Distilled water also can aid in cleansing our bladder and bloodstream and will actively absorb toxic substances from the body and eliminate them.[28]

> As a temporary detoxifier, distilled water can be used occasionally, but should not be consumed on a regular basis.

The dangers are in the long-term use of distilled water. Distilled water is devoid of nutritional and mineral content and has an acidic pH. According to Dr. Zoltan Rona, it can be dangerous because of the rapid loss of electrolytes (sodium, potassium, and chloride) and trace minerals, such as magnesium, deficiencies of which can cause heartbeat irregularities and high blood pressure.[29] The ideal water for the body should be slightly alkaline. This requires the presence of minerals, such as calcium and magnesium. The loss of these minerals accelerates the aging process and can contribute to coronary disease, hair loss, osteoporosis, and hypothyroidism.

# Over-Hydration (Special Concerns for Endurance Athletes)

Are there instances when water is too much of a good thing? Yes. Although rare, according to U.S.A. Track and Field, over the course of a long event, endurance athletes who consume huge amounts of water without taking minerals (including potassium, sodium, and magnesium) may risk seizures, respiratory failure, and even death from drinking too much. This is especially true of long-distance runners or triathlon competitors who may be gorging themselves on water throughout an event and risking hyponatremia (water intoxication syndrome), a condition where excessive amounts of water dilute blood to the point that sodium levels plummet. Electrolyte packets or supplements (not sports drinks due to their high sugar content) are the answer to this dilemma.[30]

# The Four Corners of Optimal Nutrition

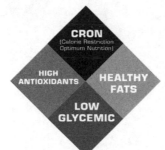

**The Four Corners of Optimal Nutrition integrate well-documented but often ignored foundations** *of nutrition and optimal health into one powerful unified theory. Adoption of this lifestyle program can enhance aerobic performance, optimize body fat, reduce stress, and lower blood pressure and blood sugar insulin levels. It can also lower cholesterol and triglyceride levels as an added bonus.*

*"He is like a man building a house,
who dug deep and laid the foundation on the rock.
And when the flood arose,
the stream beat vehemently against the house,
and could not shake it,
for it was founded on the rock."*

LUKE 6:48

SUPER
HEALTH

7 Golden
Keys to
Unlock
Lifelong
Vitality

# Ten Common Myths About Health

*Beloved, I pray that you may prosper*
*in all things and be in health,*
*just as your soul prospers.*

3 JOHN 2

My career and travels have put me in contact with a great number of people, and no matter where I go I am amazed at how many commonly held myths there are about health. When people find out I am a researcher, speaker, and consultant on optimized natural health, nutrition, and fitness, not only do I typically hear a litany of health complaints, but in the process I hear a long list of myths that people believe about health. Here are some of my favorites:

## Myth #1—Fish Is Good for You.

Without question, fish would be one of the top food sources on the planet if we hadn't destroyed it. The byproducts of energy production and Personal Care and Pharmaceutical Pollutants (see Golden Key #6—Environmental Hazards/PCPPs) have so contaminated the world's waterways with so much mercury, heavy metals, pharmaceuticals, and chemicals, such as PCBs or polychlorinated biphenyls, that most fish are no longer a health food (with the exception of sardines and anchovies, which feed on plankton and are caught young). Any food that we are told should only be eaten once a week, and not by pregnant women or small children, should not be eaten by anyone.

The Truth: eating fish other than sardines and anchovies can be dangerous. Instead, supplement with a purified fish oil together with fat-soluble antioxidants, such as a full-spectrum Vitamin E (including "mixed tocotrienols and mixed tocopherols"). (See Golden Key #2—Healthy Fats/Fish Oil.)

## Myth #2—Farm-Raised Fish Is the Answer.

Testing shows that unsafe mercury levels and other pollutants routinely contaminate commercial farm-raised fish, and they are also fed health-destroying pollutants. These fish are also virtually devoid of the vital omega-3 essential fatty acids EPA and DHA. For instance, the farm-raised salmon in your freezer was kept in ocean pens for three years, fattening up on highly concentrated unnatural protein pellets. It was vaccinated and received antibiotics to survive the diseases that are so common in these feedlots. It may have been fed pesticides to repel bloodsucking sea lice. And that lovely pink hue to its meat was gained through a steady diet of synthetic pigment (farm-raised salmon flesh would be a pale gray or white without it).

The Truth: while various governments debate at what level of consumption farm-raised fish poses no health risk, the simple fact that there is a debate tells you it's not safe.[1]

## Myth #3—Shellfish Is Healthy.

The Bible tells us in Leviticus 11:9–10 that we may eat any fish with fins and scales but to avoid fish or water creatures without them. They are called an "abomination" to the Lord. This includes the flesh of crabs, clams, oysters, lobsters, and shrimp. Why? Because they are the scavengers of the sea. Mercury and biological toxin levels abound in them, and every spring or summer we hear media warnings about them. Salmonella and campylobacter and other bacteria pathogenic to humans are some of the leading causes of food-borne illness around the world, and even parasites are found in them.

The Truth: although we are no longer bound to the Leviticus dietary law, science affirms what the Bible said centuries ago: shellfish is not healthy for human consumption. Shellfish eat the garbage, scum, and toxins in the ocean. They are the filters of the sea. Just as you probably wouldn't eat your air-conditioning filter, the same holds true for these ocean filters.

## Myth #4—Eggs Are Bad for You.

Despite all the warnings, there is no link between eating the cholesterol found in eggs and elevated blood cholesterol. Your body makes a constant supply of cholesterol, and cholesterol is found throughout your body. The small amount of cholesterol in eggs is like a drop in the pool compared to the approximately 14,000 mg of cholesterol in the body.

What can be harmful is eating eggs the wrong way. Eggs are very delicate, so avoid browning them while cooking. Browning damages them and creates toxins that are unhealthy. Do not cook eggs in vegetable oils, because heat makes the delicate oils rancid. The safest cooking oils are coconut oil, olive oil, and butter. Avoid eating only the whites, because your body needs the yolks in order to properly absorb and digest the wonderful attributes the eggs offer.

The Truth: cholesterol is primarily elevated by the over consumption of sugars and foods that convert to sugar rapidly, including fruit juices and other sweet drinks. Organic eggs are a near perfect food that should be a staple in your diet.

## Myth #5—Coffee Is Good for You.

When you hear another report that extols the virtues of coffee, you need to check out the source of the funding for the study. Here's the typical process that coffee goes through to make it into your cup.

First, unless the coffee is organic, it is one of the highest pesticide-laden crops in the world. In addition, the coffee grounds were likely ground a year or longer before the container was opened. At the moment of grinding, an oxidation process began in the coffee, which continued until it was vacuum sealed. When you hear the "pssst" after opening the container, the oxidation starts again and runs rampant through the grinds, making the grounds an oxidized fat that becomes toxic.

Then chlorinated and fluoridated tap water (which is profoundly unhealthy for us) is poured through a coffeemaker that is often lined with aluminum and gives off aluminum ions, which contributes to dementia and other health risks. This contaminated water then passes through the oxidized coffee bean fats and through a white coffee filter. The filter is generally white because it has been bleached, and thus it has dioxin in it, which is the single most cancer-causing substance ever studied by the Environmental Protection Agency.

As if that weren't enough, many of us then sweeten it with sugar or sucralose or the blue stuff or the pink stuff, which are all toxic chemicals and harmful to our bodies. To top it off, we pop the top of a dairy cream container and pour a substance that is more harmful than the coffee itself.

Consequently, this is just the beginning. The real problem begins when it enters your system and wreaks havoc in your body by raising your insulin levels and a multitude of other symptoms!

The Truth: there is some antioxidant benefit to drinking organic coffee, but there are better ways to gain the benefits. Turn to teas—green, white, or black—that are higher in antioxidants. If you must drink coffee, use highly alkaline water; coffeemakers that do not have aluminum linings; organic coffee that you grind yourself, and brown or dioxin-free or paperless coffee filters. Avoid pasteurized milk and creamers, and either do not sweeten it at all, or if you must sweeten it, only use small amounts of raw honey, brown rice syrup, stevia, or Therasweet™. Also, avoid drinking coffee on an empty stomach.

## Myth #6—Pork, the Other White Meat.

The Bible tells us in Leviticus 11:7–8 that pork is an unclean meat, and not only should you not eat it, you should not even touch it. The Hebrew words used to describe "unclean" can be translated as "foul, polluted, and putrid." Science tells us that pigs contain many toxins, worms, and latent diseases. This could be because pigs are scavengers and will eat any type of food, including dead insects, worms, rotting carcasses, excreta (including their own), garbage, and other pigs. We call that a clue.

Besides significant concerns related to pig meat and influenza, excessive quantities of histamine, and growth hormone, the pig is also the main carrier of the taenia solium worm—a tapeworm found in human intestines with greater frequency in nations where pigs are eaten. This tapeworm can pass through the intestines and affect many other organs, and is thought to be incurable once it reaches a certain stage. One in six people in the U.S. and Canada has trichinosis from eating trichina worms that are found in pork. Many people have no symptoms to warn them of this, and when they do, they resemble symptoms of many other illnesses. These worms are not noticed during meat inspections, nor are they killed by salting or smoking. Few people cook the meat long enough to kill the trichinae.

The Truth: although we are no longer bound to the Levitical dietary law, science validates the problems with pork. Pigs are scavengers, and they did not make God's list of "clean" animals for a good reason. Remember, you are what you eat, and all the garbage that the pig eats becomes part of their flesh, which winds up on your plate. There are many other delicious, healthy meats available to you, so make the better choices for a healthier you.

## Myth #7—Fruit Juice Is a Great Choice.

Don't misunderstand me on this point. Oranges and other fruits are healthy and filled with vitamins, minerals, and other nutrients that we need every day. But did you know that there is so much sugar in a glass of orange juice that, in an attempt to appear healthy, Coca-Cola® is comparing its sugar content to that found in orange juice? The obvious implication is that their soft drink is not a health risk because of its sugar levels. But just the opposite is true. Orange juice is not a healthy drink because of its high sugar levels.

An 8-ounce glass of orange juice has almost the same amount of sugar in it as a regular Coke, a whopping eight to nine teaspoons of sugar. Guess how many teaspoons of sugar are necessary in your bloodstream? Only one. Your body and brain tightly regulate one tablespoon of sugar in the bloodstream for proper brain function. So where does all that extra sugar go when you drink a Coke or a glass of fresh orange juice? The pancreas responds by secreting excess insulin to offset the sharp rise in blood sugar, and this results in the liver converting the excess sugar to LDL (or bad) cholesterol and triglycerides (a saturated fat), which is not healthy. Also, the increased insulin levels that result from such a huge inflow of sugar into your bloodstream block your body's ability to burn the newly created triglycerides, which end up as increased blood triglycerides levels and as body fat. Check your waist-line—there it is.

Your body simply can't handle the excess sugar. When you wake up in the morning, your blood sugar level should be around 87. You get to the breakfast table and drink the glass of orange juice and eat a bowl of cereal (both of which convert rapidly to sugar in the body), and your blood sugar level rockets to 120 to 130. Then your pancreas rises to protect you, secreting high levels of insulin, which then pushes your blood sugar level down into the 70s, and you feel exhausted and maybe a little shaky, so you grab a cup of coffee and a doughnut to bring it back up. This just further perpetuates the roller coaster cycle of blood sugar ups and downs, which, in turn, exhausts your organs. Over time, this roller coaster ride sets the stage for many diseases to attack and win over a weakened system. Unfortunately, America lives on this health-destroying cycle.

The Truth: eat fruit the way God made it. Fruit juice is sugar-laden, and fruit juice from concentrate is even worse.

## Myth #8—Soy Is the Ultimate Health Food.

Soy foods grew from an $800 million industry in 1992 to a $4 billion industry in 2003. After an amazingly effective marketing campaign from the soy industry, millions of Americans have jumped on the bandwagon, believing that soy is a miracle food that will fight every ailment from heart diseases to cancer and even hot flashes. Many people have made soy their primary source of protein, and hydrogenated soy oil is now found in all sorts of fast-food and packaged products—from cookies, crackers, and other baked goods to frozen French fries, TV dinners, and canned foods.

Dr. Kaayla Daniel, in her new book *The Whole Soy Story: The Dark Side of America's Favorite Health Food*,[2] not only challenges the myths that soy is a health food but also shows overwhelming evidence of harm—from the hormonal effects of soy on newborns to the antinutrients and toxins that are not removed by today's high-tech processing methods to soy allergens and digestive distress in general.

The Truth: limited amounts of organically grown non-GMO soy are not likely to hurt you. Fermented soy products, such as miso, tempeh, natto, shoyu, and tamari, can be good for you in the context of a varied diet. But unfermented soy as a dietary staple can cause health issues, and many of the highly processed soy foods we eat today are neither natural nor healthy. In fact, they can be downright harmful. Do not feed soy to infants and children.

## Myth #9—Milk Does the Body Good.

While milk is a healthy food prior to its being pasteurized (which damages proteins and destroys the precious life-giving enzymes in milk), for many, if not most, people milk is very difficult to digest. Pasteurization diminishes vitamin content, destroys Vitamin B12 and B6, kills beneficial bacteria, denatures fragile milk proteins, and promotes the rancidity of unsaturated fatty acids. The fats and proteins in pasteurized milk have also been altered, and the minerals are hard to absorb. Skim milk and reduced-fat (2% and 1%) milk are all high in lactose (milk sugar), low in fat, but more importantly, these reduced-fat milks have been created by mixing skim milk with oxidized powdered milk fats, which are toxic to the body. Drinking today's milk may increase the risk of allergies, diabetes, heart disease, and even osteoporosis (contrary to popular belief).

According to the American Academy of Allergy, Asthma, and Immunology, cow's milk is the number-one cause of food allergies in children. Evidence indicates that up to half of the children in the U.S. have some allergic reaction to milk. For these children, and for adults who are allergic to dairy foods, milk is a mucus maker and can lead to recurring problems, such as sinus infections, chronic coughs, asthma, and ear infections. Milk/dairy intolerance is the primary cause of recurrent ear infections, which are the most common complaint pediatricians face. In North America alone, 25 million children visit the doctor annually with an ear infection, which results in over 1 million surgeries on children.

When my oldest son was two years old, he had severe recurrent ear infections to the point he could not hear for four months and was scheduled for emergency surgery. My wife and I took our son to a nutritionally-orientated doctor who took him off of his favorite food, cow's milk, cheese, sour cream, and yogurt, and in seven days our son was cured. According to Dr. Michael A. Schmidt in his book *Healing Childhood Ear Infections*, the overwhelming majority of surgeries for ear infections could be prevented by taking children off of milk. More and more doctors and dieticians are realizing that removing dairy products from the diet can be a solution to many childhood illnesses, such as runny noses, constipation, colic, and ear infections.

The Truth: drinking pasteurized milk from the local grocery store is frequently associated with a decline in health, including ear infections in infants and children and sinus infections in adults. If you know of any infants or children with chronic ear infection, you can almost be certain that the cause is pasteurized milk. A healthier choice is goat's milk. A tasty but not as nutritious option is to use rice, almond, or oat beverages. Because butter is hydrolyzed (predigested), many people do well with it, even if they have problems with other dairy products. Raw butter is best.

## Myth #10—Keep Out of the Sun or You'll Get Skin Cancer.

Believe me, I am not an advocate of staying out in the sun to the point where you damage your skin. But most Americans are Vitamin D-deficient, especially African-Americans and other people with dark complexions. Because there is a widespread fear of getting skin cancer, we cover ourselves and then put sunscreens over our exposed skin. Keep in mind that most sunscreens are filled with chemicals that are absorbed through the skin into the bloodstream. Then we block the sun's ultra-violet rays that manufacture precious Vitamin D in the skin. Vitamin D is good for bone health, blood pressure, and other vital functions. According to the Vitamin D Research Council, it is also important to consume up to 1,000 to 4,000 IU per day of a high quality Vitamin D plus A supplement per day. It is a good idea to get your Vitamin D level  tested. The proper test for Vitamin D status is called 25(OH)D or 25-hydroxyvitamin D and is available at www.lef.org.

The Truth: sunlight is as important as vital nutrients to your body. The problem of a lack of sun is likely more prevalent than too much sun. If you don't want to get melanoma, just avoid getting burned. An hour a day in the early morning or late afternoon sun is critically important. As a matter of fact, years ago an effective therapy for multiple sclerosis was sunshine therapy, but it is little known and not often practiced today.

SUPER
HEALTH

7 Golden
Keys to
Unlock
Lifelong
Vitality

# The Four Corners
# of Optimal Nutrition

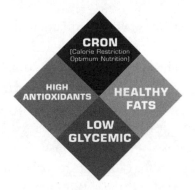

*"My people are destroyed
for lack of knowledge."*

HOSEA 4:6

Despite nearly constant warnings from the media, we as a society have been incredibly slow to recognize the serious health problems that exist all around us. Researchers at the Centers for Disease Control and Prevention (CDC) in Atlanta, Georgia, report that in 2000, 56 percent of American adults were overweight, nearly 20 percent were obese, 7.3 percent had diabetes, and about 3 percent suffered from both conditions.[3] Yet the compounding problems related to being overweight continue to soar. Recent studies predict that one in three Americans born in the year 2000 will develop diabetes in their lifetime.[4] For many of us, a simple look in the mirror reflects the need for a personal change.

Although greater numbers of people are seeking new ways to optimize their health and minimize their susceptibility to disease, never has nutritional awareness and education been a more pressing concern.

Millions of Americans are becoming casualties of one degenerative disease after another. The CDC has stated that 54 percent of heart disease, 50 percent of vascular (blood vessel) disease, and 37 percent of cancer are preventable through lifestyle changes alone. Environmental toxins are certainly part of the problem, but the bigger culprit is our ignorance and disregard of the fundamental principles of good health.

> The Four Corners lifestyle approach is for everyone from elite athletes to the health challenged who suffer from conditions such as diabetes, hypoglycemia, obesity, and eating disorders.

The Four Corners of Optimal Nutrition is one of the most well-researched nutritional approaches in existence. In fact, each element of the Four Corners concept has long been accepted by a wide variety of scientists and nutritionists, including the late Dr. Roy Walford (one of the original scientists who participated in the "Biosphere" project), Dr. Diana Schwarzbein (a foremost authority on diabetes and author of *The Schwarzbein Principle I* and *II*), Dr. Jennifer Marks (author of *Syndrome X*), and Cheryle Hart, M.D. and Mary Kay Grossman, R.D. (authors of *The Insulin Resistance Diet*).

What is unique about the Four Corners concept as presented here is that the individual four corners have been integrated into a single "unified theory" of nutrition, providing a comprehensive foundation for new levels of health awareness and life enhancement.

CORNER 1

# Calorie Restriction With Optimal Nutrition (CRON)

*Feed me with the food*
*that is needful for me.*

PROVERBS 30:8 AMP

With all its amazing complexities, the human body is easily the most amazing creation in the entire known universe. When King David asserted, "I will praise You, for I am fearfully and wonderfully made" (Psalm 139:14), he was marveling over all the intricacies of the human body and soul, including the many remarkable immunity and healing systems that we have been lovingly given by our Maker.

While our body was designed by God to keep itself in health, the fact is that we are responsible for faithfully supplying it with all it absolutely requires for health. Twenty-four hours a day the trillions of cells in our body must be receiving the right nutrition to function at an optimal level. If we deprive our body of what it requires, or if we abuse our body with what we know or don't know is harmful, we will suffer a breakdown in our health. It's the very basic, yet profound, principle that we reap *only* what we sow.

In December 2002, Mac Gober, Founder and President of Canaan Land Ministries, weighed 308 pounds and was taking heart and blood pressure medication as well as multiple insulin shots every day for his diabetes. He nearly died and was barely able to function. Starting the

Four Corners program at the recommendation of Dr. Don Colbert, Gober began by exclusively taking a whole meal super food shake instead of meals for 30 days. Then for two weeks he substituted two meals per day with the superfood and had one typical Four Corners meal per day. During those six weeks he lost over 50 pounds and was taken off his medications, including insulin. His energy returned, and he resumed a normal schedule and did not have to resume any medication.

At the other end of the spectrum, Gal Fridman is a world-class athlete who began his Four Corners diet because other athletes were getting sick on the local food while in Thailand for the World Windsurfing Championship. One week prior to competition he began eating the Four Corners way, and for the last five days of the competition he consumed only a whole meal super food instead of regular meals. He won the World Championship, then continued on the Four Corners program through the 2004 Olympics in Greece, where he won the first gold medal in the history of Israel.

## Calorie Restriction with Optimal Nutrition

The Four Corners of Optimal Nutrition revolve around the Calorie Restriction with Optimal Nutrition (CRON) concept, because *eating fewer calories has been proven to extend life span, delay disease, and promote optimal health.* Scientists agree on this, and various camps have arisen to explain the great success of the CRON concept. Some scientists think that CRON diets work because fewer calories amount to a lower glycemic (or blood sugar) effect overall (see Corner 2—Low Glycemic Diet), regardless of the type of food that is eaten. Others maintain that the relatively low amount of oxidation associated with CRON diets (because eating less calories lowers oxidative stress on the body) is why they work so well at extending life and preventing disease (see Corner 3—High Antioxidants).

On the other hand, those who eat higher calorie amounts can suffer from a wide range of symptoms, including fatigue, sleepiness, hypertension, hypoglycemia, colitis, brain fog, and more. It also affects longevity, seriously enough to subtract years from your life.

This much is certain: more than 2,000 medical studies support the astonishing conclusion that *CRON diets can increase life span by as much as 30 to 50 percent.* If we apply these percentages to the human life span, a 30 to 50 percent increase would translate into a life span between 120 and 150 years. Indeed, CRON diets have been shown to greatly enhance the life span of every species in which CRON has been studied.[5]

Is it realistic to project these life spans? In the past two years a French woman died who was verified to be 122 years old. Recently, a woman in Brazil celebrated her 125th birthday according to RankBrasil, Brazil's equivalent to the Guinness Book of World Records. With over 50,000 Americans known to be living over the age of one hundred, there's every possibility that utilizing the CRON diet can potentially extend our life span by these incredible percentages.

> **Whack the calories. Max the nutrition. Extend and enhance the quality of your life.**

CRON is thus the most researched and most effective method of life extension and optimal health in history—but why does it work? Compelling research suggests that the primary mechanism for the success of CRON-based diets may be that it helps to control pancreatic insulin response.

## Controlled Insulin Response

All food contains energy (calories) or potential fuel for the body to operate and perform its many functions. When we eat, our bodies use the calories to produce energy and various nutrients to repair and maintain body tissues. If not used, calories are stored as fat in most areas of the body. If we keep adding calories that are not being burned up, we get fat. It makes sense, then, that when it comes to calories, the key is to pack as much nutrition as possible into the lowest-calorie foods that one can comfortably eat.

Many people who struggle with excess weight or who have become diabetic have high levels of insulin in the body. Insulin is a powerful hormone that plays a critical role in regulating blood sugar (glucose) levels throughout the body and serves as a powerful fat storage hormone as well. After we eat, special cells in the pancreas secrete insulin, which acts on cellular insulin receptors and allows passage of glucose into the cells. Unchecked, high levels of blood sugar in the body lead to a loss of many vital body chemicals, such as minerals, vitamins, and water. Repeated and chronic elevations of blood sugar can cause other more long-term and potentially fatal problems, such as impairments to cardiovascular, respiratory, and immune functions.

It is important to understand the nature of this insulin/blood sugar (or glucose) connection. In a normal situation, the blood sugar (or glucose) level is maintained between 85 and 95 mg/dL, with brief increases above these levels for about one to two hours after a meal. Thus, there is ideally a tight control between consumed sugar and insulin secreted from the pancreas. Most of the cells of the body are covered with insulin receptors on their cell surfaces. These receptors come in contact with insulin and then open the cell membrane and allow glucose (sugar) to enter the cell, which is then used as a primary fuel for cell functioning.

In an abnormal situation, too much sugar consumption leads to elevated blood glucose levels, which chronically elevate blood insulin levels. As a consequence, the insulin receptors stop responding to the insulin (medically known as insulin receptor resistance or insulin resistance), and the glucose cannot enter the cell. Therefore, the blood glucose continues to increase, which further increases blood insulin, creating more insulin receptor resistance. This is known medically as negative feedback inhibition.

*So if we eat too much sugar or simple carbohydrates for too long, the insulin receptors stop listening to the increased insulin.* The situation continues to worsen in the following ways:

(1) As mentioned above, increased insulin promotes fat storage. Unfortunately, fat is not the inert blob it was once thought to be—only stored to protect us from cold and starvation. Recent research has shown that fat is the largest metabolically active endocrine organ in the entire body! Fat produces several hormones, enzymes, and proteins,

such as estrogen, aromatase, leptin, Interleukin 6 (IL6), and tumor necrosis factor alpha (TNF-alpha). Estrogen itself promotes fat storage. The aromatase enzyme converts testosterone to estrogen in women and men (thus more fat). Leptin, IL6, and TNF-alpha significantly increase inflammation, insulin resistance, and storage of fat in the liver as well as throughout the body.[6] More fat storage, especially in the abdomen, promotes more inflammation throughout the body, completing the vicious cycle. The good news is that as you lose body fat, you may see improvements on your arthritis, muscle and abdominal pains, sleep disorders, and shortness of breath.

(2) Increased blood glucose can coat blood proteins, and thereby cause the immune cells to attack them as they would a foreign invader. This immune attack can lead to still further inflammation, continuing the vicious circle from yet another direction.

(3) In the early stages, too much sugar followed by too much insulin will rapidly drop the blood sugar level. This will cause intense cravings for sugar or simple carbohydrates, since the brain is significantly dependent on glucose to maintain consciousness. Interestingly, even though the brain has insulin receptors, it is insulin-independent (with respect to glucose use)[7], so it depends on the body to regulate sugar. When blood sugar levels drop, the brain will virtually demand that sugar or simple carbohydrates be consumed to restore normal glucose levels.

In summary, insulin resistance causes a chronic increase in both blood sugar and insulin in the body, resulting in metabolic distur-bances that affect our ability to lose weight and maintain muscle mass, which in turn can lead to many serious health problems.

Unfortunately, the high carbohydrate (fat-free) diet that has been marketed so heavily in American culture actually encourages people to eat high glycemic index (GI) foods, such as bread, cookies, pretzels, etc., which are quickly converted to sugars in the body. People have assumed that if the product label says "fat-free," these foods can be eaten with impunity, as though it means it has no calories. A close com-parison of nutrition labels will show you that fat-free or reduced-fat products can have just as many, if not more, calories per serving than regular products. What has resulted is a nation of fat, unhealthy people who have been duped by the processed foods industry.[8]

## Calorie Restriction

Within our trillions of body cells we have mitochondria, or minuscule furnaces in which calories (fats and carbohydrates) are burned, changing into energy. Ironically, eating is by far the biggest single stress that we regularly put on our bodies, because the actual process of burning calories to produce energy naturally generates a large amount of damaging "free radicals"—unstable molecules that attempt to steal electrons from any available source, such as our body tissues. Free radicals cause mutations and cellular damage and are partly responsible for accelerating the rate of aging as well as a wide range of illnesses, including all the degenerative diseases, such as arthritis, cardiovascular disease, Alzheimer's, and cancer.

This is similar to the combustion process within a car engine. Fuel (calories) goes into the engine (the body), producing a controlled explosion that generates power, but also causes significant wear and tear on the engine. The more calories we make our body burn, the more free radicals are released to ravage our body cells, and the first components to be damaged are the mitochondria themselves. Each mitochondria has its own DNA, which is separate from the rest of the cell, and when damaged mitochondria reproduce, they may have genetic defects. When this happens, the body experiences a total energy drop or brown out (like a city). This is now considered to be the foundational cause of aging and many degenerative diseases.

This is why caloric restriction is one of four proven methods of actually reducing the rate of aging—not just by reducing the overall mortality rate, but also by modulating the actual rate of aging itself. In fact, as Roy Walford points out in his outstanding books *Beyond the 120 Year Diet* and *The Anti-Aging Plan,* if one actively pursues a CRON diet, it is possible to greatly extend longevity by this one dietary intervention alone.[9] The most difficult part of this dietary "treatment" is finding the appropriate low calorie, optimally nutritious foods to eat that will satisfy both hunger and individual cravings.

## Weighing In on Calorie Counting

While the benefits of a low calorie diet are high, there are hazards to avoid as well. The most obvious hazard is that as most people lower their caloric intake, they also neglect their nutrition at the same time. Many people who go on extreme low calorie diets suffer from low body temperatures, constant hunger, and depleted energy. Such diets are often difficult to sustain over the long term and can also affect the overall quality of our lives as well.

I do not advocate the extreme regimens that some practitioners of calorie restriction have taken. They meticulously measure the precise calories and weight of every morsel they eat, and some even enter the results into computer programs that keep track of everything they eat. Living on a diet of nothing but fruits, nuts, berries, grains, and vegetables, they often lose so much weight that they look as though they are starving.

> **The more food we eat, the more free radicals are created to do their damage.**

Let's face it: eating is one of our principal pleasures. My goal is a far more moderate approach that retains the enjoyment of eating. To eat well, while restricting caloric intake, is something anyone can do. You merely need a new mindset. There's never a reason to starve yourself in the pursuit of super health.

While calorie counting is an important component of optimal nutrition, calories themselves are a very limited criterion for determining the types and amounts of foods that will be the most beneficial for us to consume.

Consider, for instance, what a "calorie" is. It is the amount of energy that is required to raise one cubic centimeter of water 1°C. All food contains energy in the form of calories (or more accurately kilocalories) as potential fuel for the body to perform its many functions. The process of energy metabolism within the cell's energy factory, the "mighty mitochondrion," is a highly complex process involving dozens of steps and many biochemical reactions. Consequently, judging the foods you eat simply by counting the number of calories they contain does not account for the amount of energy that is needed to digest the food, nor does it account for the amount of food that is constantly being used in the ongoing bodily processes of breakdown (catabolism) and rebuilding (anabolism).

## Quality, Not Quantity

Calorie counting also doesn't account for food quality. It is foolish to think that the 250 calories found in a 20-ounce bottle of Coca-Cola are equal to the 250 calories found in a delicious salad of dark green vegetables and berries. The 250 calories from the Coke are comprised solely of more than 60 grams of sugar—no protein, no vitamins, no helpful minerals, no fats, and no fiber. Oh, but it does deliver an unhealthy dose of caffeine and food coloring. Those refined sugars go right into your bloodstream and cause your insulin levels to spike, and the calories you don't burn find their way to your waistline.

Another factor that calorie counting doesn't account for is the amount of food that remains undigested and is subsequently excreted from the body. Moreover, it doesn't take into consideration how the digestive process may be compromised, such as through "leaky gut syndrome." This is a condition where there is inflammation that increases intestinal permeability, usually due to medicines, stress, food sensitivities, and microbial overgrowth. In this situation, undigested food, toxins, and microbes, such as bacteria, yeasts, and parasites, enter the body through abnormal openings in the intestinal lining.

In the case of yeast overgrowth from high sugar intake and antibiotic use, long rootlike structures (rhizoids) penetrate the lining of the intestines, creating microscopic breaks that cause a highly permeable state within the intestinal membrane. This, in turn, causes undigested food particles and toxins to be absorbed directly into the bloodstream, where the immune system then initiates an attack against these "foreign" bodies, resulting in inflammation. The immune system will then attack other parts of the body that look like the undigested food (medically known as antigen mimicry). This is a major cause for autoimmune dysfunction, such as diabetes, asthma, arthritis, and dermatitis.

*The Optimal Nutrition component of CRON is about food quality and nutrient density.* "Food quality" refers to the actual quality of any given food under consideration. In short, what has it gone through on its way to your plate? Is it covered with pesticides, herbicides, and chemical fertilizers? Are these removable? Is it comprised of genetically modified organisms, even in part? Was it radiated, fortified, or heavily processed? Was it stored for inordinate lengths of time in a toxic environment? Has it been "improved" with cosmetic modifications, such as dyes or waxes? Has it been overexposed to oxygen or heat? These are some of the conditions that could lead to immune imbalance and increased biological toxicity.

> **Make the effort to get the healthy right foods, and your body will reward you!**

Is it a nutritional building block, or is it a form of nutritional "fuel" for the body? And most important . . . is it a nutritionally healthful food, which is to say, does it contribute to the body's inherent nutritional needs?

"Nutrient density" refers to the number and quality of viable nutrients in any given food, relative to the overall number of calories in it. The more nutrient dense the food is, the better it is, because it enables us to consume the greatest number of health-giving nutrients with the smallest number of overall calories.

Optimal nutrition requires that we focus, not on calories alone, but on balancing the correct macro-nutrients (proteins, fats, fiber, and low glycemic carbohydrates), so as to achieve maximum nutrient density to cover the body's most basic internal requirements.

## Food Quality Is on the Decline

A new study conducted by the University of Texas at Austin, based on U.S. Department of Agriculture data, has shown that compared to 50 years ago, today's fruits and vegetables contain smaller amounts of some key nutrients, including protein, calcium, phosphorus, iron, riboflavin, and Vitamin C. The declines included a 6 percent dip for protein and 38 percent loss of riboflavin. "This is one more reason to eat more vegetables because they are still, by far, our most nutrient-dense food," said Dr. Donald Davis, the study's lead author and researcher with the university's Biochemical Institute in the Department of Chemistry and Biochemistry.

Davis said the main reason for the fall-off in nutrients is that today's farmers breed higher yielding crops. The study of 43 fruits and vegetables looked at 13 nutrients and found that plants have a fixed amount of energy they can spend and varieties with high yields may have less energy to take minerals from the soil. Researchers found that celery, green peppers, and tomatoes lost the most protein; cantaloupe, lettuce, and tomatoes have less phosphorus than they did in the era of the space race, and eggplant and tomatoes contain less Vitamin C.

"When you irrigate and fertilize and control weeds to intensively increase the yield of a crop, it dilutes amounts of some nutrients. By encouraging a plant to grow faster and bigger, it does grow faster and bigger, but it doesn't have the ability to uptake or synthesize the nutrients at the same faster rate," Davis said.[10]

While the results are not beyond question, because the analytical techniques used 50 years ago are not the same as now, it puts a special emphasis on the quality of our food supply as well as the need for extra nutritional supplementation.

## Empty Calorie Foods

On the negative flip side are empty calorie foods—foods that are full of sugar and trans fatty acids, which come under the general designation of "junk foods." While there is no definitive list of junk foods, most authorities include in this notorious category foods that are high in salt, sugar, refined carbohydrates, or bad fat calories, and low in terms of protein, minerals, or vitamins—such as fried fast food, salted snack foods, carbonated beverages, candies, gum, and most sweet desserts. They are the high sugar, low fiber, and high fat foods that attract us like magnets and put enormous stress on the various healing systems of the body.

The sugar content of these junk foods is particularly relevant, because excess sugar in the diet quickly leads to an imbalance of the intestinal flora (microbes such as bacteria and yeasts). In the healthy intestinal tract there is a preponderance of beneficial bacteria and a minimal amount of pathogenic (disease-producing) bacteria and yeast. With increased consumption of sugar and simple carbohydrates, there will be an increase in yeast production (such as candida albicans) and possibly pathogenic bacteria as well. There are published studies showing up to a 70 percent improvement in IBS (irritable bowel syndrome) and IBD (inflammatory bowel disease, such as Crohn's disease and ulcerative colitis) when sugar is eliminated from the diet! Wouldn't the pharmaceutical companies love to have a drug that would work as effectively as sugar elimination?

Daily supplementation with beneficial bacteria (probiotics), including various species of Lactobacilli (Acidophillus, Rhamnosus, Casei, Plantarum, etc.) and species of Bifidobacteria (Brevis, Longus, Infantis, etc.), is a good idea for overall health. The beneficial bacteria crowd out unwanted species, produce natural antibiotics to kill pathogenic bacteria, help digest foods, and make many of our B vitamins and Vitamin K as well. Another recently discovered function of probiotics (another name for beneficial flora) is "crosstalk" between the flora and the intestinal lining. This occurs through uptake of parts of the bacteria and may literally be bacterial vibrations communicating with the intestinal lining itself. The result is healthy immune balancing in the intestines, which is responsible for at least 60 percent of our immunity. This is especially important in infancy and early childhood, as it has been shown to help prevent allergies and autoimmune diseases, such as asthma and diabetes.

Since it is known that we have at least ten times more bacteria than we have cells in our body, it would be wise to choose which ones we ingest to carry along with us. This is not a new concept. Humans began culturing foods with healthy bacteria (yogurt, kefir, tempeh, cheese, sauerkraut, and many others) 2,500 years ago in Iraq.

And finally, as we move into the second of the four corners, it is important to note again that optimal nutrition requires that we ingest foods that produce a low glycemic response within the bloodstream. This involves avoiding sugars and other foodstuffs that result in blood-sugar spikes and choosing foods that minimize a significant insulin response from the pancreas.

## Super Foods!

The following is a select list of the top nutrient-dense, low calorie foods that give you the most bang for the buck. Eat these foods, and live long and well!

- Grain grasses (wheat grass, barley grass, rye grass)
- Sea vegetables (spirulina, chlorella, dulse, kelp)
- Dark green vegetables (spinach, kale, broccoli, asparagus, green beans, romaine, mixed greens)
- Bright-colored vegetables (bell and hot peppers)
- Berries (blueberries, strawberries, cranberries, and raspberries)
- Eggs from free-range hens
- Grass-fed/grain-free/organic beef, bison, chicken, turkey, lamb, venison
- Rice protein and yellow pea protein
- Goat milk protein
- Non-denatured whey protein
- Stabilized brown rice bran
- Sprouted legumes and grains such as kasha (buckwheat)
- Fresh squeezed combinations of vegetable juice
- Sprouts (broccoli, alfalfa, mung bean)

It is also very important to *buy organic whenever possible.* There is an abundance of medical literature referring to the health hazards of pesticides, herbicides, fungicides, and chemical fertilizers (see Golden Key #6—Environmental Hazards). There has been a huge increase in demand for organic foods over the last five years, which will continue. If you are on a budget and cannot afford organic foods, consider growing your own organic garden or joining a co-op. If space is limited, growing sprouts or vegetables in planters may be an option. One hundred years ago, 90 percent of Americans grew at least part of their own food; now it is less than 10 percent. At a minimum, you must thoroughly wash your produce.

SUPER
HEALTH

7 Golden
Keys to
Unlock
Lifelong
Vitality

CORNER 2

# Low Glycemic Response

*Thy food shall be thy remedy.*

HIPPOCRATES

During the 1990s, nutritional scientists told us to avoid protein and all forms of *fat*—even the essential fatty acids that are necessary for life and healthy cell function. While the news and print media warned about the dangers of fat, food manufacturers were pushing their low-fat cookies, brownies, and cakes. Not surprisingly, they neglected to tell us that these processed products were filled with refined sugars and appetite-stimulating chemical additives to make us want to eat more. The result is what we are living with today—diabetes and obesity that has skyrocketed to epidemic proportions. And most of the blame has landed upon carbohydrates, so now we're actually afraid to eat carbohydrates.

But let's try to bring it back into balance. Although our body has an effective system for operating without carbohydrates (for example, there are Eskimos who are sustained on a diet entirely devoid of carbohydrates, eating mostly fish and seal), we generally need complex carbohydrates in order to survive. Just as the right amount of proteins and fats is absolutely essential for health and overall well-being, so are carbohydrates.

Carbohydrates are the major source of energy in our diet and are found in grains, legumes, fruits, vegetables, sugar, and alcohol. In fact, if you starve your body by not fueling it with the right kind of carbohydrates, you'll get to the point where you can't even think straight and you'll feel edgy all the time. But it's the right kind of carbohydrates—*low glycemic carbohydrates*—that are essential to good health.

Despite their benefits, today's diets have us consuming far too many carbohydrates. Indeed, the body's storage capacity for carbohydrates is quite limited. Excess carbohydrates are converted, via insulin, into glycogen, which is stored in the liver and muscles and easily converted to glucose as a source of energy. It is also converted to cholesterol (LDL) and into saturated fat (triglycerides), which is stored in the adipose (or "fatty") tissue.

Any meal or snack that is high in carbohydrates can cause blood glucose levels to rise much too rapidly. Insulin from excess carbohydrates both promotes fat and wards off the body's ability to lose that fat.

## Carbohydrates

Carbohydrates are derived from carbon, hydrogen, and oxygen. Sugar, starch, and cellulose are carbohydrates. During the digestion of food, carbohydrates in the food are broken down into smaller sugar molecules, such as fructose, galactose, and glucose. These are the body and the brain's favorite fuel because it helps to maintain concentration, keeps us mentally sharp, and provides the power for the brain's many supremely complex functions. Children also need sufficient levels of carbohydrates, not only because they are so active but also because they need energy to grow as well.

**Eat green rather than grain. Eat unrefined carbs as nature intended them. Avoid all refined carbs— they are killing us.**

Not all carbohydrates break down the same way. Some break down quickly (simple carbohydrates), while the molecular structure of others (complex carbohydrates) result in a gradual breakdown into glucose. This breakdown of complex carbohydrates results in slowly released energy that provides longer-lasting sustenance to the body and the brain.

Simple carbohydrates, conversely, release sugars quickly. These carbohydrates include refined white starchy foods, sugars, and alcohol. They deliver a burst of energy by the quick breakdown into glucose, which it then releases into the bloodstream, but they soon leave you exhausted and unable to concentrate. The effect of a drop in blood sugar levels can also include nervousness, hyperactivity, confusion, depression, anxiety, panic attacks, forgetfulness, headaches, palpitations, dizziness, and insomnia.

Researchers have also discovered that the constant insulin "highs" produced by fluctuating blood sugar levels lead to an increase in body weight. Insulin stimulates an enzyme called lipoprotein-lipase, which directs circulating fatty acids into fat-cell storage, which in turn increases body weight. This only reinforces why anyone who snacks on cookies, ice cream, candy, cakes, potato chips, and other simple carbohydrates will put on the weight.

The extremely high sugar content in the modern American diet has been found to directly relate to numerous degenerative diseases. Sugar now is a staple, but 50 years ago the average sugar intake was about 5 pounds a year. It has now grown to 130 to 170 pounds a year! America is locked into the sugar cycle of destruction.

**Food manufacturers know how addictive sugar is . . . and so does our waistline.**

But it isn't just plain table sugar that has this destructive effect on one's health. A high glycemic (or high sugar) biochemical response can also be created in the body by eating foods that rapidly convert to sugar in the bloodstream.

## The Glycemic Index

The Glycemic Index (GI) is just one of the many tools you have available to you to improve your dietary control. It classifies foods according to how much they raise blood glucose following ingestion of an amount of the food that contains 50 grams of carbohydrates. The GI was devised as a means to help diabetics in their food selections. One of the values of this general index is that it shows that even among carbohydrates, there is a wide variance of values. For instance, the potato is actually a high glycemic food that can spike one's insulin levels.

At the end of this chapter there is a glycemic chart based on glucose, which is the fastest carbohydrate available except for maltose. *Glucose is given a value of 100—all other carbs are given a number relative to glucose.*

For the best health results, consume a diet where most of your foods have a glycemic index of less than 45.[11] The index values are compiled from a wide range of research labs, and as often as possible from more than one study. These values will be close but may not be identical to other glycemic index lists. The impact a food will have on blood sugar levels depends on many other factors, such as ripeness, cooking time, fiber and fat content, time of day, blood insulin levels, and recent activity.

As mentioned, the GI of a food is based on an amount of that food that contains 50 grams of carbohydrates. However, a single serving of many high GI foods often doesn't contain 50 grams of carbohydrates. For instance, a watermelon has an extremely high Glycemic Index, but one slice has so few carbohydrates that the Index is irrelevant. The Glycemic Load takes into account how many carbohydrates are actually in a serving of food rather than a serving of that same food that contains 50 grams of carbohydrates. To calculate Glycemic Load you simply multiply the Glycemic Index of a food times the number of carbohydrates in a serving of food and divide it by 100. I've put a chart at the end of this chapter to show you a sample of the Glycemic Load for certain foods. A Glycemic Load of 10 or under is considered low. To learn more about Glycemic Index and Glycemic Load, go to www.glycemicindex.com.

Low glycemic foods include above-ground dark green vegetables, such as broccoli, kale, and spinach, as well as avocados, nuts, and some fruits, such as blueberries and cranberries. White bread, potatoes, rice, sugary drinks, fruits, such as ripe bananas and citrus, and below-ground vegetables, such as carrots and beets, are high glycemic foods that are known to raise insulin levels into the danger zone. Indeed, many of us have already experienced the severe "low energy letdown" that typically happens when we consume large doses of sugar or other high glycemic foods.

## Low Glycemic Foods

- Berries (blueberries, strawberries, cranberries, and raspberries)
- Broccoli

- Kale
- Spinach
- Avocados
- Nuts and seeds

## High Glycemic Foods

- Grain and grain products
- White breads
- Potatoes
- Rice
- Cooked or juiced carrots
- Cooked or juiced beets
- Soft drinks and sport drinks
- Fruit juices

**While whole fruits vary in their relative speed of sugar release, they are always better choices than juices or concentrates.**

## Benefits of Low Glycemic Response Foods

- Low GI foods cause a smaller, more gradual rise in blood glucose levels after meals.
- Low GI foods help you to stay full longer.
- Low GI diet plans can improve the body's sensitivity to insulin.
- Low GI foods can improve blood sugar control in diabetics.

## To Reduce the Negative Effect of High GI Foods in a Meal

- Eat GI foods along with high quality fiber, protein, and fats.
- Include low GI food, such as eggs, meat, or berries.
- Add vinaigrette or other acidic extras, such as lemon juice.
- Cook with or add some extra olive oil or coconut oil.

## The Munchies . . . Who's Eating Whom?

As was mentioned previously, dangerous increases in blood sugar provoke the pancreas to release a correspondingly large amount of insulin, which seriously disrupts the body. When junk foods are consumed and blood sugar is elevated, more insulin is typically released than is actually needed. The extra insulin goes on to create an uncomfortable condition known as hypoglycemia, or low blood sugar, driving us to eat more sugar. The extra insulin also goes on to add to the fat reserves of the body as well.

The extra insulin also adds to the fat reserves of the body. The result is excess weight and obesity, which, of course, lead directly to heart disease and many other degenerative diseases, including cancer. Furthermore, grains and sugars found in junk food suppress the immune system, contribute to allergies, and underlie a whole host of digestive disorders. These high glycemic foods also contribute to depression.

## Syndrome X ( Metabolic Syndrome ) on the Rise

The combination of a high glycemic diet, high blood insulin levels, and increased bodily fat reserves is responsible for creating one of the most deadly health syndromes to surface in the last century: Syndrome X, or the Metabolic Syndrome. Syndrome X is the variable combination of obesity, high blood cholesterol, and hypertension (high blood pressure) linked by an underlying resistance to insulin.[12] Essentially, Syndrome X is pre-diabetes—chronic high blood sugar and high circulating insulin.

In 2001, *Forbes* magazine documented that 70 million Americans are affected by Syndrome X. Only 15 years ago that number was at 43 million. And growing numbers are appearing among children and teenagers, especially in African-American and Hispanic communities.[13] Lifestyle, genetics, and poor nutrition all work together to create this devastating health problem.

A relatively new phenomenon in medicine, the term *Syndrome X* was first coined by Gerry Reaven of Stanford University in the late 1980s. Syndrome X owes much of its existence to the massive deterioration in the quality of our food supply in the past fifty years. Prior to World War II, most foods were "whole" in the sense of not being "processed" by high-tech machines. Foods such as whole grain breads were not being stripped of the critical, life-saving nutrients (such as B-complex vitamins and Vitamin E) found in the wheat germ—this is one of the primary reasons why heart disease wasn't anywhere near the number-one killer of Americans as it is today.

But there is a problem with wheat germ. It is highly vulnerable to spoilage. For food manufacturers this meant that the "shelf life" of these whole foods was limited at best. However, once we learned that whole grains could be refined to the point that the wheat germ could be eliminated entirely, it was discovered that the shelf life of most of these highly processed foods could be increased dramatically. And while this had a positive financial effect on all the businesses related to food production, it had a negative effect on the health of Americans.

Not only were our foods deprived of one of nature's premier antioxidants, Vitamin E, they were also deprived of all the B-complex vitamins that naturally reside within the wheat germ itself. It was at this point in American history that cardiovascular disease became the number-one killer of Americans, seemingly overnight.

As we now know, one of the chief causes of cardiovascular disease is a toxic amino acid called homocysteine, which is produced naturally within the body as the normal product of metabolism. However, the body has a built-in protective shield against homocysteine, which is comprised of the very same B-vitamins that were milled out of whole grains, such as pyridoxine (B6), folate (B9), and methylcobalamin (B12), when the "Age of Refinement" came into being. Moreover, the milling of whole grains into white flour also resulted in the loss of the fat-soluble antioxidant Vitamin E, which also has been shown to have a protective effect on the heart.

The processing and refining of whole foods was a kind of "nutritional suicide," resulting in a wave of "empty" foods, full of calories, but devoid of almost any nutritional value. Indeed, most refined foods don't even have enough critical nutrients and cofactors to enable them to be properly digested and absorbed into the body. Accordingly, when we consume these nutritionally empty foods, the body has to call upon its critical nutritional reserves just to be able to digest them. This, in turn, leads to a highly destructive cascade of events within the body.

Once these critical nutrients and cofactors are "pulled" from other parts of the body, so that they can aid in the digestive process, they are no longer available for other good uses within our body. The tragic result of this massive deficiency of B vitamins within the body is that the body has now become prone to the many potentially lethal symptoms of B-vitamin deficiency, including insanity, cardiovascular disease, hypertension, chronic fatigue, cerebral dysfunction, and even outright death.

## Syndrome X and Insulin Resistance

Syndrome X is strongly correlated with the phenomenon of insulin resistance, in that the insulin that is released by the pancreas is not used efficiently or effectively by the body, which is why progressively greater amounts of insulin are required to metabolize a certain amount of glucose. This increased amount of blood insulin wreaks utter havoc within the body, and additional fat reserves are only the beginning. The resulting health implications are profound: cardiovascular disease, diabetes, thrombosis, female endocrine disorder, acne, abnormal hair growth, infertility, impaired immunity, inflammation, and even cancer.[14]

> **High insulin levels raise blood pressure, speed up the heart, and increase the stress hormone cortisol, which then constricts or squeezes blood vessels. This is a deadly cascade.**

People suffering from Syndrome X often show a loss of energy and a general lack of vitality. They tend to lead sedentary lifestyles; they eat larger portions of food than most; and some are substance abusers, in that they consume too much sugar, alcohol, or over-the-counter drugs.

The solution to Syndrome X is mostly lifestyle related. First and foremost, one must focus on eating low glycemic foods as a matter of course.[15] As mentioned before, low glycemic foods are those that slowly and gently produce a gradual increase in blood glucose levels. These foods include nuts, meat, poultry, eggs, and low glycemic complex carbohydrates, such as broccoli, spinach, and berries.

Several additional nutrients have also been shown to help fight insulin resistance—chromium, vanadium, magnesium, and potassium. Controlled protein intake along with more liberal healthy fats, such as fish oil, olive oil, and coconut oil can have a very positive effect, as does eating a balanced diet that is high in fiber. Regular aerobic exercise is also known to reduce blood insulin levels.[16]

Some lifestyle habits should be avoided. Not only should you refrain from smoking, but you should also avoid these other addictive substances—caffeine, alcohol, over-the-counter medications, or "hidden" sources of fructose, such as soda and fruit juices. Coffee (caffeine) actually decreases insulin resistance, raises insulin levels, and increases diabetes risk.[17]

# The Glycemic Index

## BEANS

baby lima . . . . . .32
baked . . . . . . . .43
black . . . . . . . . .30
brown . . . . . . . .38
butter . . . . . . . .31
chickpeas . . . . . .33
kidney . . . . . . . .28
lentil . . . . . . . . .30
navy . . . . . . . . .38
pinto . . . . . . . . .42
red lentils . . . . .27
soy . . . . . . . . . .18
split peas . . . . . .32

## BREADS

bagel . . . . . . . . .72
croissant . . . . . .67
kaiser roll . . . . .73
pita . . . . . . . . . .57
pumpernickel . . .49
rye . . . . . . . . . .64
rye, dark . . . . . .76
rye, whole . . . . .41
white . . . . . . . .70
whole wheat . . . .72

## CEREALS

All Bran . . . . . . .38
Bran Chex . . . . . .58
Cheerios . . . . . . .74
Corn Bran . . . . . .75
Corn Chex . . . . .83
Cornflakes . . . . . .81
Cream of
   Wheat . . . . . . .66
Crispix . . . . . . . .87
Frosted Flakes . . .55
Grapenuts . . . . . .67
Grapenuts
   Flakes . . . . . . .80
Life . . . . . . . . . .66
Muesli . . . . . . . .60
NutriGrain . . . . .66
Oatmeal . . . . . . .49
Oatmeal 1 min . .66
Puffed Rice . . . . .90
Puffed Wheat . . .74
Rice Bran . . . . . .19
Rice Chex . . . . . .89
Rice Krispies . . . .82
Shredded Wheat . .69
Special K . . . . . . .54

Swiss Muesli . . . .60
Total . . . . . . . . .76

## COOKIES

Graham
   crackers . . . . . .74
oatmeal . . . . . . .58
shortbread . . . . .64
Vanilla Wafers . . .77

## CRACKERS

rice cakes . . . . . .78
rye . . . . . . . . . .63
saltine . . . . . . . .72
stoned wheat
   thins . . . . . . .7
water crackers . . .78

## DESSERTS

angel food cake . .67
banana bread . . . .47
blueberry muffin .59
bran muffin . . . . .60
Danish . . . . . . . .59
fruit bread . . . . . .47
pound cake . . . . .54
sponge cake . . . . .46

## FRUIT

| | |
|---|---|
| apple | .38 |
| apricot, canned | ..64 |
| apricot, dried | ....30 |
| banana | .62 |
| banana, unripe | ..30 |
| cantaloupe | .65 |
| cherries | .22 |
| dates, dried | ....103 |
| fruit cocktail | ....55 |
| grapefruit | .25 |
| grapes | .43 |
| kiwi | .52 |
| mango | .55 |
| orange | .43 |
| papaya | .58 |
| peach | .42 |
| pear | .38 |
| pineapple | .66 |
| plum | .24 |
| raisins | .64 |
| strawberries | .32 |
| strawberry jam | ...51 |
| watermelon | .72 |

## GRAINS

| | |
|---|---|
| barley | .22 |
| brown rice | .55 |
| buckwheat | .54 |
| bulgur | .47 |
| chickpeas | .36 |
| cornmeal | .68 |
| couscous | .65 |
| hominy | .40 |
| millet | .75 |
| rice, instant | .91 |
| rice, parboiled | ...47 |
| rye | .34 |
| sweet corn | .55 |
| wheat, whole | ....41 |
| white rice | .64 |

## JUICES

| | |
|---|---|
| agave nectar | .11 |
| apple | .41 |
| grapefruit | .48 |
| orange | .55 |
| pineapple | .46 |

## MILK PRODUCTS

| | |
|---|---|
| ice cream | .61 |
| milk | .34 |
| pudding | .43 |
| soy milk | .31 |
| yogurt | .38 |

## PASTA

| | |
|---|---|
| brown rice pasta | .92 |
| gnocchi | .68 |
| linguine, durum | .50 |
| macaroni | .46 |
| macaroni and cheese | .64 |
| spaghetti | .40 |
| vermicelli | .35 |
| vermicelli, rice | ...58 |

## SWEETS

| | |
|---|---|
| honey | .55 |
| jelly beans | .78 |
| Life Savers | .70 |
| M&M's Chocolate peanuts | .14 |
| Skittles | .70 |
| Snickers | .55 |

## VEGETABLES

| | |
|---|---|
| beets | .70 |
| carrots | .85 |
| corn | .70–85 |
| green peas | .51 |
| green vegetables | .0–15 |
| onions | .10 |
| parsnips | .95 |
| potatoes, new | ...58 |
| potatoes, russet | ..98 |
| potatoes, sweet | ..50 |
| potatoes, white | .70–90 |
| pumpkin | .75 |
| rutabaga | .71 |

SUPER
HEALTH

7 Golden
Keys to
Unlock
Lifelong
Vitality

# The Glycemic Load

| Food | GI | Serving Size | Net Carbs | GL |
|---|---|---|---|---|
| Peanuts | 14 | 4 oz (113 g) | 15 | 2 |
| Cashew nuts | 22 | 1 oz (30 g) | 9 | 2 |
| Bean sprouts | 25 | 1 cup (104 g) | 4 | 1 |
| Grapefruit | 25 | 1/2 large (166 g) | 11 | 3 |
| Pearled barley | 25 | 1 cup (150 g) | 42 | 11 |
| Kidney beans | 28 | 1 cup (150 g) | 25 | 7 |
| Pizza | 30 | 2 slices (260 g) | 42 | 13 |
| Skim milk | 32 | 8 fl oz (250 ml) | 13 | 4 |
| Low-fat yogurt | 33 | 1 cup (245 g) | 47 | 16 |
| Spaghetti, w. wheat | 37 | 1 cup (140 g) | 37 | 14 |
| Apples | 38 | 1 medium (138 g) | 16 | 6 |
| Pears | 38 | 1 medium (120 g) | 11 | 4 |
| All-Bran™ cereal | 38 | 1 cup (30 g) | 23 | 9 |
| Rye bread | 41 | 1 large slice (30 g) | 12 | 5 |
| Spaghetti | 42 | 1 cup (140 g) | 38 | 16 |
| Oranges | 48 | 1 medium (131 g) | 12 | 6 |
| Bananas | 52 | 1 large (136 g) | 27 | 14 |
| Potato chips | 54 | 4 oz (114 g) | 55 | 30 |
| Snickers Bar | 55 | 1 bar (113 g) | 64 | 35 |
| Brown rice | 55 | 1 cup (195 g) | 42 | 23 |
| Honey | 55 | 1 tbsp (21 g) | 17 | 9 |
| Oatmeal | 58 | 1 cup (234 g) | 21 | 12 |
| Ice cream | 61 | 1 cup (72 g) | 16 | 10 |
| Jelly beans | 78 | 1 oz (30 g) | 28 | 22 |

| | | | | |
|---|---|---|---|---|
| Macaroni and cheese | 64 | 1 serving (166 g) | 47 | 30 |
| Raisins | 64 | 1 small box (43 g) | 32 | 20 |
| White rice | 64 | 1 cup (186 g) | 52 | 33 |
| Table sugar (sucrose) | 68 | 1 tbsp (12 g) | 12 | 8 |
| White bread | 70 | 1 slice (30 g) | 14 | 10 |
| Watermelon | 72 | 1 cup (154 g) | 11 | 8 |
| Popcorn | 72 | 2 cups (16 g) | 10 | 7 |
| Soda crackers | 74 | 4 crackers (25 g) | 17 | 12 |
| Doughnut | 76 | 1 medium (47 g) | 23 | 17 |
| Puffed rice cakes | 78 | 3 cakes (25 g) | 21 | 17 |
| Cornflakes | 81 | 1 cup (30 g) | 26 | 21 |
| Baked potato | 85 | 1 medium (173 g) | 33 | 28 |
| Glucose | 100 | (50 g) | 50 | 50 |
| Dates, dried | 103 | 2 oz (60 g) | 40 | 42 |

CORNER 3

# High Antioxidants

*The amount of antioxidants*
*you maintain in your body*
*is directly proportional to*
*how long you will live.*

RICHARD CUTLER, M.D.

Unless you've been hibernating inside a cave for the past few years, you've heard about the importance of antioxidants in the maintenance of health and even in the prevention of degenerative disease. But what precisely is an antioxidant, and why are antioxidants so important for human health?

Simply put, antioxidants are a group of compounds produced by the body that occur naturally in many foods. They work together to protect us from damage caused by oxidation in the body. How do they do this? Let's dig a little deeper.

We all know what happens when oxygen is allowed to interact with a slice of apple. It quickly turns brown. This is due to the "oxidizing" effects of atmospheric oxygen on the slice of fruit itself. The same principle applies to the rusting of a car. When oxygen is allowed to react with unprotected metal, the metal itself becomes oxidized to the point that it becomes rusty. Oxidation is what makes oils rancid.

Remarkably, the very same process happens inside the human body. As we all know, a continuous supply of oxygen is critical for the maintenance of life itself. Oxygen is used to make energy out of the food we eat through a complex biochemical series of reactions called the Krebs Cycle.

However, there are toxic byproducts of this energy-making process that are inevitably produced when oxygen is used to produce energy inside the cell's built-in energy factory, the "mighty mitochondria." These toxic byproducts are called free radicals, and they are dangerous because they tend to wreak all types of biochemical mischief inside the body, in an ever-increasing "domino effect," unless they are "mopped up" by substances designed to stop their toxic spread throughout the body. These invaluable substances are appropriately known as "antioxidants," because they soak up the toxic free radicals that are produced by the oxidation process. Think of them as free-radical scavengers.

## Free Radicals—Inside the Body and Out

Some free radicals are generated from normal body functions, such as breathing, metabolism, and exercise. Others are created by the immune system to neutralize viruses and bacteria. But it is important to note that not all free radicals are naturally generated within the body in response to normal body metabolism. On the contrary, the vast majority of free radicals come from our toxic environment, whether from pollution in the air and water, radiation, herbicides, cigarette smoke, or the ingestion of delicate oils overexposed to oxygen or heat.

> **Antioxidants can mean the difference between life and death. They are a protective shield that insulates the body from aging and disease.**

These externally acquired free radicals then go on to add to the internal damage that is caused by the body's own pool of naturally produced free radicals. These free radicals attack healthy cells, weakening them and making them more susceptible to deterioration and disease. In short, as Lester Packer points out in his groundbreaking book, *The Antioxidant Miracle*, they "fast-forward the aging process."[18]

The overall proportion of oxidants to antioxidants within the body has even been shown to be responsible for the vast majority of human diseases. The noted California biochemist Stephen A. Levine was the first individual to build a comprehensive theory of health and disease on the pervasive existence of free radicals within the body. In 1984, his landmark book, *Antioxidant Adaptation*, showed how one's propensity for illness is directly related to the balance of oxidants to antioxidants within the body.

When the balance is upset in favor of oxidants over antioxidants, the body will attempt to adapt to the new situation until adaptation is no longer physiologically possible. This is when the various degenerative diseases begin to set in. But even when the number of oxidants is roughly balanced (and hence neutralized) by the number of antioxidants, and a state of health is achieved, the body is still quite vulnerable to further degeneration.

## Oxidation and Aging

There are two ways of controlling free radicals—through CRON (a low calorie diet) or through the use of a full range of health-protecting antioxidants—so that the disease process caused by free radicals can be quenched to the greatest possible degree.

The importance of supplementing one's diet with appropriate antioxidants cannot be overemphasized. There are several reasons for this. First, it is difficult, if not impossible, to get the optimal level of antioxidants through food alone. Also, as we age, our ability to synthesize antioxidant enzymes within the body diminishes markedly, as do the various hormonal markers of aging. Moreover, age greatly diminishes the body's ability to detoxify the various poisons that it ingests unintentionally on a daily basis, thus leading to a steady accumulation of free radical-producing toxins with each passing day.

This is the "free radical theory of aging" in its simplest form, and it says essentially that we age because free radicals tend to accumulate within the body in ever-increasing amounts. This, in turn, leads to all manner of biochemical mayhem within the body.

These destructive effects include "cross-linking" the skin's different layers to one another, which produces wrinkles. This cross-linking stiffens tissues that were formerly flexible or elastic. The process happens gradually, so that cross-links accumulate over the years on the longest-lived proteins that do not get recycled very often. Part of cross-linking is due to glycation, an oxidation-like process that involves the harmful linking of proteins with sugar molecules in the blood, which renders the proteins ineffective (in much the same way as a chicken browns in the oven). Left unchecked, glycation can result in the neutralization of as many as one-third of the body's protein by the end of one's life.

Glycation is not as well known as its cousin oxidation, but it is just as destructive. I predict that in the years to come that glycation will be as well known as oxidation. The only way currently known to block glycation is through use of the amino acid supplement, Carnosine (a supplement I highly recommend for every adult), and a low glycemic diet.

## Antioxidants to the Rescue

This "free radical theory of aging" and disease can actually be used therapeutically to help counter the disease process. For if disease is simply caused by a significant imbalance of oxidants to antioxidants within the body, then it will be of major benefit to introduce a wide variety of antioxidants into the body, in the hope that they will help quench the many disease processes that have been initiated by the initial onslaught of free radicals. This is why the medical use of an intravenous Vitamin C drip can be effective in fighting a whole host of different diseases—because all the extra Vitamin C goes toward quenching the huge number of disease-causing free radicals within the body.

**Free radicals—avoid them, minimize them, and counteract them before they start the disease process.**

As 95 percent of all cancers are thought to be caused by the free radicals that are contained in our diet and the environment, it makes sense to consume a protective mixture of antioxidants, so that self-propagating free-radical reactions can be quenched before they have a chance to alter our DNA and create disease.

The quantity of each person's exposure to these environmental poisons is also critical, because antioxidants don't function indefinitely to quell free-radical production. On the contrary, they are used up, and hence become worthless, when they neutralize any given free-radical reaction within the body. This is why it is imperative to consume enough antioxidants to effectively neutralize all the toxins and free radicals within the body.

A good rule of thumb is to try to balance the amount of toxins one is exposed to with the amount of antioxidants that one consumes on a daily basis. Particularly heavy toxic exposures within the environment should thus be treated with an even higher dosage of antioxidants, because this will minimize the free radical-mediated disease process within the body.

## A Bold Defense Against Degenerative Diseases Related to Aging

Many people are skeptical of using antioxidants to battle the major degenerative diseases of aging, largely because they don't understand how free radicals themselves can actually cause disease. In the case of cancer, for instance, free radicals actually attack the genetic machinery inside the DNA molecule, by stealing away electrons from within the DNA itself. This, in turn, leads to a chain reaction "domino effect," by forcing each newly created free radical to steal yet another electron from amongst its neighbors. If this terribly destructive process isn't quenched immediately, it goes on to cause catastrophic alterations within the various "base codes" of the DNA molecule itself.

It is this type of damage to the information content of each DNA molecule that causes the cell to begin to grow wildly, without any control. Fortunately, the intake of various antioxidants is able to intervene positively in this extraordinarily destructive process, by quenching the various free radicals that are causing all of these DNA-altering chain reactions in the first place.

A similar mechanism applies to cardiovascular disease. The propagation of free radicals within the body damages the inner lining of our blood vessels (which is called the intima), by stealing electrons from them, thus causing them to become unstable. These damaged areas of the intima are then plugged with oxidized cholesterol and other fatty deposits, and this process continues unabated until atherosclerotic "plaques" are formed on the inside of our blood vessels. These plaques not only cause the diameter of the blood vessels themselves to shrink (hence leading to a full-scale blockage of blood flow), it also causes the blood to become "hyper-coaguable," by increasing the blood's propensity to clot.

> **A person's propensity for illness is directly related to the balance of oxidants to antioxidants within the body.**

The clots that are formed in this manner contribute to blocking the blood vessels entirely, which in turn leads to the symptoms of ischemia, or of low oxygen and nutrient supply to the target tissues that are involved. If this situation is occurring in the brain, a stroke is the typical result, and if the target organ is the heart, a classic heart attack is generally the result.

Fortunately, this degenerative process can also be arrested in the early stages by the oral administration of various antioxidants. For by quenching the free radicals that cause the initial damaging of the inner lining of our blood vessels, antioxidants help to stop the original cause of cardiovascular disease. This is good news indeed, for not only does it give us the ability to actually prevent heart disease many years down the road, it also helps to increase the flow of blood throughout the body in the here and now, which in turn leads to a better functioning body today.

Oxidation can be reduced by eating nutrient-dense, high antioxidant foods, by eating less food, and by supplementing with antioxidants.

## The Quest for Antioxidants

Fortunately, we have available to us today a wide range of very potent antioxidants, which can scavenge and neutralize free radicals before they have a chance to cause disease.

For instance, there are flavonoids, part of a larger group of molecules called polyphenol compounds, that are found in abundance in plants, fruits, vegetables, plant-based beverages, and notably in the pigments of leaves, barks, rinds, seeds, and flowers. The best sources include tea leaves, oranges, citrus fruit, apples, onions, red grapes, berries, and pine bark.[19] Flavonoids:

- Improve memory and concentration and are used to treat attention-deficit disorder.
- Are powerful free-radical scavengers that can boost the effectiveness of Vitamin C in the antioxidant network.
- Regulate nitric oxide, a potent free radical that is a regulator of blood flow.
- Keep your heart healthy in three important ways. They prevent blood clots, protect against oxidation of LDL cholesterol, and lower high blood pressure.
- Improve sexual function in men.
- Reduce inflammation and bolster immune function.

Other well-known antioxidants are Vitamin A, Vitamin C, full-spectrum Vitamin E, including tocotrienols and tocopherols, along with zinc, selenium, manganese, alpha lipoic acid, N-acetyl cysteine, and glutathione.

Clearly, through the work of Packer, Levine, and others, we are discovering just how incredibly pervasive the benefits of antioxidants are. The benefits include bolstering immune and detoxification systems, regulating genes, keeping the brain healthy, retarding and controlling the aging process.

## The Top Antioxidant Foods

1. Small red bean (dried)
2. Pinto bean
3. Blueberry (cultivated)
4. Cranberry
5. Artichoke (cooked)
6. Blackberry
7. Prune
8. Raspberry
9. Strawberry
10. Red Delicious apple
11. Granny Smith apple

12. Pecan
13. Sweet cherry
14. Black plum
15. Russet potato (cooked)
16. Black bean (dried)
17. Wild blueberry
18. Red kidney bean (dried)

SUPER
HEALTH

7 Golden
Keys to
Unlock
Lifelong
Vitality

CORNER 4

# *Healthy Fats*

> *Low-fat diets are associated with greater feelings*
> *of anger, hostility, irritability,*
> *and depression. These mood changes appear*
> *to be biological consequences of inadequate*
> *dietary fat in the central nervous system.*
>
> BRITISH JOURNAL OF NUTRITION

Of the Four Corners of Optimal Nutrition, healthy fats is the most universally misunderstood. In the late 1950s, the American Heart Association advised us to limit our fat intake—implying that all fat is bad. From the mid '60s through the '80s, the message was to eat polyunsaturated vegetable fats and to avoid bad saturated fats. When the bad news about trans fatty acids (TFAs) could no longer be hidden, the message in the '90s changed for us to eat good fats (olive oil, fish) and to avoid bad fats (saturated and trans fats).

Contrary to popular opinion and despite all the confusing messages and warnings, healthy fats are essential to optimal health and do not make you fat. A University of Buffalo study found that a moderate 33 percent fat diet was equally effective for weight loss as a low-fat 18 percent diet, but better at reducing the risk of heart disease and diabetes.

Let's take a quick look at three major types of fat: unsaturated, saturated, and trans. We might think of these fats as "The Good," "The Misunderstood," and "The Ugly."

## The Good—Unsaturated Fats

Unsaturated fats (usually soft at room temperature and often called oils) are of two varieties—polyunsaturated and monounsaturated—and are found in products derived from plant sources. Polyunsaturated fats are found in high concentrations in chia seeds, flaxseeds, fish oil, and borage seed oil. Monounsaturated fats are found in high concentrations in olives, nuts, and avocados. Omega-3s and omega-6s are types of polyunsaturated fats that are essential for normal growth and may play an important role in the prevention and treatment of coronary artery disease, hypertension, arthritis, cancer, and other inflammatory and autoimmune disorders. Most people eat too much omega-6 and are deficient in omega-3s.

> **Fats are the major component of all cell membranes. Fats are to the cell membranes as our skin is to our body.**

## The Misunderstood—Saturated Fats

Saturated fats are mainly animal fats found in meat, dairy products, poultry skin, and egg yolks. Over the years saturated fats have become the dietary scapegoat for nearly everything. They have gotten a bad name because it was once thought that in excess they tend to worsen blood cholesterol levels. However, saturated fats have gotten their bad reputation unfairly, and in fact they have many health benefits. Coconut and coconut oil are plant-based medium chain saturated fats that have been shown to provide extraordinary health benefits.

## The Ugly—Trans Fats

While they exist in nature, trans fatty acids are also produced by heating liquid vegetable oils in the presence of hydrogen, in a process known as hydrogenation. This process increases the oils' firmness and resistance to oxidative spoilage. These are fats that the body cannot easily break down and often lead to blocked arteries and heart disease. Most of the trans fats in the American diet are found in foods such as French fries, onion rings, shortening, margarine, donuts, partially hydrogenated oils, dressings, puffed cheese snacks, potato chips, tortilla chips, burgers, chicken nuggets, ice cream, candy, cookies, and cakes. Unlike saturated fats, trans fats do not produce any good HDL cholesterol, and they raise bad LDL.

## It's Still a Potato Chip

It may say "low fat" and even "organic" on the label, but let's get real . . . a potato chip is a potato chip no matter how you "slice it." While the trans fatty acids may give potato chips and many other products unusually long shelf lives, they're also exceptionally damaging to every organ system in the body, and they're the most damaging to cells of the nervous system and, in particular, the brain. Trans fatty acids damage the body because they displace, and thus supplant, the natural *cis* fatty acids from the body's various cell membranes, with the tragic result that their essential functionality is profoundly damaged relative to the not-found-in-nature "trans"-configuration.

> Some of the most damaging foods to the body are donuts, French fries, potato chips, and other foods deep fried in delicate oils.

This damaged functionality displays itself in the form of a vastly altered permeability of the cellular membrane itself, which in turn results in unwanted molecules making their way inside our cells, while the "right" molecules for optimal health are not absorbed properly. One of the physiological consequences of this is severe and unrelenting inflammation, which itself leads to all sorts of degenerative diseases within the body. So think again before reaching for that Dunkin' Donut.

## What's All the Fuss About Fats?

Americans tend to have a knee-jerk reaction to the word *fat*, even when it's a healthy fat. The low-fat food craze has left behind a terrible misperception in the minds of Americans—that "low in fat" means healthy, and that fats in general are bad. Yet this is far from the truth!

From her work with insulin-resistant patients with Type II diabetes, Dr. Diana Schwarzbein has concluded that:

- Low-fat diets cause heart attacks.
- Eating fat makes you lose body fat.
- It's important to eat high cholesterol foods every day.[20]

According to Schwarzbein, the high carbohydrate, low-fat, moderate protein diet that most dieticians and disease-prevention organizations recommend is the culprit that turns people into diabetics, makes them age faster to the point of acquiring degenerative diseases, and it also keeps them fat and unhealthy as well. She supports her theory with case studies of people who were sick and unhealthy on high carbohydrate, low-fat diets, but who sprang back to life when they "balanced" their diets with more fat and protein.

> **Good fats supply the body with its most concentrated source of energy, which is so lacking in most diets.**

Schwarzbein recommends avoiding "man-made carbohydrates"—processed carbohydrates—in favor of those you can "pick, gather, or milk." She advises patients to eat "as much good fat as their body needs." This means eggs, avocados, flaxseed oil, butter, mayonnaise, and olive oil. Fried foods and hydrogenated fats are, of course, "bad fats," or "damaged fats," as Schwarzbein calls them. You can eat as many eggs a day as you want on this plan, plus meat, saturated fat, cream, and nonstarchy vegetables.

However, remember that every person is an experiment of one. Be honest with yourself and pay attention to how you feel for hours to days and weeks after making any significant change in your diet. Genetically, some people do better with more or less animal products, especially meats.

## Omega-3—The New Vitamin C

As Andrew L. Stoll, M.D. points out in his book *The Omega-3 Connection*, omega-3s may be this millennium's Vitamin C. Historically, humans have been slow to recognize nutritional deficiencies. We now know that Vitamin C deficiency can lead to scurvy. But the nations of Europe didn't really make the connection until the mid

1700s, when an English naval surgeon discovered that oranges and lemons could cure sailors of the disease.[21]

Natural lipids (fatty acids) of the omega-3 EPA/DHA variety are derived from cold water oily fish as well as from wild animals and plants. Omega-3 fatty acids began to disappear from the typical Western diet in the twentieth century, and only recently have we begun to see the health concerns that their absence has caused. Omega-3 fatty acids control many of the most basic functions of the cell. Omega-3 oils are a major constituent of brain cell membranes and are converted to critical brain chemicals.

One can easily see, then, how essential they are for normal nervous system function, and how their deficiency might be linked to mood regulation, attention, memory, and mental health.

Stoll documents that one can see the effects of omega-3 deprivation or loss at every developmental stage of life. Deficiency in infants results in sub-optimal cognitive and visual development. In children, it can result in lowered attention, impulse control, and susceptibility to depression. In teenagers and adults, it can cause a greater tendency toward violence and hostility. And in aging adults, it puts them at higher risk for stroke, memory problems, and dementia.[22]

Omega-3 fatty acids also benefit the body by increasing insulin sensitivity. We tend to think of circulation as the process of flow through arteries and veins; obviously this is the case, but the major part of circulation is what goes into and out of the cell itself, by crossing the all-important cell membrane.

Regardless of what nutrient is delivered to a cell in the blood, it will have no effect at all if it can't get into the cell itself. Cellular circulation is deeply affected by the intake of fatty acids, which in turn affects the fluidity of the cell membrane. Increasing the omega-3 content of one's diet significantly increases cell-membrane fluidity and hence allows more nutrients to reach the cells themselves.

One of the more profound uses of omega-3 fatty acids is in the treatment of a wide range of mental illnesses, including bipolar disorder, unipolar major depression, postpartum depression, schizophrenia, and attention-deficit disorder. The brain does not function well unless adequate amounts of omega-3s are circulating in the bloodstream and are incorporated into cell membranes. It appears that increases in omega-3 dietary intake raises the levels of the neurotransmitter dopamine, which is related to motivation and ambition, qualities often lacking in depressed people.[23]

## Time for an Oil Change

The bottom line is that healthy fats (i.e., essential fatty acids) are critical to life. The body is designed to manufacture most of the fats it needs. However, there are two major classes of fats that the body needs but cannot manufacture on its own; hence they must be obtained through diet alone. These fats are the essential fatty acids (EFAs).

> Omega-3 fatty acids are essential for normal growth and may play an important role in the prevention and treatment of coronary artery disease, hypertension, arthritis, cancer, and other inflammatory and autoimmune disorders.

The EFA classes are called omega-3 and omega-6 fatty acids. There are two categories of omega-3: plant sources, such as flaxseed that contains alpha linolenic acid (ALA), and marine sources, such as salmon, tuna, mackerel, sardines, and anchovies. The most effective forms of omega-3s are EPA (eicosapentanoic acid) and DHA (docosahexaenoic acid). Scientists agree that less than 15 percent of ALA converts to DHA and with little or no conversion to EPA. Due to this poor conversion, plant omega-3, such as flaxseed, cannot on its own meet our body's nutritional requirement for omega-3.

Fish oil from cold water fish is a direct source of EPA and DHA. In fact, fish oil has been shown to significantly increase life span and delay disease where no other dietary changes are made.[24] One would assume that eating fish regularly would be prudent; however, it is unsafe to eat fish, as virtually every species has been shown to contain unsafe levels of mercury and other contaminants.

Similar to omega-3 EPA/DHA, gamma linolenic acid (GLA) is one of the most powerful forms of omega-6. When GLA (found in borage seed oil and evening primrose oil) is combined with EPA, beneficial prostaglandins (short-lived local anti-inflammatory hormones derived from specialized essential fatty acids) are produced.[25]

## Where to Find Omega-3s?

So is it as easy as taking a fish oil supplement? Unfortunately, it's not. While high dose fish oil (equivalent to a piece of fish) has extraordinary health benefits, it is extremely susceptible to oxidation/lipid peroxidation within the body unless therapeutic doses of fat soluble antioxidants (tocotrienols and full-spectrum Vitamin E) are taken along with the fish oil. Most commercially available fish oils contain miniscule amounts of Vitamin E, which addresses the issue of shelf life, but has no protective effect within the body. *Purified antioxidant protected fish oils appear to be the only wise choice.*

The body must receive a continuous supply of EFAs in proper ratios in order to ensure proper production of prostaglandins. Prostaglandins are beneficial hormone-like compounds that affect virtually every system in the body. They regulate pain and swelling, help maintain proper blood pressure and cholesterol levels, and promote efficiency in the nervous system.

Because the American diet is rich in omega-6 foods and salad dressings (sesame, sunflower, corn, peanut, and soy, to name a few) and low in cold water fish, most people tend to eat far too much omega-6 and are dangerously deficient in omega-3. Both the level of omega-3 and the ratio of omega-6 to omega-3 fatty acids are critically important, and a healthy ratio of omega-6 to omega-3 fatty acids is thought to be approximately 3:1. But many Americans have an imbalance of 20:1. The answer is usually as simple as taking fewer omega-6s and adding antioxidant protected fish oil to your diet. Also, as I will note later, grass-fed meat and poultry has higher levels of omega-3 and is much healthier for you. It's well worth the price.

Remember . . . antioxidant protected fish oil is fish oil that contains sufficient fat soluble antioxidants (tocotrienols and tocopherols) to block the risk of lipid peroxidation of the delicate fish oil within the body.

## What You Need to Know About Fish Oil

1.  The purest forms of fish oil are derived from sardines and anchovies and purified through a flash-molecular distillation process.

2.  Fish oil must be rigorously tested to ensure that it is free of impurities, including PCBs, heavy metals, or oxidized contaminants.

3.  The most beneficial omega-3 is EPA and DHA, which can only be found in high concentration in fish oil. Plant-based omega-3 from flaxseed oil cannot give you all the benefits of fish oil.

4.  When taking fish oil, use a high quality full-spectrum Vitamin E with tocotrienols and tocopherols to protect against lipid peroxidation, which is toxic to every cell in the body.

5.  Fish oil will retain its original flavor and aroma. If not, the oils have been over-processed.

6.  What to AVOID:

-   Every species of commercial fish has been shown to contain unsafe levels of mercury and other contaminants.
-   Farm-raised fish are contaminated for different reasons (they are fed toxins).
-   Super concentrated fish oils are reconstructed into an unnatural etherified form.
-   Liquid fish oils due to risk of oxidation. Fish oil should be oxygen protected in a gelatin capsule (buffalo gelatin is the safest).

## Summary of the Four Corners of Optimal Nutrition

In summary, the Four Corners of Optimal Nutrition can be likened to a team of four players. When all are used in harmony and synergy with the right balance, the results will be greater than the total of the four taken separately. Let's review it for a final time:

1.  Calorie restriction decreases free-radical damage all the way down to the mitochondria, and thereby allows them to reproduce in a

healthy fashion, protecting our energy supply and production.

2. Consuming low glycemic foods ensures that we do not elevate blood sugar, forcing the release of excess insulin, promoting insulin resistance, with the negative consequences of inflammation and fat storage.

3. Healthy fats are essential to maintain cellular membrane function. This allows cells to efficiently exchange nutrients and wastes and to protect themselves from free-radical damage.

4. Antioxidants work throughout the cell and even down into the mitochondria to protect our energy supply from free radicals.

Implementing the Four Corners Program of Health and Vitality can add life to your years, and maybe years to your life.

**Hundreds of studies have shown that fish oil reduces inflammation and the occurrence of chronic diseases and cancers.**

# The Four Corners Nutritional Program

*The rest of your life begins today—*
*and what a great day it can be!*
*The power you need to create anything*
*you desire already lies within you.*

STU MITTLEMAN

Finding the foods that fit into the Four Corners approach is a lot easier than you might think!

## How to Get Started

### CHANGE YOUR BREAKFAST, CHANGE YOUR LIFE

Breakfast is the meal where most people make the biggest nutritional mistakes, ranging from not eating anything to eating sugars, grains, pasteurized dairy products, pork products, or fried foods. Don't let the breakfast food paradigm force you into making poor breakfast choices. It is nutritionally proper to eat lunch and dinner foods for breakfast (i.e., leftover chicken or steak and salad from dinner). The goal is to get protein, healthy fats, fiber, and low glycemic carbs at *every* meal. Organic eggs with steamed or sautéed vegetables are an excellent choice.

### DRINK LOTS OF FRESH, PURIFIED SPRING WATER

You should drink 8 to 12 glasses per day, which can be as much as 1 quart per 50 pounds of body weight per day. Do not regularly drink distilled water and do not drink water in cloudy plastic containers.[26]

Those who drink water exclusively seem to experience the best results. However, occasional drink alternatives can include organic herbal teas (dioxin- and caffeine-free) served hot or cold, lemon water, or lemonade sweetened with Stevia, Agavi, or TheraSweet™—excellent natural sweeteners with virtually no glycemic index. If you choose a sweet-tasting beverage, it's best to drink it with food. (See Golden Key #1—Hydration.)

## LEARN WAYS TO BALANCE A NEGATIVE WITH A POSITIVE

Recognize that there are only two reasons why people should eat and at least three reasons why we actually do. The two essential reasons are Foundational in nature (i.e., physical building blocks of the body) and Fuel. The third reason why people eat is for Fun. Most people are not going to give up eating for fun, so the trick is to discover those fun foods that are the best for your health.

> **Adopt a few good changes in your diet and you'll feel so much better you'll want to adopt more!**

Learn how to reduce the negative impact that some of these fun foods have on the human body. For instance, if you choose to consume a high starch meal, a sweet dessert, or an alcoholic beverage, then eat high fiber foods, such as a large dark green salad or other greens, or eat quality fats and proteins beforehand, or you can get all three by having a Living Fuel shake. It is also helpful to drink water with lemon or have olive oil and vinegar on your salad. All these steps help to slow the pace at which sugar enters your bloodstream, thereby reducing the harmful insulin response from the concentrated sugars.

## HAVE A SNACK STRATEGY AND INVENTORY ON HAND

Great snack choices are smoothies, berries, salads, above-ground raw vegetables, soft-boiled eggs, raw nuts, and seeds (walnuts, almonds, macadamia nuts, Brazil nuts, coconuts, chia seeds, and pumpkin seeds). Eat organic whenever possible.

## What You Should Eat

Even if you are not ready to make radical nutritional changes, there are simple steps you can do that can dramatically impact your health:

- Eliminate all sweet drinks and stimulants and drink 8 to 12 glasses of water per day.
- Minimize all sugars, high GI foods, and grains (replace with raw and minimally cooked vegetables). Grains can be a good choice if they are sprouted.
- Minimize pasteurized dairy products.
- Take antioxidant protected purified fish oil daily.
- Minimize heat in preparing foods.

> Discover easy, natural strategies that God has created for you to live in super health, and start with the purest, freshest foods He has made.

### EAT A VARIETY OF SALADS, GREEN VEGETABLES, AND BRIGHT-COLORED (ABOVE-GROUND) VEGETABLES

Some good choices include broccoli, spinach, kale, mustard greens, collard greens, mixed greens, asparagus, green beans, peppers, cucumbers, Brussels sprouts, barley greens, radishes, and onions. These vegetables deliver the most nutrition when they are raw, juiced, or slightly steamed, as cooking decreases the nutrient quality. You can't get too many of these!

### EAT EGGS

Eat eggs from organically raised free-range or free-roaming hens that are not grain-fed. Look for high DHA on the label. Buying organic eggs is important, because processed or "tricked-chicken" eggs, where farmers trick the chickens into laying more eggs by using lights 24/7, are not as nutritious. A natural free-roaming hen lays approximately 80 eggs per year, whereas a tricked chicken lays as many as 250 eggs per year. Don't be afraid to add more eggs to your diet. Contrary to popular belief, eggs do not significantly increase blood cholesterol levels.[27] Excess sugar and high GI foods are the cause of high cholesterol levels. Additionally, eat only eggs that have been prepared with low heat, such as soft-boiled, poached, over-easy, or even raw[28] eggs. If your eggs have been burned, do not eat them, and if they are not organic, do not eat them raw!

## EAT CHICKEN, ORGANIC TURKEY, AND WILD GAME

If you are not eating organic foods and grain-free/grass-fed meats and eggs because of their compromised omega-6 to omega-3 ratios, then it is even more critical that you take antioxidant protected fish oil, in doses equivalent to the oil from eating a medium-sized piece of fish.

## EAT FISH (BUT ONLY FISH CERTIFIED TO BE FREE OF MERCURY)

Testing shows that unsafe mercury levels and other pollutants contaminate most fish, including farm-raised fish.[29] Therefore, you may want to minimize your fish intake and take an antioxidant protected fish oil such as Living Fuel's Omega-3&E. If you choose to eat fish, the fish with higher levels of the essential fats EPA and DHA include Pacific salmon, summer flounder, haddock, anchovies, and sardines. Avoid commercial farm-raised fish, as they are fed pollutants and are virtually devoid of omega-3 EPA/DHA essential fats.

## EAT OTHER EXCELLENT SOURCES OF PROTEIN

These include grain-free, grass-fed lamb, bison, or beef (commercial beef has numerous problems and should be minimized). In his book *21 Days to a Healthy Heart*, Al Watson provides this insight into the meats we are eating. "Starting in the 1950s, the meat industry began taking animals off pasture and grass and putting them into feedlots and on grain. Grass is high in omega-3. In humans and in cattle, omega-3 promotes leanness. Grains are high in omega-6. In humans and cattle, omega-6 promotes obesity. More omega-6 and less omega-3 is a recipe for obesity and inflammatory conditions such as blood vessel damage and cancer. Cattle put on weight more rapidly on a high grain diet than they will in the pasture, even when they consume exactly the same number of calories. The omega-6 rich grain diet creates more fatty acid synthetase, an enzyme that promotes fat production. Meat from grain-fed animals contains as much as 20 times more omega-6 than omega-3. Grass-fed beef has an n-6/n-3 ratio of 3:1, ideal for human health."[30]

Look for pasture-fed, grain-free, hormone-free meat at your local health food stores or check out www.eatwild.com.

## EAT APPROPRIATE SOUPS, BROTHS, AND STEWS

These items are also healthy as long as their ingredients are consistent with the above.

## How You Should Eat

First, it's critical to eat smaller portions, smaller bites, and to minimally cook or eat raw foods when appropriate. Also, you may hear your mother's voice whispering in your ear when I say this, but *chew your food!* Try to masticate your food to a liquid form and then swallow it. This will predigest your food with the enzymes in your saliva. It also provides neurological stimulation of your stomach and pancreas to increase their acid and digestive enzyme production.

## What You Shouldn't Eat

The foods to avoid are the majority of foods that most people eat and by their nature are highly addictive. This part of the Four Corners approach may require some "won't power" at first, even though you will not be hungry. However, realize that you will be making better choices and learning new habits. Most people overcome their unhealthy cravings and food addictions to coffee, dairy, grains, and sugar after only one to four weeks.

### TOP 7 WORST FOODS

1. Sugar and White Flour
2. Doughnuts
3. French Fries (and Nearly All Deep Fried Foods)
4. Soft Drinks, Coffee, Sports Drinks & Fruit Juices
5. Alcoholic beverages
6. Pasteurized Dairy
7. Peanut Butter

## MINIMIZE SUGAR AND FOODS THAT TURN TO SUGAR QUICKLY AFTER EATING[31]

Such items include all grains, syrups, pasta, potatoes, white rice, oatmeal, breads, and cakes.[32] A good rule when considering these types of carbohydrates is "If it's white, it ain't right." This rule is generally accurate; exceptions include cauliflower, radishes, garlic, and onions. Regular consumption of sugar and high glycemic foods causes chronic hyperinsulinemia, which is the root cause of most diseases of aging.[33]

## MINIMIZE SNACK FOODS, DESSERTS, MOST FRUITS, SOFT DRINKS,[34] SPORTS DRINKS, FRUIT JUICES,[35] SWEET DRINKS,[36] COFFEE,[37] AND ALCOHOLIC BEVERAGES[38]

Alcohol is essentially liquid sugar and is extremely high glycemic, and it adversely raises insulin levels and compromises sleep patterns. If you must have a drink or juice or other "destructive carbohydrate," then treat each such food or drink as if it were a dessert and govern yourself accordingly.

## AVOID PORK PRODUCTS, SUCH AS BACON, SAUSAGE, AND HAM, AND SHELLFISH, SUCH AS LOBSTER, SHRIMP, AND CRAB

Pigs can be a breeding ground for potentially dangerous infections, and shellfish have been found to contain high mercury levels. (See Ten Common Myths About Health/Pork).

## MINIMIZE OR AVOID ALL PASTEURIZED DAIRY PRODUCTS[39]

Only use such foods if you get them raw, right from the farm, prior to the pasteurization process (eggs are poultry *not* dairy). Raw organic butter from grass-fed cows is very nutritious and an exception to the no-dairy rule, but minimize all pasteurized dairy products.

## MINIMIZE UNFERMENTED SOY PRODUCTS

Soy is not healthy for most people because of its anti-nutritional properties (unless it is non-GMO and fermented soy, such as soy sauce, miso, or tempeh); 98 percent of the soy crop worldwide is genetically modified, which has been shown to have negative health consequences.[40]

## AVOID ALL JUNK FOOD,[41] FRENCH FRIES,[42] FRIED FOODS,[43] PIZZA,[44] AND MARGARINE[45]

Following the Four Corners guidelines can have a profound impact on your health, life, and performance. It is a lifestyle program that works best when complemented by regular exercise, sleep, meditation, and prayer. Give yourself some time to become acclimated to the dietary changes you've made and to enjoy the incredible variety of health benefits that are derived from a low calorie, low glycemic, high antioxidant, and healthy fats diet. Eating intelligently and well is a pleasure . . . it will not only make you feel better . . . in very little time it will start to taste better too. My hope is that as you begin to implement these powerful health changes in your own life, you will begin to discover new and creative ways to enjoy the foods that will help you live longer and better.

# At-a-Glance Foods to Eat and Avoid

## BEVERAGES

- Drink 8 to 12 glasses of spring or purified water a day.
- Drink caffeine-free organic herbal teas.
- Eliminate all soft drinks and fruit juices.
- Minimize coffee, alcoholic beverages, and artificial sweeteners.

## FOODS

- Eat a variety of salads, green vegetables, and bright-colored, above-ground vegetables. Some good choices include broccoli, spinach, kale, mixed greens, asparagus, green beans, peppers, cucumbers, barley greens, radishes, garlic, and onions.
- Eat organic, free-range eggs.
- Eat berries (cranberries, strawberries, raspberries, and blueberries).
- Eat organic chicken, turkey, and wild game, such as grass-fed beef, venison, buffalo, lamb, and deer.
- Eat antioxidant protected fish oil and certified mercury-free Pacific salmon, summer flounder, haddock, anchovies, and sardines. See www.vitalchoice.com.
- Use virgin coconut oil, virgin olive oil, GLA, conjugated linolenic acid (CLA), and raw organic butter.
- Use Celtic Sea Salt or Real Salt brand mineral sea salts.
- Eat nuts (almonds, cashews, and macadamia) and organic coconut.
- Minimize all grains (bread, rice, and cereal); avoid junk foods, anything deep fried, such as French fries and pizza.

- Minimize pasteurized dairy products, such as milk, cheese, and cream.
- Minimize unfermented, genetically modified soy products.
- Minimize grain-fed, commercial beef, pork products, and shellfish.
- Avoid farm-raised fish, such as catfish or salmon, and other fish with high mercury levels, such as tuna.
- Avoid hydrogenated oil found in commercially prepared baked goods, margarines, snacks, and processed foods.
- Minimize all sugars (candy, cookies, cakes, and syrups) and chips.

SUPER
HEALTH

7 Golden
Keys to
Unlock
Lifelong
Vitality

# Four Corners Shopping List

## Vegetables
Asparagus
Avocado
Beets
Bell peppers
Broccoli
Brussels sprouts
Cabbage
Carrots
Cauliflower
Celery
Collard greens
Cucumber
Eggplant
Fennel bulb
Garlic
Green beans
Green peas
Kale
Leeks
Mustard greens
Olives
Onions
Parsley
Romaine lettuce
Root vegetables
Sea vegetables

Spinach
Squash, summer
Squash, winter
Sweet potato, with
skin
Swiss chard
Tomato, fresh
Turnip greens
Yam

## Fish *(only Certified Mercury/PCB-Free)*
Anchovies
Fish oil with
antioxidants
Sardines

## Fruits
Apple
Apricot
Banana
Blueberries
Cantaloupe
Cranberries
Fig
Grapefruit
Grapes
Kiwi fruit

Lemons and limes
Orange
Papaya
Pear, Bartlett
Pineapple
Plum
Prune
Raisins
Raspberries
Strawberries
Watermelon

## Dairy and Eggs
Cheeses, soft raw
milk
Organic eggs,
free-range
Milk, raw goat
or cow
Yogurt, raw goat
or cow

## Beans and Legumes
Black beans
Dried peas
Garbanzo beans

Kidney beans
Lentils
Lima beans
Miso
Navy beans
Pinto beans
Tempeh

Poultry and
Lean Meats
(organic)
Beef, lean, grass-fed,
    grain-free
Bison
Chicken, free-range
Lamb
Turkey, roast
Venison

Nuts, Seeds,
and Oils
Almond Nut Butter
Almonds
Cashews
Chia seeds
Coconut
Living Fuel Rx™
    CocoChia™
Living Fuel Rx™
    Extra Virgin
    Coconut Oil
Garden of Life®
    Extra Virgin
    Coconut Oil
Flaxseed
Macadamia Nut
    Butter

Macadamia
Olive oil
Pumpkin seeds
Valencia peanut
Walnuts

Grain Grasses
Barley grass
Oat grass
Rye grass
Wheat grass

Sprouts
Quinoa
Spelt

Other
Acceptable
Grains
Buckwheat
Rice, brown
Steel-cut Oats

Spices and
Herbs
Basil
Black pepper
Cayenne pepper
Chili pepper, red,
    dried
Cinnamon, ground
Cloves
Coriander seeds
Cumin seeds
Dill weed, dried

Ginger
Mustard seeds
Oregano
Peppermint leaves,
    fresh
Rosemary
Sage
Thyme, ground
Turmeric, ground

Natural
Sweeteners
Blackstrap molasses
Brown rice syrup
Living Fuel Rx™
    Therasweet™
Raw honey
Stevia

Other
Green/white/black
    teas
Celtic Sea Salt™ or
    Real Salt™
Soy sauce (tamari),
    organic

Foundational
Foods
Whole Meal Super
    Foods
Living Fuel Rx™
    Super Greens
Living Fuel Rx™
    Super Berry™

**Green Drinks**
Garden of Life®
  Perfect Food®

**Protein Supplements**
Garden of Life®
  Goatein® (pure
  goat's milk protein)
IMUPlus™ non-
  denatured whey
  protein

Living Fuel Rx™
  Living Protein™
RenewPro™ non-
  denatured whey
  protein

**Foundational Supplements**
Living Fuel Rx™
  Omega 3&E™
Living Fuel Rx™
  Pure D&A™

**Foundational Supplements for Athletes and People Over 40**
Carnosine
CLA (conjugated
  linololeic acid)
CoQ-10
Phosphatidylserine
Antioxidant complex
Creatine

Also, see www.makersdiet.com for other Four Corners foods and supplements.

# Exercise

**Regular exercise is critically
important to one's health.**
*Studies show that exercise reduces the risk of heart attacks
and strokes, improves lung and immune system function,
increases mental vitality, and lowers blood pressure,
blood glucose, cholesterol, and triglyceride levels. Exercise
can dramatically affect "secondary aging"—the incidence
and severity of diseases associated with aging, such as diabetes,
osteoporosis, and muscle and bone strength loss. Lifelong
exercise has been shown to reduce mortality and increase
life expectancy. People who exercise feel better, perform better
in both work and leisure activities, and enjoy life more than
people who do not exercise regularly.*

*But I discipline my body and bring it into subjection...*
1 CORINTHIANS 9:27

# Exercise

> *Food fuels the furnace of metabolism;*
> *exercise stokes its fire.*
>
> MAJID ALI, M.D.

If you're waiting for a magic pill that will melt the fat away and keep the weight off and your body in the fullness of health, you've wasted enough time. Along with the proper hydration and nutrition, God has designed your body to naturally burn the fat and build muscle as you exercise it. Your body is a gift from God that keeps on giving if you treat it right. It is possible to achieve a strong, healthy, beautifully shaped body that is full of energy and vitality for a lifetime.

But if you're among the 50 percent of Americans who live a totally sedentary lifestyle, you're not giving your body a chance to function in the healthy way God designed it. Despite repeated warnings from the Surgeon General and the National Center for Chronic Disease Prevention, millions of Americans are suffering from illnesses that can be prevented or improved through regular exercise. Far too many of us continue to pay the price for consuming more calories than we burn and for abusing our body through lack of care.

There's a simple reason why exercise is such a powerful key to weight loss. Exercise burns calories, and when you burn calories, your body must compensate for the extra energy being used. To compensate, the mitochondria, or power plants, inside your body cells divide, which burns twice as many calories. Nothing else will do that.

And there's a simple reason why exercise is so key to health. "Every time you work out and sweat, you stress your muscles, draining them of energy stores; you actually injure them a little bit. It's not enough to do long-term damage, but enough to stimulate repair and growth and to make muscles a little stronger. Enzymes and proteins from those muscles enter your bloodstream, where they start a powerful chain reaction of inflammation, or decay, then repair, and finally growth. And what an incredible process this is: the proteins that control inflammation and growth are called cytokines, and they regulate crucial metabolic pathways in almost every tissue and cell in your body. . . . Even moderate exercise will stimulate the good guys—growth cytokines—who will eventually overwhelm the agents of decay. . . . Every joint, bone, organ, and even the far reaches of your brain get a dose of healthy, rejuvenating chemistry each time you sweat."[1]

Studies show that the benefits of exercise are nearly unlimited. It reduces the risk of heart attacks and strokes, improves lung and immune system function, increases mental vitality, lowers blood pressure, blood glucose, cholesterol, and triglyceride levels. How's that for starters? Exercise can dramatically lower the incidence and severity of diseases associated with aging, such as diabetes, osteoporosis, and muscle and bone strength loss.

Lifelong exercise has been shown to reduce mortality and increase life expectancy. People who exercise feel better, as exercise causes the release of endorphins, which are the body's natural feel-good hormones. Exercise also helps remove the adrenaline that gets pumped into our bloodstream through stress, and thus it helps keep stress under control. People who exercise perform better in both work and leisure activities and enjoy life more than people who do not exercise regularly.

Exercise throughout life is optimal, but studies have shown people in their 90s can improve strength and increase muscle mass after only two weight training sessions per week for six weeks. Clearly, it is never too late to start, and there's no excuse for couch potatoes. Research has even suggested that otherwise sedentary individuals can increase strength by mentally visualizing exercise without any physical exercise. That's the power of the brain.[2]

## Specific Research on the Benefits From Exercise

Keep in mind as you read this research that the results can be even more dramatic when exercise is combined with the other six Golden Keys, starting with good hydration and nutrition.

## DEPRESSION AND AGE-RELATED MENTAL DECLINE

Researchers found that walking for 30 minutes each day quickly improved the patients' symptoms—faster, in fact, than antidepressant drugs typically do. The results indicate that, in selected patients with major depression, aerobic training can produce a substantial improvement in symptoms in a short time. In one study that compared exercise with antidepressants among older adults, investigators found that physical activity was the more effective depression-fighter.[3] In a separate study, researchers found that an hour of aerobics reduced tension, anger, and fatigue among their study participants, with the benefit being significantly greater among those who felt depressed before the exercise bout.[4]

There is growing evidence that regular physical activity helps ward off mental declines as people age and may even protect against Alzheimer's disease. A study out of Canada suggests that exercise cuts the risk of Alzheimer's and less-devastating mental losses, particularly in women. In a five-year study of men and women aged 65 and older, researchers found that exercisers were less likely to develop Alzheimer's and other forms of dementia and were less likely to see a drop-off in their mental abilities.[5]

## LONGEVITY

A study of more than 115,000 female nurses found weight and activity levels are both powerful predictors of longevity, and that being either overweight or sedentary independently increases the risk of death. Being obese triples the risk of heart disease as well as produces a tenfold increase in the chance of developing diabetes. Women who were obese and inactive had a 2.5 times higher mortality rate than women who were lean and active, while obese women who were active were twice as likely to die a premature death. Obese women who worked out for at least 3.5 hours a week experienced a death rate that was 91 percent higher than lean women who exercised similarly. While physical activity improves health, it by no means erases the high health risks associated with excess weight.[6] Centenarian studies show virtually all people who live over one hundred years live active lifestyles and are not overweight.

## DIABETES, SYNDROME X, HEART DISEASE, AND HDL

The Diabetes Prevention Program is the first large study to show that losing weight and exercising can effectively delay diabetes in a wide range of overweight men and women who are just a step away from having full-blown diabetes. This study demonstrates that lifestyle changes can actually prevent diabetes in nearly 60 percent of those who are poised to develop the disease. Type II, or adult-onset, diabetes is the most common form of the disease, accounting for 95 percent of cases in the United States. It is the leading cause of kidney failure, limb amputations, and new blindness, and it contributes to heart disease and stroke—two of today's major killers.[7]

Exercising, even moderately, can significantly reduce the risk of Syndrome X (metabolic syndrome), a condition that increases heart disease and diabetes risk among older adults, according to a study. Some 43 percent of participants had metabolic syndrome when the study began. At the end of six months among the exercise group, no new cases of metabolic syndrome developed, and metabolic syndrome was resolved in nine people for a total reduction of 41 percent. In the control group, eight people had their metabolic syndrome resolved, while four new cases of metabolic syndrome developed, resulting in a total reduction of 18 percent.[8]

A study of nearly 40,000 women found that walking, even at a moderate clip, reduced heart disease risk, including among those who smoked, were overweight, and had high cholesterol. Women who spend as little as one hour walking each week can cut their risk of heart disease in half.[9]

Certain obese men can increase their levels of "good" cholesterol through regular extended endurance exercise, a new study has found.

All four groups in the study experienced small reductions in body fat during the training period, with the greatest losses seen in men and women with high triglycerides and low HDL cholesterol.[10]

## CANCER

Women who stay highly active throughout life are less likely to develop ovarian cancer, according to a new study. Researchers studied more than 2,100 women and found that those who exercised more than six hours per week were 27 percent less likely to develop ovarian cancer than women who exercised less than one hour each week.[11]

Exercise reduces bowel transit time and thereby the duration of contact between fecal carcinogens and the mucosal lining of the colon, which is critical in colon cancer development. Physical activity may also reduce the risk of breast and endometrial cancer through its normalizing effect on body weight and composition. Athletes show lower levels of circulating testosterone than non-athletes, and testosterone influences the development of prostate cancer, leading to the hypothesis that physical activity may protect against prostrate cancer.[12]

> **One pound of muscle is thought to burn 35 calories a day, whereas 1 pound of fat burns only 2 calories!**

## LEPTIN, THE OBESITY HORMONE

The results of a recent study suggest that lifestyle changes may lower levels of leptin, the "obesity hormone" thought to be involved in appetite regulation. The investigators also found that leptin levels declined significantly in men and women who made changes in diet, exercise, or both. When the researchers took into account the amount of fat lost during the study, they found that leptin levels dropped more than expected.[13]

## IMPOTENCE

Men who burned at least 200 calories a day through exercise were less likely than inactive men to become impotent. Exercise may ward off impotence for the same reasons it can prevent heart attacks, by keeping blood vessels clear.[14]

## MUSCLE IS INVALUABLE

Without resistance exercises, studies tell us that between the ages of 20 and 30 we begin to lose muscle, and this continues as we age. Loss of muscle slows our body metabolism, leading to fewer calories burned naturally by the body. Keep in mind that one pound of muscle is thought to burn about 35 calories a day, whereas 1 pound of fat burns only 2 calories! So, typically, as we age we lose muscle and gain fat simultaneously, often without noticing it. We may eat the same number of calories and just keep adding the pounds because of the change in our body composition. This shows how extremely important it is to exercise and build muscle.

Think about it. There are 3,500 calories stored in a pound of fat. If you were to gain 10 pounds of muscle or lean body mass through exercise, you increase your metabolic rate by about 350 calories a day (10 x 35 calories). Over a period of just 10 days, those 10 new pounds of muscle will burn off 1 pound of body fat naturally. Think of the new you that's possible and how much better you would feel, and it all happens naturally. Even if you add only 5 pounds of muscle, that's 175 extra calories burned a day and 63,875 calories or 18 pounds a year.[15] Moreover, when you follow the Four Corners Program, along with the other Golden Keys, you will greatly compound the results! I am going to show you how to accomplish increased muscle mass with relative ease.

# The Masters of Physical Fitness

We live in an era dominated by weightlifting for strength, but I believe that the true masters of physical fitness over the past one hundred years used a far more effective form of exercise: Isoflexion™ and isometric resistance exercises. Unlike weightlifters who pack on massive muscle bulk, these masters of physical fitness are sculpted like Greek statues and routinely perform amazing acts of strength and flexibility that men twice their size cannot achieve. And yet these individuals train without using weights! This may sound absurd to you, but their method of exercise delivers all the strength development you'll ever need *without* the stress on your joints, ligaments, tendons, and nerves that tends to lead to significant loss of flexibility and injury over an extended period of time. The Seven Tiger Moves that I am about to show you will develop tremendous strength and flexibility with a lot less effort than you might imagine, regardless of your level of fitness or lack thereof.

I know many athletes and health enthusiasts who have been very successful with their weightlifting programs for long periods of time and who are very comfortable with what they are doing. I was one of them! But I discovered that I had maxed out in strength and had therefore lost much of my flexibility and range of motion. Flexibility is critical for everyone and is a measure of youthfulness, regardless of fitness level. Getting your flexibility back after a dramatic loss in your range of motion requires good information and a tremendous amount of dedication.

When aging athletes are said to have lost a step, I believe they have simply lost flexibility through the wrong types of exercises, or a lack of variety in their exercises and a lack of proper rest, coupled with poor stretching techniques and a poor diet. The Seven Tiger Moves naturally accomplish wonders for both strength and flexibility. Nevertheless, if you need to go further with flexibility, I have seen athletes have amazing transformations using optimal nutrition and the advanced flexibility techniques set forth in Bob Cooley's book, *The Genius of Stretching,* and Meridian Stretching (www.meridianstretching.com). If you are one of these people, I challenge you to incorporate the system I am about to present, either by incorporating it into your present training regimen or by doing it alone, in order to see if you can increase your strength, flexibility, and muscle definition. You will!

## EARLE E. LIEDERMAN

Liederman was probably the most instrumental person in creating America's awareness of strength and physical conditioning. Utilizing a brilliant series of ads throughout the late 1910s and all of the 1920s, he built a huge following by offering his exercise course through mail-order. He was the undisputed First King of the Mail-Order Bodybuilders. Many people still feel that his original books were the most thorough and well-conceived books *ever published* on this subject.

The Liederman exercise course was primarily *free hand* resistance exercises. He placed great emphasis on the push-up as the key to upper body strength and development, and the single knee bend as the key to the lower body development. He also challenged his students to do a wide variety of chinning exercises, and he had a few exercises that required his elastic chest expander. The entire course was written so that anyone could train at home and attain the same physical development that he did.

## CHARLES ATLAS

In 1917, Earle Liederman met the young man, Angelo Siciliano, who had changed his name to Charles Atlas, and the two men put together a vaudeville act that showcased their strength, hand-balancing skills, and physical development. Young Atlas had transformed his physique using similar weight-resistance exercises that Liederman himself had taught. Atlas had learned the secret of stretching his muscles with great tension through watching the big jungle cats at the Brooklyn Zoo. He then added push-ups, sit-ups, and deep knee bends to develop his own physical training system.

**The best health-building exercise systems prevent injury, speed healing, and are not a source of injury.**

Charles Atlas went on to become a legend, and his mail-order bodybuilding course literally transformed hundreds of thousands of young men from the 1930s to the 1960s. And among those thousands of students was my friend, young John Peterson, who determined at the age of ten to never allow another Goliath-like bully to beat him up again. It is ironic that Atlas began his career in a similar fashion, by getting sand kicked in his face by a beach thug at the young age of sixteen.

## ROCKY MARCIANO

The world has seen some extraordinary heavyweight boxing champions in the past, but Rocky Marciano, at only 5 foot ten and 184 pounds, was a class unto himself. After taking a beating for twelve consecutive rounds, Rocky's explosive knockout of Jersey Joe Walcott in the thirteenth round during his first title shot has to be seen to be believed. If you see the video of that shattering right blow to Walcott's jaw, you'll realize that pound for pound, "The Rock" was the strongest and best-conditioned fighter in history. Where did his strength come from? It came, of course, from his teacher and mentor, Charles Atlas, who was pleased to claim Rocky as one of his students. It was the body-resistance exercises and hundreds of push-ups of Charles Atlas's training system that gave Rocky his phenomenal strength and punching power.

## JOHN McSWEENEY

John McSweeney was a master of the martial arts. He was one of legendary Ed Parker's first martial arts students, and he ultimately became a superior martial arts professional and teacher. His seven "Tiger Moves" system is literally second to none, which is why I'm recommending them in this book. McSweeney tried just about every exercise system imaginable—weightlifting, calisthenics, isometrics, yoga, Tai Chi, and Qi Gong. But in terms of strength benefits, physique development, and the acquisition of vibrant health, he was adamant that nothing compared to his remarkable "Tiger Moves" system. Even when he was in his 70s, he had retained so much of his strength and incredibly powerful physique that he could throw an overhand right with the power of a young Rocky Marciano.

## MATT FUREY

Matt Furey was a national and world title martial artist and wrestler, who had studied with Karl Gotch, the world's foremost authority on the lost art of "Catch-As-Catch-Can." Using the body-weight exercise technique that was taught by Gotch, Furey could hardly believe how far his strength, endurance, and flexibility powers had leaped forward. In 2002, Furey published his groundbreaking bestseller, *Combat Conditioning,* which turned the world of strength training and physical conditioning on its ear. Not only did this program excel over all other systems, many people who had been previously injured using incorrect training methods discovered that their bodies could actually begin to heal while using his exercises. From the Furey training method, I will introduce you to the Furey Push-up and the Furey Bridge.

## JOHN PETERSON

John Peterson is a friend of mine and, in my opinion, is today's Charles Atlas. He is a walking encyclopedia on the history of physical fitness. John's personal story in *Pushing Yourself to Power* is worth the price of the book alone. The fact that he is the most physically fit man I know, yet he's in his early 50s, is amazing enough. But the fact that he contracted polio in 1956, which left his legs dreadfully misshapen, and was the target of a bully's torture is the stuff of legends. He was fortunate to have gone on to be schooled in the Earle Liederman course and the Charles Atlas course, which truly took him from being a 94-pound weakling to the man he is today.

> The first essential exercise is the deep breathing of pure air.

John built his system of Isoflexion™ resistance and high tension isometrics by taking *the best of the best* exercises from the Masters and integrating them into one comprehensive program. He has never used weights in his training methods, because he has relied exclusively on his mentors' use of body-weight resistance exercises only. His one goal: *results!* When it comes to strength, all-around good health, radiant energy, youthfulness, and well-being, John is the perfect example that his system produces maximum results!

## An Exercise Program That Works Wonders

For years I have been looking for an exercise program I could do and recommend for *anyone* that would require minimum time and effort and yield maximum results, and I've finally discovered it. Despite all the astounding benefits of exercise, I know the reasons most people hold back. Most of us procrastinate and fear the consequences of what it takes to get in shape, and the truth is that most exercise systems are too hard and intimidating for people. We also tend to convince ourselves that it will take too much time out of our already overcommitted days and evenings. And for many of us, the cost of a club membership or expensive exercise equipment is simply too much.

That's why I'm thrilled to introduce a system that is the perfect answer to these common issues. It is a system of exercise that utilizes time-tested body-sculpting Isoflexion™ techniques, along with high tension isometrics that literally allow you to become your own gym. It is so natural, so simple, and so powerful that it actually heals the body as it energizes it. You can use it to achieve the level of fitness and vitality you've always wanted to have, without joining a gym or buying any equipment or wasting a minute of your day. It covers every muscle group from your neck to your toes, and you can do these exercises anytime and virtually anywhere. And, best of all, you won't do anything that compromises your body, causing pain or injury or creating overuse symptoms.

This may sound a little too good to be true, but I have to tell you that I have done countless exercise programs over the years, and I've trained in the martial arts for much of my life, holding a black belt in a Christian martial arts system called Yon Ch'uan. Peterson's system delivers on its promises. I know this to be true because I am using it today. It has enhanced my strength, increased my range of motion and flexibility, and it had an almost immediate impact upon my body.

With the assistance of John Peterson and his associate and coauthor, Wendie Pett, I am going to outline some primary facets of their exercise program that will help you build muscle, as well as slim, sculpt, and strengthen your entire body if you devote 15 to 30 minutes a day, one to five times per week. Exercise sessions do not have to last long to be productive, particularly if you exercise correctly, and they do not have to be completed in a single session.

It is my experience that the first thing people do when they want to get in shape is go to the gym, which generally is short-lived because their bodies are fighting against poor nutrition and compromised metabolism. *My firm belief is that the last place people should go to get into shape is the gym or to begin a strenuous exercise program. The first step is to get your hydration and nutrition under control and your metabolism back on track.* Your body will then experience such a rise in energy that you will actually want to work out.

You should check with your doctor before beginning any exercise program—period. If you are in poor health and over 40, a treadmill test is highly recommended. Checking your blood pressure and monitoring your heart performance are vital. If you ever have symptoms of chest pain or pressure, heart irregularities, or unusual shortness of breath, call your doctor immediately.

## Deep Breathing Exercises

The first essential exercise is the deep breathing of pure air. This sounds simple, and it is, but it is profoundly effective in reducing stress in the body. All the most successful courses on physical fitness throughout history made deep breathing the primary vitality building method of exercise. Martin "Farmer" Burns, for example, was the preeminent teacher of catch wrestling in the 1910s and is famous for saying, "*Deep breathing alone* has made many a sick man well, and many a weak man strong."

Here's what deep breathing provides: increased energy, mental alertness, and creativity, strengthened abdominal muscles, improved digestion and elimination, purified lungs, enhanced relaxation, and enhanced power throughout the entire body due to increased oxygenation of the tissues. Yet it is reported that most people barely use one-fifth of the lung's capacity.

The secret to deep breathing is to copy the way babies breathe, using the diaphragm to create suction that pulls the air into the lungs. When the diaphragm expands and flattens moving downward, it produces suction within the chest cavity that causes the inflow of air into the lungs. When the diaphragm relaxes and rises, air is forced out of the lungs. Both operations are of equal importance . . . inhalation to bring in life-giving oxygen . . . exhalation to expel every bit of carbon dioxide.

Here's what you do. In the morning, while still in bed before arising, consciously relax your entire body. Inhale deeply through your nose and fill your entire lungs with life-giving oxygen. Feel the inhale all the way to the maximum and let yourself expand, hold for a count of seven seconds, then exhale slowly. During the exhale, squeeze your abdominals from the top down to the bottom (great for the abs). As you squeeze, make a "ssss" sound until you have forcefully completed your exhale. Practice this deep breathing exercise 10 times every morning. You will be amazed at your energy level.

I also recommend you do this exercise throughout the day, especially when you want to energize and recharge your thought processes or to get rid of mental or emotional stress.

## Cardiovascular Exercises

Working out with the Seven Tiger Moves will result in a dramatic increase in both strength and lean muscle mass as you shed unwanted body fat. But I also recommend that you add an aerobic element to your life as well. Cardiovascular exercise is any activity that uses large muscle groups, is rhythmic in nature, and can be maintained for a period of time. Done consistently, aerobic activity trains the heart, lungs, and cardiovascular system to process and deliver oxygen in a more efficient manner.

There is walking, running, rowing, biking, swimming, elliptical training, tennis, basketball, and so forth to pick from. Walking is a wonderful starting point, because it is very doable, and the health benefits are marvelous. Most experts agree that 3 to 5 aerobic sessions per week for a duration of at least 20 minutes at 60 to 85 percent of your age-specific maximum heart rate is a good place to begin (see chart). You will want to do an average of 45 minutes per day, 5 or 6 days per week, and increase this by 15 to 30 minutes for maximum fat loss.[16] Contrary to popular belief, you do not have to complete your exercises in a single long session. Research shows that you get the benefits of prolonged exercise sessions even when you break it up into multiple shorter sessions throughout the day.[17]

> The secret to building strength is contracting and extending your muscles with great tension while thinking into them.

| AGE | 70-80% OF MAX RATE | 60% OF MAX RATE |
|-----|--------------------|-----------------|
| 20 | 140–160 | 120 |
| 30 | 133–152 | 114 |
| 40 | 126–144 | 108 |
| 50 | 119–136 | 102 |
| 60 | 112–128 | 96 |
| 70 | 105–120 | 90 |

To prepare and better endure your workouts, bring some spring water to keep you hydrated and protect you from mineral imbalances (see Golden Key #1—Hydration). Do not train too long and too hard. One well-known effect of exercise is that it raises oxidative stress and increases free-radical production. Though exercise has been shown to improve antioxidant mechanisms, these defenses can be overwhelmed over time, and the risks of increased free-radical production are well known, such as damage to DNA and a host of pathologies that are best avoided. Eat foods that are high in antioxidants and consider taking supplements, as antioxidants have been shown to dramatically speed up muscle and tissue recovery (see Golden Key #2—Nutrition/Antioxidants).

Most people can reach the recommended exercise goals by simply making it part of their daily routine. The key is to make exercise a habit and figure out what time of the day works best for you, such as before going to work, during lunch hour, right after work, or in the evening with a friend.

## The Seven Tiger Moves— Foundational Exercises

The following exercises are the Seven Tiger Moves that John Peterson learned from the legendary master of the martial arts, John McSweeney. Repetition for repetition, they deliver more benefits than virtually any other form of exercise. While they can certainly build a powerful and beautifully developed physique, as with many forms of exercise they also help slow the aging process as well as accelerate healing. This is due mainly to the fact that Tiger Moves teach you to conserve and use your nerve force to your best advantage.

Many exercise systems can actually cause more pain and injury than benefit. It is possible for free-weights and exercise machines to tear muscles and stress joints. Too much of these wrong methods can make you feel far older than your actual years.

The Seven Tiger Moves are completely natural. The secret to the system, said McSweeney, is "nothing more than contracting and extending your muscles with *great tension* while thinking into them. Tigers and lions stretch their entire body with a tension so great that their limbs actually quiver. The tiger's stretch is so powerful that it actually builds incredible strength and muscle. The inner resistance produced by the tension builds muscle fibers as much as the external resistance produced by weight or machines. However, since the resistance is perfectly controlled at all times throughout the entire range of motion, there is no jerking, no compression, and no harm to the body."[18]

Let your body be your guide by starting your program with moderate tension and 7 or more repetitions. Do additional repetitions and an additional set as you can comfortably perform them. The key to the system is the amount of tension used while performing every exercise. Vary the amount of tension until it feels comfortable. If you use only moderate tension, you will maintain muscle tone, but not dramatically increase the size of your muscles. If you use higher amounts of tension, you will perform repetitions and sets as indicated in the chart below. The Seven Tiger Moves should be performed slowly with great tension. Breathe using both the nose and mouth, inhaling on the way back or up and exhaling on the way forward or down. Don't forget to breathe.

| REPETITIONS | | SETS |
|---|---|---|
| MODERATE | 8-10 | 3 max |
| HEAVY | 6-8 | 2-3 max |
| VERY HEAVY | 3-5 | 2 max |

Please read all descriptions carefully and follow these photograph sequences of John Peterson and Wendie Pett. You can also go to **www.superhealth7.com** for more information.

## FULL RANGE PECTORAL CONTRACTION

Primary focus: Chest

### STEP 1

Stand with your left foot about a pace forward. Left knee is bent and back is straight. Hold your hands facing each other just a couple inches apart. Powerfully flex all the muscles of the arms, shoulders, chest, and upper back before movement begins.

### STEP 2

Bring your hands back slowly under great tension and continue until the back muscles are fully flexed. Hold this position for a count of "one tiger one."

### STEP 3

While maintaining tension in the muscles, slowly move your hands forward until they are facing each other once again just a couple inches apart. Hold this position for a count of "one tiger one," then repeat the entire sequences for 7 to 10 more repetitions.

### ☞ Points to Remember:

▪ Be sure your arms remain parallel to the floor throughout the entire range of motion.

▪ Shoulders should be held naturally and not lifted.

▪ Using both your nose and mouth, breathe *in* on the way back and *out* on the way forward.

*tiger move* 1

## SHOULDER ROLL
Primary focus: Deltoids

### STEP 1

Stand with your right foot forward about one pace. Your right knee is bent and your back is straight.

### STEP 2

Start with your arms bent and hands in fists. Powerfully flex all the muscles of your forearms, biceps, triceps, pectorals, and deltoids before movement begins.

### STEP 3

While maintaining tension in the muscles, slowly move your arms back with your forearms remaining parallel to the floor throughout the entire range of motion until the back muscles are powerfully flexed. Hold this position for a count of "one tiger one."

### STEP 4

Return to the starting position by simply reversing the motion and retracing the exact same plane of motion. Repeat the entire sequences smoothly and fluidly for 7 to 10 repetitions.

### ☞ Points to Remember:

■ Forearms remain parallel to the floor throughout the entire range of motion.

■ Shoulders remain low and not lifted.

■ Using both your nose and mouth, breathe *in* on the way back and *out* on the way forward.

*tiger move* 2

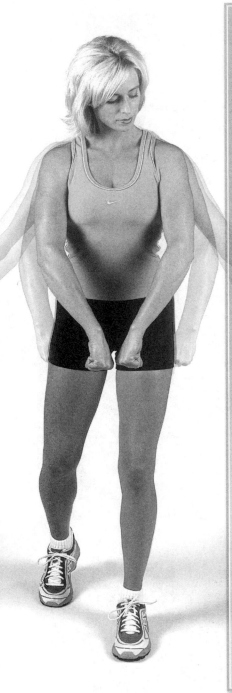

## WRIST TWIST

### STEP 1

Stand with your left foot one pace forward. Left knee bent, back straight, arms in front close to your body with fists turned in. Back of hands almost touching.

### STEP 2

Powerfully flex the muscles of your forearms, upper arms, pectorals, and shoulders. While maintaining tension, slowly rotate your arms back, turning the fists gradually until they turn out. Flex your back muscles and triceps powerfully for a count of "one tiger one."

### STEP 3

While maintaining tension slowly rotate your arms forward to starting position while turning your fists gradually until the backs of your hands are almost touching.

### ☞ Points to Remember:

▪ Keep your arms pointing down throughout the entire range of motion.

▪ This exercise works the triceps with great intensity but also works the deltoids and pectorals.

▪ Keep movement smooth from beginning to end.

*tiger move* 3

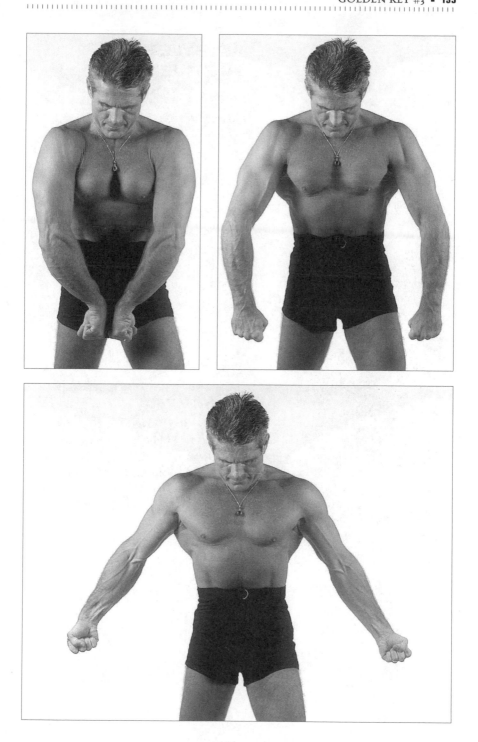

# McSWEENEY HIGH REACH

### STEP 1

Stand with your feet shoulder-width apart.

### STEP 2

Begin with both arms at shoulder height. With your right arm slowly reach as high as possible with great tension. As your right arm comes down to your shoulder, your left arm is reaching up with great tension.

### STEP 3

Do 7 to 10 reps with each arm.

### ☞ Points to Remember:

▪ Arms move independently under great tension in both directions.

▪ Reach as high as is comfortably possible.

▪ This is the movement that John McSweeney believed to have curative powers. Many people have used it to restore full mobility to injured shoulders.

*tiger move* 4

*"This is the exercise that rehabilitated my shoulder!"* —Wendie Pett

# ONE ARM CHIN

### STEP 1

Stand with your feet side by side and shoulder-width apart. Your left arm is above your head, your right arm at shoulder level.

### STEP 2

While exerting great tension in the forearms and biceps of both arms, slowly start to pull your left arm down while moving your right arm to the "up" position.

### STEP 3

As each arm comes down, bring them as close to the center line of the body as possible.

### ☞ *Points to Remember:*

■ Maintaining tension in both directions.

■ Come down the center line of the body as much as possible.

■ This exercise builds and strengthens biceps, forearms, inner pectorals, and especially the latissimis dorsi of the upper back for that classic V-shape.

• • • • •

One of John Peterson's students from Boulder, Colorado, used this exercise exclusively to improve his pulling strength and went from a maximum of 4 pull-ups to 10 in just a matter of weeks. Bottom line: This is a powerful strengthener and V-builder.

*tiger move* 5

## ABDOMINAL CONTRACTION

**STEP 1**

Stand with your feet side by side and shoulder-width apart. Arms in position shown, performing the Liederman chest press.

**STEP 2**

Press your abdomen down as hard as possible with great tension as you exhale powerfully. Hold for "one tiger one."

**STEP 3**

While inhaling to the maximum, consciously try to draw your abdomen in and up and try to feel as though it is touching the spine. At the point of greatest contraction, hold for "one tiger one."

### ☞ Points to Remember:

▪ This is a great energizing exercise that can be performed anytime during the day.

▪ It improves both digestion and elimination.

▪ John McSweeney once told John Peterson that he had seen several people whom he knew lose several inches from their abdomens by learning how to powerfully contract both the "down" and "up" positions as indicated with this exercise.

▪ This is also a great breath control exercise.

*tiger move* 6

# HALF KNEE BEND

### STEP 1

Stand with your feet side by side. Arms as shown, performing the Liederman Chest Press contraction.

### STEP 2

While thinking into your leg (thigh) muscles and powerfully contracting them, slowly bend your knees and descend only halfway while maintaining maximum muscle tension.

### STEP 3

Slowly reverse direction and come back up to the starting position while maintaining tension in upper body and legs.

## ☞ Points to Remember:

■ By maintaining an aerobic isometric contraction of the upper body muscles (approximately 50 percent of maximum perceived effort), you will discover that it is much easier to contract the thigh muscles (quadriceps) very powerfully.

■ Breathe deeply, exhaling while going down and inhaling while coming up.

■ No need to go deeper than halfway unless you want to. But be careful not to harm the knee joint.

*tiger move* 7

## Advanced and Specific Muscle Group Isolation Exercises

If you are an athlete or are in good shape or have been doing the previous Foundational exercises long enough to get in shape, you may now be ready to integrate some of the following supplemental exercises. Women should note Wendie Pett's **women-specific additions** to the Seven Tiger Moves as found in *Every Woman's Guide to Personal Power* by Wendie Pett.

## BALANCE SQUAT

Stand with feet slightly wider than shoulder-width apart, toes turned out and hands in prayer position. Pull navel into spine. Keeping back straight, bend knees into a squat until thighs are almost parallel to the ground. Arch up high on toes to strengthen calves and practice balance. At the same time, with your hands in a prayer posture at the center of your chest (see photo #1) and with both hands applying extra heavy resistance, slowly extend your arms. After acheiving full extension, return to the start position while maintaining the tension.

## LIFT WITH A KEGEL CONTRACTION

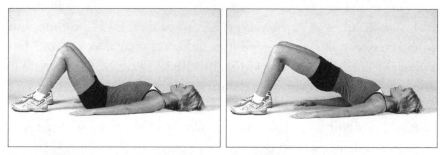

Lie down and bend both legs keeping both feet on floor. Then press up with your hips as far as possible with a Kegel contraction for 5 to 10 seconds. This exercise is very important for women to practice routinely.

## PRONE LEG KICK

Lie face down on the ground, resting chin on hands. Keeping hips on the ground, slowly raise your left leg. Return to start. Repeat, alternating legs.

## THE FUREY PUSH-UP

One of the key exercises Matt Furey teaches is the Furey Push-up. In his book, *Combat Conditioning*, he calls it the Hindu Push-up, but John Peterson calls it the Furey Push-up because if it were not for Matt Furey the entire Western world would be unaware of this incredible exercise. It exercises every muscle from your neck to your toes and on both front and back sides of the body, delivering the highest level of strength, flexibility, and endurance. Follow the complete photographic sequence as demonstrated by John Peterson.

Photo #1. Start with your hands on the floor, shoulder-width apart, and your head tucked in and looking directly at your feet. Your feet are shoulder-width apart or slightly wider. Your legs and back are straight, and your butt is the highest point of the body.

Photos #2-3-4-5. Bend your elbows while descending in a smooth circular arc almost brushing your chest and upper body to the floor as you continue the circular range of motion until your arms are straight, back flexed, and hips almost, but not quite, touching the floor.

Photo #6. At the top of the movement, look at the ceiling while consciously flexing your triceps and exhaling.

Photo #7. Raise your hips and buttocks while simultaneously pushing back with straight arms, causing a complete articulation of both shoulder joints.

Photo #8. Arrive at the starting position with your legs and back straight, your head tucked in, and eyes looking at your feet.

Continue as smoothly and as fluidly as possible for as many repetitions as you can do.

At the beginning, anywhere from 5 to 25 repetitions is excellent. Once you can routinely do sets of 50 or more, you will have superb shoulder, chest, arm, and both upper and lower back development.

## THE ATLAS PUSH-UP

In the world famous Charles Atlas Dynamic Tension Training Course, only one type of push-up was recommended, and here Wendie Pett demonstrates it. Notice the built-in stretch.

With two chairs side by side (between 18" and 26" apart, depending upon your shoulder width and arm length), place a hand on the seat of each chair (photo #1). Your body is extended in a sloping position with your feet on the floor. Now perform a push-up between the chairs, allowing your chest to descend as close to the floor as is comfortable (photo #2). Do not force yourself to descend beyond what is comfortable. In time your range of motion will naturally increase. Smoothly extend your arms to complete extension for one complete repetition. Anywhere from sets of 5 to 25 is great, and sets of 50 will build an awesome physique.

## THE ATLAS PUSH-UP #2

To create even more intensity, you may want to experiment with elevating your feet above your hands as Wendie demonstrates here. Do as many as you can and as smoothly as possible. This is a superb deep breathing and pectoral development exercise. Atlas recommended that a total of 200 be performed if you want superb chest development. It is also a great exercise for the triceps of the upper arm and the latissimus dorsi muscles of the upper back. If you can perform sets of 25 or more, you are doing great.

## THE STANDARD PULL-UP

Please Note:
1. **ALL PULL-UPS** are performed with palms facing away from the body.
2. **ALL CHIN-UPS** are performed with palms facing the body.

This represents the distinction between a pull-up and a chin-up.

## THE FUREY BRIDGE (For Super Athletes Only Or Those Who Want to Be)

Photo 1 shows the starting position. As strength and flexibility increase, weight is shifted slowly to the forehead until you finally reach...

Photo 2 shows the ***Furey way***. I know it seems extreme, but once you work up to it, your flexibility will be nothing less than incredible and wall walking will seem like child's play—because, by comparison, it is!

## THE SUPERMAN WHEEL PUSH-UP

Over the years I've been asked by many friends if there isn't a single ab exercise that does it all. Just one "silver bullet" that if practiced consistently would do the job. Well, truth to tell, there is! And it's the exercise you see John Peterson performing here. It's called "The Superman Wheel Push-up." This one exercise truly does it all.

But there is a problem with it. Guess whom you have to be in order to do it even once. Hint: "It's a bird . . . it's a plane . . ."

# *Stress*

**Stress is synonymous with change
and refers to anything that causes us to
react to a physical, mental, emotional, social,**
*or spiritual stimulus. As we adjust to the continual fluctuations
and startling threats that are a normal part of life, the effects
can be emotional as well as physical, negative as well as positive. Even good change can be stressful, but imagined change
(worry and fear) can be extremely stressful. Chronic worry and
fear have devastating consequences to our health. The body has
its own natural ability for preventing disease and dealing with
stress. All we have to do is tap into that innate potential while
we are learning how to harness the inappropriate affects of that
stress. How we handle stress has a major impact on our health.*

*Be anxious for nothing, but in everything by prayer and supplication,
with thanksgiving, let your requests be made known to God;
and the peace of God, which surpasses all understanding,
will guard your hearts and minds through Christ Jesus.*

PHILIPPIANS 4:6–7

SUPER
HEALTH

7 Golden
Keys to
Unlock
Lifelong
Vitality

# Stress

*"A stress-free life is an impossible goal—*
*we need some stress to be alive.*
*After all, we call it blood pressure.*
*Without some pressure, we are dead."*

DR. HANS SELYE

We all know the story of the hapless cave dweller, who confronts a saber-toothed tiger in the jungle and must choose in an instant whether to face the threat with his spear or to cut his losses and make a run for it. This classic fight-or-flight stress response is one we have all experienced at one time or another. To maintain our equilibrium, or *homeostasis*, we modify our systems to meet a perceived danger or threat. Although it is unlikely that any of us will ever come face to face with a saber-toothed tiger, the chronic pressures and traumas of the modern world are every bit as distressing and potentially life-threatening. Today's stressors undermine our health, our happiness, and our longevity, if we let them.

What actually happens to us in a high stress or emergency situation? A typical stress response sets off approximately 1,500 biochemical reactions in the brain and body. Our heart rate elevates. Our muscles constrict. Our lungs expand. We breathe faster. And we experience an adrenaline rush that sends quick energy to our muscles. Almost all body functions and organs react to stress. Like our caveman friend, this flood of adrenaline allows us to move and think faster and can help save our life. Our hearing and vision become more acute; we are amazingly alert; and we may even have an unexpected surge of seemingly supernatural strength.

Inside a small part of our brain called the *hypothalamus*, a signal has been sent to our pituitary gland to start adding a hormone called *corticotrophin* into our bloodstream. Corticotrophin, in turn, tells our adrenal glands to release other stress hormones, *glucocorticoids*, which stimulate the *hippocampus*—one of the parts of the brain related to memory—so we are able to deal with similar threats should they occur again. Once glucocorticoids are released into the bloodstream, the hippocampus signals the hypothalamus to stop releasing corticotrophins, ending the stress response. All of these stress responses are automatic and allow us to effectively and safely rescue ourselves.

## Adrenal Fatigue

We aren't meant to experience these high stress threats often, however. They should be the exception rather than the norm. If stress becomes chronic and long-term, which it does in many of our lives, our feedback loops become degraded, and we experience "adrenal fatigue"—the result of racing through life with a constantly aroused sympathetic (fight-or-flight) nervous system. Just ask the person who is stuck in freeway traffic when he's late for a meeting or the person working on an assembly line with increased quotas despite recent layoffs of personnel.

When the stress response does not automatically turn off, our hippocampal brain cells become weakened. Prolonged increased levels of adrenaline can compromise the nervous system and contribute to brain aging and cognitive impairment. In a study published in the November 29, 2004 issue of *Proceedings of the National Academy of Sciences*, scientists found that chronic stress affects three biological factors involved with cellular aging: telomere length, telomere activity, and oxidative stress. In addition, excess levels of cortisol raise blood sugar and insulin levels, resulting in increased triglyceride and LDL (bad) cholesterol levels, while depleting our immune systems.[1] This chronic situation combined with the standard American diet and lifestyle can result in chronic fatigue, anxiety, and panic attacks.

> The same physiological alarm mechanisms that helped save the caveman's life are killing us today.

As an antidote, Jesus told us, "Therefore I say to you, do not worry about your life, what you will eat or what you will drink; nor about your body, what you will put on. Is not life more than food and the body more than clothing? Look at the birds of the air, for they neither sow nor reap nor gather into barns; yet your heavenly Father feeds them. Are you not of more value than they? Which of you by worrying can add one cubit to his stature?" (Matthew 6:25–27).

## What Is Stress?

Simply put, stress is synonymous with change and refers to anything that causes us to react to a physical, emotional, social, or spiritual stimulus. As we adjust to the continual fluctuations and startling threats that are a part of life, the effects can be emotional as well as physical, negative as well as positive. Anything that causes change in our lives causes stress. Even good change, such as falling in love or a promotion at work, can be stressful, but imagined change (worry and fear) can be extremely stressful. Science tells us that chronic worry, fear, unforgiveness, and bitterness have devastating consequences to our health.

Dr. Hans Selye (1907–1982), the Canadian endocrinologist who is considered the "father of the stress field," did the vast majority of his groundbreaking work on stress in the 1930s. His legacy lives on until the present day. He defined stress as "the non-specific response of the body to any demands made upon it. Each demand made on the body is unique in that there is a definite response: when we are cold, we shiver; when we are hot, we perspire; a great muscular effort increases the demands upon the heart and vascular system. However, whatever the specific response, there is also activated a non-specific response which is independent of the cause. For example: the woman who is told that her husband died in battle suffers a terrible mental shock. If, years later, he walks into the room alive and well, she experiences extreme joy. The specific results of the stress are opposite, but the non-specific effect on the body is the same. The accumulation of stressors, whether good or bad, if intense enough, will ultimately cause physical disorders."[2]

## The Sources and Signs of Stress

Stress comes in all shapes and sizes. There is emotional stress, such as a disagreement with a friend or grief over a loss. There are physical stresses, such as illness or a lack of sleep or pushing our body to extremes. There are external stresses, such as climatic extremes and environmental toxins. And there are internal stresses, such as anxiety over a speech or fear of punishment. Hormonal shifts and allergic responses are stresses. Relentless work pressure, financial worries, excessive caffeine, alcohol consumption, smoking, and unresolved traumas from the past—all of these are stresses, and they can exact a grim toll on our body and our psyche.

Dr. T. H. Holmes of the University of Washington has devised a Social Readjustment Rating Scale in which he has given numerical values to many different types of stressful situations. He has been able to correlate, with a remarkable degree of accuracy, the number of stress points a person has accumulated in any two-year period, along with the degree of seriousness of the disorder which that person is then likely to suffer.

**Our response to stress when it occurs determines how the stress will affect us.**

For example, the death of a spouse equals 100 stress points; divorce equals 73 points; marital separation, a jail term, and the death of a close family member all result in 63 points. Personal injury or illness scores 50 stress points, as does getting married. Marital reconciliation, on the other hand, gets 45 stress points, as does retirement. A change to a different line of work equals 36 points; an outstanding personal achievement equals 28 points; trouble with your boss equals 23 points; a change in residence equals 20 stress points, and even a vacation gets a score of 13 stress points.

Remarkably enough, getting married is almost as stressful as a jail term! Retirement is more stressful than changing to a different line of work, and marital reconciliation is only slightly less stressful than a formal separation. It's revealing that Christmas, which should be a joyous time of year, is equivalent to the stress associated with violating the law—both score 12 stress points!

According to Dr. Holmes, more than 250 points within a two-year period is likely to be followed by a life-threatening illness; 150 points is likely to be followed by an illness which may be serious, but not life-threatening. With 20 to 50 points, recurrent bronchitis, cold sores, or other illnesses may result.[3]

## The Symptoms of Stress

There are both physical and emotional symptoms of stress.

The physical symptoms include:

- Thyroid gland malfunctions
- High blood pressure
- Itchy skin rashes
- Decreased resistance to infection
- Flus and colds
- Gastrointestinal problems, such as ulcers, cramps, diarrhea, colitis, and irritable bowel
- Fatigue
- Hair loss
- Jaw pain
- Irregular heartbeat, palpitations
- Shortness of breath
- Obscure aches and pains
- Insomnia
- Tension headaches

> **The accumulation of stressors, whether good or bad, if intense enough, can ultimately cause physical disorders.**

Emotional symptoms include:

- Depression
- Moodiness
- Nervousness
- Irritability, frustration
- Memory problems, cognitive impairment
- Lack of focus
- Substance abuse

- Phobias
- Over-reactions
- Anxiety attacks (panic)

In addition, stress can lead to antisocial behaviors and signs, including argumentativeness, social isolation, conflicts with coworkers, road rage, domestic or workplace violence, and frequent job changes.

## The Negative Effects of Stress

The National Institute of Mental Health reports that 19 million Americans between the ages of 18 and 54 are afflicted by anxiety- and stress-related illnesses per year.[4] The effects of this stress are profound. They impact not only our susceptibility to disease, but they also affect the progression of disease and our ability to recover from it. In fact, virtually every major physical disorder is caused by, or greatly exacerbated by, stress, from migraine headaches to asthma. The toll it takes on the body is every bit as severe as smoking, obesity, and genetic predisposition.

> It is not stress that is harmful— it is *dis*-tress. Distress occurs when unresolved emotional stress is prolonged and not dealt with in a positive way.

Stress is also extremely costly. Each year the United States spends more than $300 billion to cover the healthcare costs brought on by stress in the workplace. And occupational experts report that workers who admit they are stressed cost companies an average of $600 more per person than other employees. This is because they incur 46 percent higher healthcare costs.[5]

Some physicians estimate that stress and anxiety may be a contributing factor in 90 percent of all illnesses. Many psychiatrists believe that most back problems are related to stress. Accumulated stress can predispose patients to medical conditions such as hypertension, ulcers, and heart disease, but that's just the beginning. Here are just a few of the many links between stress and physiology:

- *Stress is a major factor for infections.* Research in humans has found that psychological stress can take a toll on the immune system by reducing the concentration of *cytokines*, proteins that help to ward off infections.[6]

- *Stress worsens our immune systems.* It was recently discovered that people under chronic stress had above-normal levels of *interleukin*-6 (IL-6), an immune-system protein that promotes inflammation and has been linked with heart disease, diabetes, osteoporosis, rheumatoid arthritis, severe infections, and certain cancers. Without a properly functioning immune system, our body is vulnerable to invasion by opportunistic germs, such as fungi, viruses, and bacteria.[7]

- *Stress intensifies flu and cold symptoms.* Researchers believe that *interleukin*-6 may also be a biological link between psychological stress and the severity of cold and flu symptoms.[8]

- *Stress can lead to infertility and affect the success of fertility treatments.* Women who report high levels of stress at the outset of fertility treatments had fewer eggs retrieved and fertilized, compared with women who expressed optimism that they would become pregnant.[9]

- *Prenatal stress can cause learning problems and brain deficits.* Stress can affect many of the body's systems, including the nervous system, cardiovascular system, endocrine system, and immune system, and there is evidence that severe emotional stress can cause birth defects, especially during the early stages of pregnancy when development is occurring at the fastest rate.[10]

- *Stress alters our physical appearance.* Stress affects our bodies, not just in terms of the way we feel, but also in terms of the way we appear. It leads to overeating, weight gain, and increased fat around the abdomen. It can cause weaker muscles and bone loss, as well as skin problems, such as eczema, psoriasis, hives, and premature wrinkles. Stress often coexists with depression, substance abuse, and eating disorders, such as bulimia, anorexia, and obesity.

- *Stress literally rewires the brain.* There is a strong link between stress and depression. According to the National Institute of

Mental Health, the damage caused by a combination of the two can be profound. Developments in brain imaging and neurology have shown that stress actually "rewires" the brain's emotional circuitry, altering its connections in such a way that it affects the way the brain functions.

Stress triggers a "fear center" in the amygdala sector of the brain that takes over emotions and affects thinking. Usually, when a stressful event occurs, our body's response to it fades away. But when combined with depression, the chemical imbalance in the brain holds on to the stress, keeping the feelings active. Brain-imaging scans have shown that those who suffer from long-term stress may fail to feel any positive feelings in the prefrontal cortex, the region of the brain that maintains and originates emotions. The depressed brain's rewiring means that dread and fear can flow unimpeded from the amygdala to the prefrontal cortex.[11]

## Stress and Anxiety Disorders

As we discussed before, there are various sources and indicators of anxiety and stress. Anxiety ranges in severity from mild anxiety, which does not impair performance, all the way to a severe form of anxiety known as Generalized Anxiety Disorder, which makes a person almost totally dysfunctional. The five major anxiety disorders that follow are more extreme forms of stress and are usually serious enough to require medication and/or professional treatment.

Some physicians estimate that stress and anxiety may be a contributing factor in 90 percent of all illnesses.

Balance in your life is critical, and this is where I cannot overemphasize that the other six Golden Keys can have a profound effect on coping with stress. Hydration, nutrition (in particular the use of fatty acids and amino acids and the limitation of sugars), exercise, controlling and eliminating environmental toxins, achieving restorative sleep, and meditation and prayer are all tremendous stress busters. Incorporating these into your life is critical in dealing with or avoiding any of these disorders. There are often deep-rooted spiritual issues to problems involving the mind, will, and emotions (the Soul).

## GENERALIZED ANXIETY DISORDER (GAD)

GAD is much more serious than the daily anxieties most of us feel. It involves chronic, excessive worrying about health, finances, work, daily tasks, schedules, and family. It is distinguished by fatigue, difficulty sleeping, irritability, muscle tension, headaches, trembling and twitching, and lightheadedness.

## PANIC ATTACKS

Panic is characterized by repeated episodes of intense fear that appear suddenly and often without warning. This type of anxiety holds our mental processes captive, while it simultaneously paralyzes our entire gastrointestinal tract. Symptoms of panic disorder include chest pains, tingling extremities, heart palpitations, hot and cold sensations, shortness of breath, sweating palms, intense perspiration, dizziness, a feeling of unreality, and an irrational fear of dying. Attacks usually last a couple of minutes, but can occasionally be much longer. It is my experience that panic attacks are directly related to adrenal exhaustion and to overconsumption of sugars and other high glycemic foods and stimulants. This causes hyperglycemia (high blood sugar levels), resulting in high insulin levels followed by severe hypoglycemia (low blood sugar levels). Panic attacks seem to be triggered when blood sugar crashes to its lowest levels, so it is important to avoid blood sugar spikes. Chronic sleep deprivation can also be a significant factor as well.

## PHOBIAS

Phobias are seemingly inexplicable fears that may be either specific (fear of heights) or social. Social phobias are an intense fear of humiliation in a public situation and may be characterized by a feeling of dread beginning weeks in advance of a social event. People who suffer from this disorder feel that they are constantly being watched, evaluated, and judged.

## OBSESSIVE-COMPULSIVE DISORDER (OCD)

OCD is characterized by obsessions or anxious thoughts that a person wishes to control through compulsive behaviors or rituals.

These rituals provide temporary relief. An example of an OCD is an obsessive fear of germs that results in constant hand washing.

## POST-TRAUMATIC STRESS DISORDER (PTSD)

PTSD results from a traumatic event or events and can be severely debilitating. Typically the symptoms of this disorder are related to traumatic experiences originating in childhood, such as sexual, emotional, or physical abuse. They also can be related to the experience of trauma as an adult, such as rape, natural disaster, crime, or war. These traumatic experiences become internalized, remaining forever present and painful. People diagnosed with PTSD may relive the event in nightmares or have disturbing recollections (flashbacks) that may result in a loss of reality and feelings of helplessness, causing them to believe the event is happening all over again. These experiences can affect the developing personality. To make sense of these overwhelming experiences, many people with PTSD will create entire belief systems or world views that cause them constant stress.

> The Seven Golden Keys are critical in dealing with or avoiding any of these disorders.

These five anxiety disorders often require more serious treatment options, such as psychotherapy or cognitive-behavioral therapy. Even if we've never experienced one of these disorders, all of us have experienced free-floating anxiety, the kind that exists most of the time, or acute anxiety and stress associated with certain places or events, such as a traffic jam or an altercation with our boss.

## Stress Management

Some people believe we should avoid stress entirely, as though all stress is harmful. Research has shown that active stress—the kind we experience in competition or just before a bungee jump or an important deadline—can actually boost our immune system, improving our ability to fight off infection.

In fact, there are two kinds of stress. Bad stress (or *distress*) occurs when unresolved stress is prolonged and not dealt with in a positive way. Good stress (called *eustress*) compels us into action and results in greater awareness, emotional intelligence, and resiliency. Meeting a goal, problem solving, excelling in competition, working through a conflict with a coworker, and even grief can be important learning experiences that enrich and broaden our lives.

Without the challenges of daily life, we cannot mature and become complete human beings in a healthy way. Instead of eliminating stress, we need to learn how to *manage* it and increase our tolerance for it by following the Seven Golden Keys!

The benefits of stress management are pervasive and profound. Stress management can help lower blood sugar as well as our risk for heart disease; and it can make us less susceptible to colds and flu as well. It can reduce violence, accidents, and poor job performance. It allows us to rebound faster (both physically and mentally). It can literally alter our appearance, taking pounds off our body and years off our age—increasing our longevity and dramatically improving our overall quality of life.

> **Stress management doesn't mean eliminating stress. It means changing how we react to it so that we don't feel overwhelmed by it.**

## Attitude and Positive Self-Talk

A positive attitude, particularly a positive attitude rooted in faith in Jesus Christ, directly correlates with an increased ability of the immune system to fight pathogens. The ability to handle stress positively and proactively in everyday life can alleviate the constant activation of the endocrine system. Studies have shown that optimists tend to have better coping skills and rely on more supportive social networks, which gives them a greater capacity for growth and a positive reinterpretation of negative events.

Stress management doesn't mean eliminating stress. It means changing how we react to it so that we don't feel overwhelmed by it. If we believe a situation is too overwhelming, to the point that we can't cope with it, that stress can damage us.

There are several attitudinal modifications that can help us monitor and manage stress whenever it rears its ugly head:

- *Acknowledge the stress.* Dismissing how you feel or ignoring your problems won't make them go away. In fact, to repress or deny your emotions only compounds stress. Notice what the stress is doing to your body, and the meaning and interpretation you are giving to the stressful event.

- *Decide what you can change.* Once you've acknowledged the stressor, you can more effectively deal with it. Perhaps the stressor can be eliminated or solved, or perhaps all you have to do is ignore it because it's not that important. Perhaps you can simply reduce the intensity of the stressor or your exposure to it. Decide what you can do to alleviate the impact of the stress on your life. See the section on Meditation and Prayer at the back of this chapter.

- *Gauge and monitor your emotional reactions to stress.* Are you overreacting? Are you viewing your stressors in exaggerated terms? In short, are you making a mountain out of a molehill? Are you reacting rather than acting? Decide how much of the stress is coming from the outside, and how much you are contributing to it yourself. Perhaps your perfectionism or your need to please everyone is making the situation a lot worse than it needs to be. Learn how to prioritize; this means deciding what is truly critical and what is not. Then finish your priority before pursuing another goal. By moderating and tempering your responses, you are taking control of the situation rather than allowing the situation to take control of you.

- *Gauge and moderate your physical reactions to stress.* Breathing and relaxation techniques can take you from those agitated, white-knuckled stress responses to a place of calm and stability. Take a time out, pause to monitor your body's responses, and exercise or massage away the places of muscular tension.

- *Build your physical reserves.* Eating healthy, exercising regularly, getting enough sleep, avoiding self-destructive behaviors, and allowing time for leisure activities will give you the physical stamina you need when stress begins to make excessive demands.

- *Nurture your emotional self.* Supportive friendships, realistic goals, and being fair to yourself when you confront disappointment or failure will ensure you have an emotional safety net in place that will protect you from life's harder falls.
- *Each week, make sure you give yourself a day of rest and relaxation.*

## Exercise

The most effective techniques for fighting stress are the Seven Golden Keys, including regular and effective exercise and optimal nutrition. Exercise causes the brain to release natural endorphins, neurotransmitters in the brain that have pain-relieving properties akin to morphine. Exercise also is a detoxifier, useful in removing the byproducts of the stress response. The very act of exerting our muscles and breathing aerobically delivers a wide range of stress-combatants to the body. It alleviates muscular tension. It makes us more robust and better equipped to fight stress and disease. It helps us to fall asleep more easily and to sleep more soundly.

Competition and higher risk activities, such as bungee jumping, are also examples of *good stress;* they allow us to gradually take on higher and higher loads of stress and to learn how to manage them effectively. Welcome these stresses as working in your favor. Exercise is also a useful outlet for anger and hostility—a healthy way of releasing pent-up negative energy. Because it involves breathing and repetitious movement, exercise can have a similar effect on the body as meditation (which is why many people speak of feelings of tranquility and calmness after they exercise). Exercise elevates self-esteem, as it allows us to improve our appearance, our health, and to master new challenges. Some activities, such as running or doing laps in the pool, also provide temporary escapes— places of solitude and introspection—while others, such as basketball or golf, offer opportunities for social support and companionship.

Remember . . . *regular exercise* is more important than intense exercise. Working ourselves into a state of exhaustion while exercising can actually intensify feelings of anxiety, while regular, moderate exercise lowers anxiety and relaxes the body (see Golden Key #3—Exercise).

Exercise, if done at the same time on a frequent basis, will become a healthy habit.

## Talk It Out

Many people who suffer from chronic stress and anxiety have benefited from traditional talk therapy. This can be with your spouse, a psychotherapist, a minister, a counselor, or even a wise and trusted friend. Research has shown that when individuals talk about a tragic or stressful event, they show an elevated immune response and are generally healthier than those who are emotionally inhibited and non-disclosing. Therapy has been shown to decrease the number of sick days and to lower healthcare costs.

In turn, individuals with an effective social support network have also been shown to have stronger immune abilities.

## Dietary Options and Supplements

**Tell yourself the truth. Are you making mountains out of molehills? Learn how to prioritize; this means deciding what is truly critical and what is not.**

One of the chief problems with the body's stress response has to do with the "auto-oxidation" of the very stress hormones that our bodies naturally release in order to help us deal with the stress. What this means is that our stress hormones *themselves* can become oxidized once they are released by our adrenal glands, which in turn means that they then go on to create a cascade of dangerous free radicals within the body. This is one of the main reasons why chronic stress is such a killer—because of all the excess free radicals that are produced by the very release of these stress hormones.

*Warning: Do not self-prescribe supplements if you are taking prescription drugs.*

### OMEGA-3s WITH VITAMIN E

This is where antioxidants, such as full-spectrum Vitamin E and the essential mineral selenium (which is a vital mineral cofactor for the cancer-fighting enzyme glutathione peroxidase, which prevents your cell membranes from oxidizing and becoming rancid) can be of tremendous help, since they can scavenge and quench these free radicals before they can do significant harm to the body. Omega-3 fish oils (EPA and DHA) combined with natural, full-spectrum Vitamin E (i.e., mixed tocopherols and tocotrienols, including gamma tocopherol) can safely boost the essential fatty acid levels in your body, which in turn are instrumental in preventing depression and also can help to elevate mood at the same time (see Golden Key #2—Nutrition/Healthy Fats).

## SEROTONIN

Serotonin is a type of neurotransmitter known as a *monoamine*. Neurotransmitters are chemicals that send messages from one nerve cell to another. In short, a neurotransmitter helps different parts of your brain "talk" to each other. The food you eat has the potential to raise or lower your serotonin levels. The protein in the food you eat is made up of "strands" of amino acids. Your body can't make serotonin without the help of the essential amino acid *tryptophan*, which is now available in the U.S. without a prescription.

If you were to eat just tryptophan by itself, it would enter the blood, flow into the brain, and raise serotonin levels. But if for some reason you cannot get tryptophan itself, you can get the next best thing, which is known as *5HTP*, or 5-hydroxytryptophan, which is the immediate precursor to tryptophan in the body. A number of foods also offer high trytophan levels, including free-range turkey and chicken, berries, bananas, almonds, cashews, and sunflower seeds, to name a few.

Richard and Judith Wurtman, researchers from the Massachusetts Institute of Technology, have shown that meals high in carbohydrates can actually "help" tryptophan to enter your brain.[12] When you eat a food high in carbohydrates, your body releases insulin. Insulin helps to clear the competing amino acids from your blood. However, insulin has no effect on tryptophan. Consequently, once insulin has cleared the competing amino acids from your blood, tryptophan is free to enter your brain. Most people have a problem with too much insulin in the

**Warning: Do not self-prescribe supplements if you are taking prescription drugs.**

bloodstream, and thus increasing carbohydrates is not an option.

Serotonin-raising foods include:

- Lentils
- Omega-3&E
- Free-range turkey
- Organic cheese and yogurt (unsweetened)
- Low glycemic fruit
- Low glycemic leafy greens, such as spinach, romaine lettuce, broccoli, green beans, peppers, and onions

## AMINO ACIDS

Sometimes the stress in our lives can be so paralyzing that we may need extra medicinal help in combating it. The tranquilizing amino acid GABA can be a great natural aid to help eliminate the physical symptoms of stress in the body, as can the active calming ingredient in green tea, known as *theanine*. Fortunately, both are available as nutritional supplements to help you deal with stress.

*Tyrosine* is an amino acid found in protein foods, and it boosts two important brain chemicals—dopamine and norepinephrine. Together, these two amino acids stimulate the central nervous system, increasing energy and improving concentration, alertness, and performance.[13] A depletion of these amino acids can contribute to Post-Traumatic Stress Disorder.

## VITAMIN C

A high dietary intake of Vitamin C may help reduce the effects of chronic stress by inhibiting the release of stress hormones, thus preventing these hormones from dampening the immune response.

## FOODS TO AVOID

There are also certain foods you should try to avoid, as they exacerbate stress symptoms. Try to wean yourself off of coffee, non-herbal tea, or any substances, such as chocolate, that contain caffeine, which can cause the development of insulin resistance. Avoid grains, fruit juices, and sugars, such as candy, which offer a temporary high (the blood sugar rush) followed by a distressing crash or bottoming out. As you are aware from the Nutrition chapter, stay away from processed foods, artificial sweeteners, junk foods, fried foods, pork, shell fish, and foods containing preservatives. Smaller, frequent meals are better than three large meals, particularly for those who suffer from hypoglycemia (low blood sugar). Hypoglycemia is generally caused by hyperglycemia (high blood sugar) and the subsequent blood sugar crash. If your blood sugar falls to an uncomfortable low within a couple of hours of eating, you likely ate something that was high in glycemic content.

## Breathing/Relaxation

When facing a stressful situation, relaxation and deep breathing exercises deliver immediate and direct benefits to the body, including lowering our heart rate and blood pressure and improving our sleep. Relaxation and creative visualization exercises, aromatherapy, meditation and prayer—all these techniques relax the mind and spirit, allowing us to feel and think better.

### MAKE FUN AND R&R A PRIORITY

How many of us pause long enough in our busy lives to smell the roses? Instead, we often choose to overwhelm our spirits and minds with noisy and often negative clutter, from cell phones to television to the Internet. We need to take a break from our hectic, technology-driven schedules and stop taking life so seriously. Why not go for a long walk or replenish our spirits with a good book or an afternoon playing with our children?

Find ways to nurture yourself. Schedule a massage. Take a luxurious bath—it's a cheap mini-vacation. Light some candles and listen to your favorite Mozart concerto. Plant some flowers, draw a picture, or enjoy a leisurely meal with some friends. Learn to laugh. Creative activities, such as expressive writing or "journaling," have been shown to reduce stress and alleviate the symptoms of asthma and rheumatoid arthritis in patients with these chronic illnesses.[14]

## BECOME BODY AWARE

We like to joke about "knowing our bodies," but the truth is, most of us go through the day completely unaware that we are hurting and that our bodies are in distress. We don't pay attention to our breathing, which is often shallow; our posture, which is often stooped or cramped; our muscles, which are tense and making us sore and tired. Increasing our somatic awareness (becoming more in tune with our body) is very important, as it reacquaints us with our emotional and physical needs. Monitor your bodily responses regularly—your respiration, muscular tension, and heart rate. Your body will "red-flag" you when something is wrong through tell-tale signs, such as a rapid heart beat, dizziness, or unusual body aches. Pay attention . . . ignoring these signals over time can actually be lethal.

> The bow always strung... will not do.
>
> GEORGE ELIOT

Activities such as meditation and prayer, massage, acupuncture, biofeedback, chiropractic therapy, and physiotherapy exercises can help us stay clued in to what is happening with us, inside and out. In fact, people who regularly practice meditation and prayer experience increased mental and physical energy, higher levels of satisfaction, fewer sleep problems, and show less of an inclination toward aggressiveness and emotionality.

## Prayer and Meditation—*See Golden Key #7*

And finally, one of the most important ways to manage stress is through exploring our spiritual beliefs and relying on our faith in times of anxiety and distress. After the 9–11 crisis, pollsters reported that among 560 Americans interviewed, 90 percent indicated that they had turned to religion, 60 percent had participated in group activities or vigils, and 36 percent had donated clothes, money, or blood.

Turning to God during periods of apprehension and worry is important because we learn to trust in God's power rather than ourselves. It is easy to get caught up in the materialism and egocentrism of our lives today. Spirituality gives us a broader perspective. While prayer provides a place of respite and calm during trying times, it is also an intimate conversation with God that allows us to see beyond our everyday realities and concerns, putting our stresses and anxieties into proper perspective.

Someone asked a Christian how he managed to deal with stress. He replied, "God means for us to live our lives a day at a time. He is in control of my situations, and I know that He won't let anything come my way that He and I can't handle. Even when it all seems to go wrong, He can turn the bad into good. I do all that I can do, and God has to do the rest. After all, the apostle Paul said, 'And we know that all things work together for good to those who love God, to those who are the called according to His purpose' " (Romans 8:28). This type of faith is a marvelous stress buster. Cast your burdens upon Him. Stay "prayed up," so that significant stress doesn't cause you to react in a deleterious manner.

The benefits of religious and spiritual beliefs are many:

- Religiously active people tend to have better coping strategies and are able to face the emotional challenges associated with bereavement, divorce, unemployment, and serious illness.
- Religious and spiritual beliefs are associated with reduced anxiety, anger, and depression, and with greater life and marital satisfaction, intact and stable families, well-being, and self-esteem.
- People who attend religious services have lower blood pressure and half the risk of heart attack as non-attendees. Religious beliefs may be as important in heart disease as traditional risk factors, such as homocysteine, cholesterol, and smoking!
- Several studies have discovered that individuals with greater spiritual involvement exhibit stronger immune systems.
- Religious beliefs are associated with fewer unhealthy behaviors, such as smoking and drinking.[15]

## REACHING OUT TO OTHERS

Spiritual practice also teaches us compassion for others and the importance of good deeds and right actions. It fosters forgiveness and tolerance of the imperfections in oneself and others, along with empathy and altruism. Helping others in need can distract us from our own troubles and encourage us to see that all people everywhere struggle and experience pain and frustration. As we mentioned earlier, socializing with others helps to reduce feelings of isolation and loneliness. An active spiritual life usually provides a rich social support network and promotes volunteer activities and a sense of community.

Two excellent books that help people deal with stress are *Deadly Emotions* by Don Colbert, M.D., and *The Secret to Navigating Life's Storms* by Dr. Terry Lyles.

## REACHING TOWARD INNER PEACE

Dr. Herbert Benson of Harvard Medical School maintains that religious beliefs and prayer may be health enhancing because they elicit the relaxation response, an inborn quieting reaction. He suggests that when we pray, we enter a relaxed state that enhances feelings of joy and contentment.[16] Relaxation, calming ritual, and quiet reflection are all aspects of spiritual meditation, prayer, and worship, and they go very far in mitigating the stresses of modern life.

# Sleep

**Sleep is almost as important
as breathing for your health.**

*Sleep restores energy to the body, particularly
to the brain and nervous system. The heartbeat
and breathing rate slow down, blood pressure falls,
muscles relax, and the overall metabolic rate
of the body decreases. Sleep allows the body to rest
and repair itself, having a major impact on every cell
in our body. Simply put, the better we sleep, the healthier
we are, the better we perform, and the longer we live.*

*It is vain for you to rise up early,
to sit up late,
to eat the bread of sorrows;
for so He gives His beloved sleep.*

PSALM 127:2

# The Vast Importance of Sleep

*Sleep that knits up*
*the ravel'd sleave of care . . .*

WILLIAM SHAKESPEARE

Sleep is one aspect of our daily routine that many of us take for granted . . . until we have a couple nights in a row of either not enough sleep or interrupted sleep. Yet it is without doubt one of the most important aspects of our daily routine as far as the maintenance of health and prevention of disease is concerned. After all, sleep is when the body regenerates itself, thereby making it ready for a whole new day of activity. Sleep gives our body a chance to rebalance itself. People who sleep well feel better, look younger, live longer, and are more energized and motivated throughout their days.

Therefore, when the body is deprived of sleep, even a little bit, one's overall degree of health can easily become compromised without one even knowing it. When you wake up tired, you feel irritated through the day. Combine a lack of sleep with high stress at your job, caring for a newborn or a sick child, a heavy study load at school, or going through menopause, and we start to feel like a basket case. You can't "burn the candle at both ends" and not pay a price.

Regularly catching only a few hours of sleep can hinder metabolism and hormone production in a way that is similar to the effects of aging and the early stages of diabetes. Chronic sleep loss may lead to depression and anxiety and speed the onset or increase the severity of age-related conditions, such as Type II diabetes, high blood pressure, obesity, and memory loss. Sleep debts are sort of like stress (see Golden Key #5—Stress). Most sleep-deprivation research has focused on what it does to the brain, but it is likely that sleep has many functions. In one study, subjects' blood sugar and hormone concentrations were restored after the sleep-recovery period.[1]

How serious can it get? Drowsiness accounts for 200,000 to 400,000 automobile accidents every year and is responsible for two-thirds of all industrial mishaps, most common among shift workers in the early morning hours. People who take sleeping pills on a regular basis are 50 percent more likely than other people to die in accidents. Sleeping pills are also the third most commonly used means in suicide.[2] Many people go to bed late and get up early to exercise to try to be healthy, but the reality is that in most cases those people would be better off to sleep more and exercise less. That is how important a good night's sleep is.

## Sleep Deprivation

If you feel you are among the sleep deprived, you are among a large group. According to the National Commission on Sleep Disorders, one in three Americans do not get enough sleep. Other experts estimate the number of chronically sleep-deprived people in this country to be closer to one in two (around 100 million people).[3]

> **Sleep is not a luxury. It is an essential key to Super Health. Make it a priority in your life.**

Sleep deprivation has long been used as a wartime torture, yet we often voluntarily inflict that same torture upon ourselves through our diet and lifestyle choices. *Torture* means "excruciating physical or mental pain; agony: *the torture of waiting in suspense.*" And that describes life for those who don't get enough sleep.

Here's why sleep deprivation is such an effective means of torture. After two sleepless days, one's concentration becomes difficult to maintain. A person may be able to perform well for short periods of time, but will be prone to mistakes and slips of attention. Stretch that to three sleepless days, and most people will have a difficult time thinking, seeing, and hearing clearly. Some will begin to hallucinate, seeing things that are not there. They will also lose track of their thoughts and confuse their daydreams with reality. At three days one can start to experience mild personality changes.

Beyond three days, a person will begin to lose contact with reality, becoming paranoid and fearful.

Thus, it behooves us to do everything possible to ensure that we get as much sleep as our bodies naturally require, which for most adults is between seven and eight and a half hours per night. The average American sleeps roughly six to seven hours a night. A century ago, people were sleeping about one and a half to two and a half hours longer. Many people sleep less as they get older, which can be an indication of a compromised hormone production, including melatonin and growth hormone (GH or HGH).

There is no magic number for how many hours of sleep you need, because every individual's requirements are different. You need as much sleep as you need to feel rested in the morning. If you don't feel refreshed, you won't be able to function at peak efficiency throughout the following day.

## REM Sleep

"Sleep is one of the most mysterious of all human activities. Exactly what happens during sleep is still not completely understood. By studying brain wave patterns, sleep researchers have identified four separate stages in a normal period of sleep. Stage 1 begins when we first fall asleep. Stage 1 is light sleep. Muscles relax and the heart slows down in stage 1. During stage 2, the heart rate increases. Stage 2 sleep is called *REM* sleep because of the rapid eye movements that occur during this stage. The autonomic nervous system is active in REM sleep, causing rapid breathing and increased stomach acid secretion. Stage 2 is the period when we dream. During deep sleep (stages 3 and 4), no dreaming occurs. In a normal sleep period, a person cycles from stage 1 to stage 4 in about 90 minutes."[4]

One of the most critical parts of the sleeping process is the REM sleep. This is the stage of sleep in which people dream, and when they dream, their eyes dart about underneath their eyelids, as though they are watching the events of a dream. While there is much about the phenomenon of dreaming that is not understood, this is the time when most of the psychological stressors of the mind and body are dealt with.

Accordingly, anything that interferes with REM sleep is bound to cause problems the next day. A large number of substances are known to interfere greatly with REM sleep, including alcohol, benzodiazepine tranquilizers (such as Valium), caffeine, and other mood-altering drugs. This can ultimately become catastrophic for the person who is regularly deprived of REM sleep, since the lack of this form of sleep gradually accumulates in the mind, day after day, until a critical "breakthrough moment" occurs during the *daytime*. This is when all the REM sleep that one has been deprived of accumulates together and breaks through into one's conscious mind while one is awake!

This can be catastrophic in the extreme, because it represents the accumulation of weeks and months of psychological stressors that would have otherwise been dissipated during REM sleep. However, if you deprive yourself of REM sleep on a routine basis, say through the routine use of alcohol, there will eventually come a day when all of these accumulated psychological stressors will break though into consciousness, with the tragic result that you can become mentally ill. This REM rebound effect has been known to cause visual and auditory hallucinations, extreme anxiety, and panic attacks.

> Since we spend one-third of our entire lives asleep, we need to consciously do everything possible to improve our sleep patterns.

The solution to this problem is straightforward—the individual must do everything in their power to eliminate the drugs, including caffeine, alcohol, or other substances that are blocking REM sleep at night and focus on improving all of the Seven Golden Keys. Once this is done, the problem will eventually take care of itself, although a period of extremely vivid dreaming may ensue while the brain seeks to retain internal equilibrium within itself.

## Human Growth Hormone as Well as the Immune System

If you need a few more reasons for committing yourself to a good night's sleep, consider that by guarding your sleep you can increase your production of the human growth hormone (GH), which repairs cell damage and is now being marketed as an anti-aging substance.[5] The body produces its highest amounts of GH during the first two hours of sleep. Don't be fooled by companies that market the benefits of human growth hormone (GH/HGH) in a pill, as it is mostly unsubstantiated hype. The benefits of growth hormone are well established, but what these companies are selling is not GH/HGH—it is what is known as amino acid *secretagogues,* or nutrient hormone precursors that the body uses in its production of GH/HGH. There is a thread of truth to the hype—certain amino acids taken in high dose on an empty stomach at bedtime can increase production of GH/HGH in the body. The products I have seen that claim GH/HGH benefits have a mere fraction of the dosages recommended in the studies.

Additionally, recent studies by Nigel Curtis, a senior researcher at the Murdoch Children's Research Institute and head of infectious diseases at the Royal Children's Hospital in Sydney, Australia, suggest that a sleep-deprived person has a weakened immune system and a higher risk of becoming sick. In a paper published in *Nature Review Immunology,* he and his colleagues at Melbourne University drew this conclusion, after reviewing all studies on sleep and immunity over the past ten years: chronic sleep deprivation, rather than a short-term interruption, was damaging to the immune system.[6] Clearly, our immune system is revitalized during our hours of sleep.

## Insomnia—the Enemy of Sleep

One of mankind's oldest complaints and the greatest enemy of restful sleep is the plague of insomnia, or habitual sleeplessness. For a wide variety of reasons, many people just can't get to sleep at night or can't fall back to sleep if they wake up. If you're one of them, you're not alone. It affects more than one in ten Americans and about 30 percent of healthy seniors.[7] Failure to get an entire night's sleep on most nights over a one-month period is considered chronic insomnia and threatens the well-being, productivity, and safety of all who suffer with it.

One cause of insomnia that affects about 20 million Americans is sleep apnea.[8] The person with apnea actually stops breathing altogether for about 10 seconds at a time while they are asleep. When the breathing stops, the level of oxygen in the body drops, then the person wakes up with a start, and the breathing resumes. This phenomenon may occur up to 200 times a night, and it's not a surprise that they wake up feeling exhausted. Sleep apnea is associated with an increased risk of high blood pressure, heart attack, congestive heart failure, stroke, and Type II diabetes.

Sleep apnea occurs most frequently in those individuals who have a snoring problem, and, indeed, snoring by itself can cause oxygen deficits within the body, which reveal themselves the next day in persistent sleepiness. It keeps a person from entering into sleep at the REM level, which can lead to catastrophic problems.

Unfortunately, there are no truly good remedies for either snoring or sleep apnea, as sleep medicine is in its infancy. Nevertheless, it is critical to work toward optimal health by addressing all Seven Golden Keys. Sometimes these issues will resolve themselves once food intolerances are addressed and optimal fitness and body weight are obtained. Conventional medical approaches address symptoms and rarely get to the root of the problem. Sleep apnea is extremely serious and can be a death sentence if it is not taken seriously.

One conventional route is to first go through a formal sleep study, in which a person sleeps in a controlled environment, where they are constantly being monitored for various abnormalities. Once these abnormalities are documented, you will generally be given two surgical options and a device called Continuous Positive Airway Pressure (CPAP)—a mask you wear while you sleep that keeps your airway open through continuous air pressure.

## Melatonin

One way that many people have found to improve their sleep is to take the neurohormone called *melatonin*, which is released by the pineal gland from within the center of the brain when one is asleep.

The pineal gland is influenced by the amount of light seen by our eyes each day, and production of the hormone is cyclical.

Throughout early life, melatonin is produced in abundance, but shortly after puberty the production begins to drop and continues to decrease steadily as we age. The changes in sleep quality that often come with age seem to trigger shifts in the endocrine system, altering hormone levels and metabolism. Researchers say that a good night's sleep may be a natural form of hormone therapy, particularly for older adults.[9]

Scientists have found increased blood levels of stress hormones in people with chronic insomnia, suggesting that these individuals suffer from sustained, round-the-clock activation of the body's system for responding to stress.[10] Melatonin helps produce a substance called arginine vasotocin, which inhibits an adrenal gland stress hormone called cortisol. Cortisol has multiple functions, including protein, carbohydrate, and fat metabolism. Cortisol production is increased during periods of stress, causing the body to feel agitated. Melatonin helps induce sleep by providing arginine vasotocin to inhibit the cortisol production. Immune functioning is also improved when cortisol production is cut back.[11] Melatonin is also thought to be an antiaging hormone.

Melatonin helps to regulate REM sleep, just as it also helps to make us drowsy so that we feel like sleeping. This is especially important for insomniacs. Melatonin is also extremely effective for restoring sleep cycles when you change time zones. My favorite way of taking melatonin is to take it one hour before the time I want to be asleep.

It is wise to begin with the smallest dose of melatonin (say 1 mg or even less), so that you slowly test and adjust yourself up to the most effective dose for you as an individual. A good reason to start with smaller doses is that when some people take too high a dose of melatonin they develop extreme sleepiness or fogginess the next morning, and it may take longer than usual to clear their heads. This effect typically doesn't last very long, and it could easily be a sign that one is using too high a dose of melatonin for one's own idiosyncratic sleep needs.

Numerous research studies have shown melatonin to be extremely potent in the fight against cancer. For not only is it a very powerful antioxidant in its own right, it helps to turn off the various cancer pathways within the body, and this is a very important finding indeed. Melatonin is one of the few antioxidants that can penetrate the mitochondria, our cells' "power plants," and it seems to protect the mitochondria from free-radical damage.

In fact, a recent study proved the effectiveness of melatonin in preventing breast cancer. Two groups of women were examined during this study—those who worked the night shift, and those who did not. Remarkably, those women who worked the night shift had a much higher rate of breast cancer than those who worked regular daytime hours. The reason for this is that the nighttime lighting of working the nightshift suppresses melatonin production, and thereby makes a person susceptible to the very same cancers that melatonin prevents.[12]

**Warning: Do not self-prescribe supplements if you are taking prescription drugs.**

One way to deal with this problem, particularly for nightshift workers, is to take a melatonin supplement as soon as one eventually goes to bed. However, the single most effective way of reaping the many health benefits of melatonin is to sleep normal hours, in total darkness, so that the pineal gland in the brain can produce its own melatonin, in just the right amounts that the body needs to remain healthy. As a side note, night workers are virtually assured of being dangerously Vitamin D deficient and should strongly consider being tested and taking a supplement containing Vitamin D3 and Vitamin A. The proper test is called 25(OH)D or 25-hydroxyvitamin D and is available at www.totalhealthtests.com and www.lef.org.

However, there is an important caveat that must first be heeded before this natural melatonin production can take place. It is now known that melatonin production can only take place in total darkness. Even a tiny nightlight or the light from an alarm clock can greatly interfere with natural melatonin production. This being the case, you can either make sure that you are sleeping in a pitch black bedroom, or you can use the very handy "eye pillows" that are available through a variety of outlets. They block all light from entering the eyes, and in the process, they ensure that the greatest amount of melatonin will naturally be produced within the brain, but darkness is the best.

## Other Natural Remedies to Help You Sleep

There are several natural remedies to help you sleep. Millions of doses of sleeping pills are prescribed every year, and sleeping pills should be avoided because they are addictive. They interfere with your body's normal sleeping rhythms because they temporarily alter the activity of the brain.

Moreover, sleep problems such as insomnia are symptoms of other problems that often can't be treated with sleep medications. Researchers note that doctors could be missing these underlying problems, even to the point of compounding them by turning instead to sleep medications as an inappropriate solution.[13]

Again, *do not self-prescribe supplements if you are taking prescription drugs. Also, don't mix supplements. Try one at a time and see how it works for you.*

### SUPER HEALTH KEY #3—EXERCISE

For starters, you can begin a regular exercise program, because nothing has been shown to improve sleep quality as effectively as regular exercise. It relieves stress and leads to relaxation. But don't work out within three hours before going to bed because your metabolism needs time to slow down.

### CREATE A SLEEP SANCTUARY

Keep your bedroom completely dark. Wear ear plugs if you are easily awakened by small noises. Keep the bedroom comfortable and quiet, with beautiful drapes and pleasant, peaceful pictures. If it is too quiet, listen to a recording of nature sounds or soft music. Find a temperature that is most conducive to your sleeping—many people find that cool temperatures help to find a restful sleep (70°F has been shown to be conducive for sleep). Don't allow the air to get stuffy. Keep the air circulating with a fan in your bedroom. Wake up naturally with sunlight or a light alarm.

Invest in a comfortable bed. After many attempts to find a bed that was comfortable to both me and my wife, we discovered the Tempur-Pedic Swedish style memory foam mattress and pillows (www.tempurpedic.com). One word of caution: to avoid out-gassing of the foam, allow this mattress to fully air out before using it, then use a mattress cover that seals the top surface of the mattress.

## TRYPTOPHAN

The calming amino acid tryptophan, which I previously mentioned in the stress chapter, is also a terrific natural remedy for sleep disorders. Tryptophan is commonly thought to be the reason why people think they feel so sleepy after eating their Thanksgiving turkey dinner—because turkey contains a large amount of tryptophan. The reality is that almost no one eats a sufficient amount of turkey to get enough tryptophan to cause drowsiness. The truth is that the consumption of high glycemic foods, such as stuffing, potatoes, cornbread, and pie, cause such an insulin response that people actually get sleepy from the spike of insulin after eating Thanksgiving dinner.

> Optimal Nutrition is probably the single best thing that one can do to help improve the quality of one's sleep.

As we saw earlier in the Stress chapter, tryptophan is now available over the counter. However, if for some reason you have trouble getting tryptophan by itself, you can get the next best thing, which is known as 5HTP (or 5-hydroxytrytophan). This is the immediate precursor to tryptophan in the body, and it can definitely help to mitigate the effects of insomnia within the body. It is most effective if it is taken with Vitamin B6, since this vitamin cofactor helps in the conversion of 5HTP to bona fide tryptophan. My experience is that if you take high dose Vitamin Bs (particularly Vitamin B12) over a number of days it can result in making you dream in such vivid color that it can actually shock you awake!

## SUPPLEMENT WITH GABA

Another way to improve your sleep quality is to take a GABA supplement before you retire at night. GABA (gamma amino butyric acid) is a natural inhibitory neurotransmitter within the brain, and it helps to induce a state of calm throughout the brain and body. Another relaxing supplement is the amino acid *theanine*, which is found in green tea. However, you wouldn't want to drink a cup of green tea before bedtime because of the caffeine it contains (unless one uses a decaffeinated variety). Fortunately, theanine is now available as a nutritional supplement all by itself, and it not only helps to induce a state of calm and tranquility within the mind, it also helps to improve your overall mood during the day as well. If none of these sleep solutions, together with the other six Golden Keys, are working, be sure to consult a specialist in this field to rule out a medical situation that needs attention. My preference is to get a diagnosis from a conventional medical practitioner and then seek a natural medical practitioner to be treated.

## VALERIAN AND KAVA ROOT

Many people like to take the herb known as valerian before sleeping, because it does indeed induce a state of drowsiness in most individuals, probably because it binds in the same brain receptors that Valium and other benzodiazepines do. The very same thing applies to the Polynesian relaxant known as kava root.

## SUPER HEALTH KEY #2—OPTIMAL NUTRITION

In addition to exercise, embarking on the Four Corners Program for Optimal Nutrition is probably the single best thing that you can do to help improve the quality of your sleep. By changing your diet for the better, as the Four Corners Plan explains in detail, the body will naturally begin to operate more naturally, including detoxifying the toxic substances that help to keep us up at night. This is what internal toxins do—they prevent sleep because they disrupt the entire brain and its concomitant neurological functioning.

Moreover, by providing your body with the many natural substances that it needs to operate at peak efficiency, through superior nutrition, you will naturally encourage your brain and body to operate normally for a change, and this can naturally result in far better sleep patterns.

Indeed, sometimes the cause for insomnia can be the toxic load on the body of all sorts of environmental toxins and neurotoxins within the body. In this case, consider the detailed instructions in Golden Key #6—Environmental Hazards.

## GET OUT OF BED IF YOU CAN'T SLEEP

**Looking for the Fountain of Youth? Start by getting enough sleep tonight!**

Another effective tip on beating the insomnia problem is to never lie in bed if you are not sleepy. Get up and begin to do other things instead of tossing and turning all night. For as long as you associate the bed with sleep, and only with sleep, it will help to encourage you to sleep once you've "taken to bed." However, if you want to sleep but can't, do not engage in activities that stimulate you to be more awake, such as exercise, staring at a computer monitor, or watching TV. Consider sitting in a chair and reading the Bible.

## DON'T DRINK BEFORE GOING TO BED

For obvious reasons, stay away from liquids in the late evening. Getting up in the middle of the night to go to the bathroom breaks your sleep cycles. If you do drink, make it chamomile herbal tea, which has long been used as a sleep inducer. It contains tryptophan as well as calcium.

Despite the fact that alcohol may make you feel sleepy, it disrupts deeper sleep cycles. You'll wake up feeling lousy, even if you've slept a long time.

## ESTABLISH NORMAL SLEEP PATTERNS

World-class athletes whom I know stress the importance of establishing a daily rhythm for eating, exercise, and sleeping to maximize their training. The human body loves routine, and setting our habits and following them consistently will go a long way toward establishing a healthy sleep cycle.

## STAY AWAY FROM CAFFEINE

Always avoid caffeine in the late afternoon and evening. Whatever source you are getting it from—coffee, tea, hot cocoa, chocolate, and some pain killers and antihistamines—caffeine can remain in your system for six hours and keep you awake.

## WIND DOWN BEFORE GOING TO BED

Another time-honored remedy for insomnia is to read for a while before going to bed. The very process of reading helps the mind to unwind itself, and many insomniacs find themselves dozing off within a few minutes of beginning to read.

Don't watch television or work on the computer right before going to bed. And don't work on paying the bills or trying to solve work problems as you're heading toward bed. Find ways to unwind.

Get the worries out of your head. If you have matters that need to be taken care of the next day, write them down and leave the anxiety on the sheet of paper. Keep a pad or journal or hand recorder next to your bed and record anything you have to remember, then forget about it.

## AVOID SNACKS BEFORE GOING TO BED

Minimize late-night eating. The process of digestion is the heaviest energy demand on the body and can interfere with deep sleep. Try to eat a satisfying evening meal two or three hours before bedtime.

## RELAX WITH A BATH

Take a hot bath before going to bed. Put several drop of a soothing essential oil such as chamomile in the water for even better relaxation.

## CONSIDER SOCKS—WARM FEET = DEEP SLEEP

Don't laugh. Warm feet—a sign of healthy blood flow—may help induce restful sleep. Thermoregulation—the body's heat distribution system—is strongly linked to sleep cycles. Even lying down increases sleepiness by redistributing heat in the body from the core to the periphery.

## SUPER HEALTH KEY #7— PRAYER AND MEDITATION

Finally, both prayer and meditation have been proven to greatly assist the sleeping process. The vast importance of prayer cannot be overestimated, because it is the miraculous process of talking directly with your very own Creator. This is the single most vital "connection" in the entire universe—that of the created individual "hooking up" with his or her Creator. God loves us beyond our wildest dreams, and this very realization can help to alleviate the many anxieties that can easily keep us awake at night.

Meditation is also an extremely effective means of unwinding, so that you can sleep better. Meditation has been shown to increase the natural relaxing power of the brain itself, as documented through hundreds of EEG (electroencephalogram) studies.

# Environmental Hazards

**Without becoming paranoid
or obsessive about environmental hazards,**
*the reality is that we all face them every day and in almost
countless ways. Polluted air, contaminants in the water,
food additives and preservatives, and pesticides and herbicides
are only a few issues on an increasingly extensive list.
Gradually, over time we have been exposed to steadily
increasing numbers of toxic poisons, which can compromise
our immune system and lead to disease. It is critical for us
to understand that we are truly under attack from unseen
hazards, and this is magnified by poor diet and lifestyle choices.
We must educate ourselves regarding environmental hazards
and effect change in our own homes to counteract
and prevent them from doing their damage.*

*The heaven, even the heavens, are the Lord's;
but the earth He has given to the children of men.*

PSALM 115:16

# Environmental Hazards

*Then God blessed them, and God said to them,*
*"Be fruitful and multiply; fill the earth and*
*subdue it; have dominion over the fish*
*of the sea, over the birds of the air, and over*
*every living thing that moves on the earth."*
*And God said, "See, I have given you every herb*
*that yields seed which is on the face*
*of all the earth, and every tree whose fruit*
*yields seed; to you it shall be for food.*
*Also, to every beast of the earth, to every bird*
*of the air, and to everything that creeps*
*on the earth, in which there is life, I have given*
*every green herb for food"; and it was so.*

GENESIS 1:28–30

The earth is a living organism with built-in self-organizing and self-regulating systems. The earth's intricate and elegant design reflects the creativity and imagination of an intelligent Creator, and everything in our world was fashioned with purpose and reason. God gave mankind dominion over His creation, with an eye toward our cooperating with Him as good stewards of our natural environment. However, "dominion" does not mean the earth is ours to treat as we please. While we can enjoy and benefit from the amazing bounty all around us, we also have a responsibility to uphold and protect it.

What we see today is mankind's failure to be accountable to God's purpose. The delicate ecological balance of our planet has become terribly compromised. We have contaminated our air and water, and we are overconsuming resources that are not well managed. Overworked land has resulted in soil loss, drought, famine, and eventually desertification. Pesticides and herbicides and hormone-enhancing drugs, chemical additives and preservatives, chemical sprays and food processing damage our foods to a truly profound extent. We are surrounded by asbestos, formaldehyde (in particle board, plywood, paints, and plastics), vinyl chloride, and radioactivity—all of which are dangerous. Polluted air, noise pollution, traffic congestion, radiation hazards, and psychological stress, are just some of the byproducts of today's obsessive technological growth and expansion. It is amazing that anyone is healthy. It is truly incredible what our bodies can endure.

You will learn things in this chapter that can be frightening, such as the toxicity of many of the personal care items and cosmetics you are using right now. The bottom line is that we must take control of what is controllable and help our bodies withstand the constant attacks from sources we cannot control. We can do this by maximizing our health and following the Super Health principles. There are some things we cannot change, but most of our health issues result from nutrition and lifestyle decisions that we have made. I challenge you to start to make better decisions. This chapter will provide helpful suggestions and safer alternatives. A few of these hazards are deemed controversial, with passionate scientists on both sides of the issues. Nevertheless, my challenge to you is that you examine the evidence presented here and assess the risks for yourself. Remember the old adage: it is far better to be safe than sorry.

## When the Troubles Began

In her landmark 1962 book, *Silent Spring,* Rachel Carson noted that many of our troubles began with the introduction of large quantities of pesticides into our environment in the 1930s to protect agricultural crops. This was followed by the post-World War II registration and introduction of nearly 25,000 pesticide products into our food supply and environment in the name of money and waste management. Yes, waste management! Our government needed something to do with the chemicals that were produced and used in the war, which created an industry in and of itself. Unfortunately, poisons were allowed to be registered and used in our environment to create jobs and commerce.

Carson forecasted, quite accurately, that the indiscriminate use of pesticides would haunt us for generations to come by disrupting health and ecological processes fundamental to life on earth. Countless other books and scientific research have chronicled the devastating effects of these chemicals on our health, and the problem is getting worse. *There are approximately 77,000 chemicals produced in North America alone. More than 3,000 of these are added to our food supply, and 1,000 new chemicals are introduced each year.* They are absorbed into groundwater, rivers, lakes, and oceans, spewed into our air, and quite intentionally added to our food supply.[1]

In addition, a radical change in farming methods has led to a decline in the quality and nutritious content of our foods. In the past, farmers would plant different crops every year, rotating them so that a balance in the soil was preserved. Pesticides weren't needed, because insects attracted to one crop would disappear with the next. Instead of using chemical fertilizers, farmers enriched their fields with manure, returning organic matter to the soil to continue the biological cycle. These respectful, earth-friendly farming methods changed drastically when farmers switched from organic to synthetic products. The massive use of chemical fertilizers and pesticides changed the whole fabric of agriculture and farming. Yields were tripled . . . but at a devastating cost.[2]

In addition to the way food is grown, there are many other problems with the quality of our food today. We have chemical additives, irradiated produce, fat substitutes, chemical sweeteners, chemicals leached from packaging, and new "designer" (genetically modified and engineered) foods. These prepared foods are coming to us from big industry because of our demand for it. We no longer grow our own produce, gather fruit in season, or purchase our meat from a local farmer or butcher. What we have lost is the pristine quality and richness of vital nutrients from our foods. Although the impacts of these choices are catching up with us as adults, the far greater impact is on those who are being born today. In the March 2004 PBS documentary

"Trade Secrets," commentator Bill Moyers stated: "Today, not a single child is born free of synthetic chemicals," and "If breast milk were regulated like infant formula, it would commonly violate FDA levels for poisonous substances in food."[3]

## The Link to Our Health

In December 2004, doctors in the Ukraine confirmed that dioxins were the cause of the poisoning that ravaged the skin and health of Viktor Yushchenko, a presidential candidate. Dioxin is a chemical that is predominately a byproduct of human industry and comes to us slowly through what we eat. They bio-accumulate in the food chain, and a high exposure to them can increase our risk of cancer by 40 percent as well as create a litany of other effects (such as Yushchenko's severe skin problem and twenty years of near-instant aging).

What assaulted Yushchenko's health, almost overnight through extreme exposure in the poisoning, is simply a more dramatic example of what we do to ourselves by choosing to eat fried foods, hydrogenated oils, pesticide-laden, processed foods, and exposing ourselves to numerous environmental hazards. We are aging ourselves prematurely and opening a door to diseases, which is unlikely we would otherwise get. Here's the point: we can make a few simple choices that make a dramatic change in our lives. The body is an incredible design, capable of fending off numerous attacks from a plethora of directions, but overload is imminent if we don't make good choices.

> The challenges we face are not insurmountable. Take control and bring change to what you allow in your own home.

Gradually, over time we have been exposed to steadily increasing numbers of toxic poisons. Because our bodies have never encountered these toxins before, we lack the innate ability to detoxify and eliminate many of them. Most are fat-soluble poisons that have been accumulating and persisting in our own fat tissue, most likely from the point of conception onward, which is why we are seeing such high levels in breast milk. Breast milk is still the healthiest food for infants; however, this is another example of the importance of managing the hazards over which we have control. These environmental toxins are not only stored endocrine disruptors, but they also circulate throughout the body, stressing detoxification systems and organs, disrupting enzymatic functions, energy metabolism, and cellular communications. Once cellular communication is disrupted, the immune system's innate surveillance capabilities break down, resulting in deficiencies and disease. And worst of all, these internal toxins are all carcinogenic by nature. There is little wonder that we've experienced such a huge increase in cancer cases in the last few decades. Back in the 1960s, only one in five people eventually developed cancer in their lives; now the odds are an astonishing one in every two people.

Given the heavy implications of environmental pollution and toxins, it is easy to feel helpless and without recourse. The problem seems too enormous in scope for us to change anything. The magnitude of the problem may seem overwhelming, but it is not insurmountable. We all have the capacity to effect change on a personal and a local level. It may sound overly simple, but the first place to begin making these changes is in our own homes.

Read on to learn about the most dangerous "environmental culprits," and the types of damage they cause. Each environmental issue is followed by suggestions and recommendations for alternative products or steps to take to mitigate these dangers.

## Plastics

*Phthalates (DEHP), bis-phenol A, polycarbonates, nonylphenols . . .* they just roll off the tongue, don't they? These are just a few of the chemicals found in *all* plastics—from water bottles, carpets, and Tupperware™ to car parts, perfumes, and cling wrap. Next to pesticides, plastic is the most pervasive and persistent "personal use" product around today. Plastic is everywhere and used in everything, and yet few of us understand how toxic it really is. We store our leftovers in it; we microwave our meals in it; our favorite drinks (water, juice, or soda) are bottled and stored in it; and our brand-new cars are out-gassing it for up to two years.

As a consumer of water that is bottled in plastic, you have no idea how long the fluid has been sitting on the store shelf or in a warehouse before transport. Why is this such a problem? Because water that has been sitting in hot warehouses is contaminated with plasticizers. Plasticizers leach into the water over time as the flexible, malleable plastic degrades. In addition, people will often reuse plastic bottles. This is also dangerous, as oxidation occurs after a bottle has been opened. When air has been introduced into the bottle, plastic degrades much more quickly and hence becomes much more toxic.

*Phthalates* are universal in our environment and can be found as contaminants in just about anything. International use of phthalates includes softeners of plastics, oily substances in perfumes, additives to hair sprays, lubricants, wood finishers, and millions of other manufactured products. They have been known to cause genital abnormalities in males and are contributing to the rise in *hypospadia*, a birth defect. Phthalates, such as those found in perfumes, are also toxic (poisonous) to both the fetus and babies.

Often found on the bottom of plastic bottles, other containers, and shopping bags, the numbers and letters shown with the chasing-arrows "recycling" symbol mean the following[4]:

- #1 PETE or PET (polyethylene terephthalate): brighter than PVC plastic, very transparent, and almost looks like glass. PET is generally considered the safest *single-use* plastic bottle choice. There has been some research to suggest, however, that long-term storage of beverages in PET containers may increase the levels of DEHP, an endocrine disrupting phthalate and a probable human carcinogen. Therefore, experts recommend this water not be stored for long periods of time, and that the containers never be reused.
- #2 HDPE (high density polyethylene): used for "cloudy" milk and water jugs, opaque food bottles.
- #3 PVC or V (polyvinyl chloride): used in some cling wraps (especially commercial brands), some "soft" bottles.

- #4 LDPE (low density polyethylene): used in food storage bags and some "soft" bottles.
- #5 PP (polypropylene): used in rigid containers, including some baby bottles, and some cups and bowls.
- #6 PS (polystyrene): used in foam "clam-shell"-type containers, meat and bakery trays, and in its rigid form, clear takeout containers, some plastic cutlery and cups. Polystyrene may leach styrene into food it comes into contact with. A recent study in *Environmental Health Perspectives* concluded that some styrene compounds leaching from food containers are estrogenic (meaning they can disrupt normal hormonal functioning). Styrene is also considered a possible human carcinogen by the World Health Organization's International Agency for Research on Cancer.
- #7 Other (usually polycarbonate): used in five-gallon water bottles, some baby bottles, some metal can linings. Polycarbonate can release its primary building block, *bisphenol A*, another suspected hormone disruptor, into liquids and foods. In 1998, the Japanese government ordered manufacturers there to recall and destroy polycarbonate tableware meant for use by children because it contained excessive amounts of bisphenol A. Other sources of potential bisphenol A exposure include food can linings, dental sealants, plastic food containers, refrigerator shelves, juice and milk containers, microwave ovenware, film, sheets of laminate, water main filters, nail polish, automobile parts, enamels, varnishes, and adhesives. Bisphenol A was invented in the 1930s during the search for synthetic estrogens. Some health effects of bisphenol A are: breast tissue development, reduced sperm count, increased rate of sexual maturation, adipogenesis (contributing to obesity), prostate health problems (including benign prostate hypertrophy and prostate cancer), and chromosomal damage. Most people are being educated that the #7 plastics are the safest. I propose that this is not so, and that one should minimize drinking out of, heating in, or storing food in plastics of any kind.

Unfortunately, many plastic products are not labeled with a number or initials. When in doubt, you can call the manufacturer directly. On food products, there is usually a toll-free question/comment number listed.

## ALTERNATIVES TO PLASTIC

- Lead-Free Glass—See www.glashaus.com, which makes lead-free glass canning jars and storage containers.
- Ceramic or stainless steel cooking implements and storage products, such as lead-free Corning Ware (www.corningware.com).
- Pyrex containers (www.pyrexware.com).

## OTHER TIPS

- Buy your water in glass water bottles (see Golden Key #1— Hydration, for recommended waters).
- Use cellophane or waxed paper for packing your children's lunches, along with small lidded glass containers.
- Do not allow the dentist to put plastic sealant on your children's teeth.
- Choose a pacifier made of silicon, rather than plastic.

# Food Processing, Pesticides, Irradiation, and GMOs

## FOOD PROCESSING/PESTICIDES

In addition to plastics, the food processing industry adds more than 3,000 chemicals to our food annually. These are chemicals that you cannot pronounce, much less understand why they are in your food. They are not there to prevent deficiency and disease, but are added for the convenience and profit of both manufacturer and grocer. Chemical food additives and preservatives have been put there by manufacturers to increase shelf life. Many of these manufacturers sell synthetic products instead of healthy organic foods and then try to make up for the lack of nutritious content by adding artificial coloring and flavoring.

But additives and preservatives are just part of the problem. According to the EPA, 60 percent of herbicides, 90 percent of fungicides, and 30 percent of insecticides are known to be carcinogenic. Pesticide residues have been detected in 50 to 90 percent of U.S. foods, increasing our risk for cancer, Parkinson's disease, miscarriage, birth defects, nerve damage, and more.[5]

The FDA, USDA, the World Health Organization, and the USEPA all assert that our food supply is the safest in the world. No need to worry, right? Wrong! Consider reading Lynn Lawson's research in her book *Staying Well in a Toxic World.* She reveals how studies by the EPA, the FDA, and countless other agencies demonstrate the impact our polluted environment is having on our food supply and well-being. Lawson shows the numerous pesticides that are missed in testing, along with the different pesticides that are linked to cancer and that are legally allowed on food, and how few food shipments are tested for illegal residues. One can

> **An essential key to health and reversing aging is identifying and eliminating the toxins from our life.**

understand why Dr. Richard Jackson, California's chief of communicable disease control, said in 1993, "Placing your trust in the FDA's monitoring of (pesticide) residues is a lot like standing in a downpour holding a teacup over your head; you have no way of capturing all that's coming at you."[6]

To learn more, read: *Diet from a Poison Planet* by David Steinman. This book discusses pesticide residue in foods and rates them by content.

## FOOD IRRADIATION

Food irradiation is used to extend the shelf life of our foods by eliminating or controlling pests, sprouting, and rapid ripening. This is done by exposing the foods to certain levels of gamma radiation, the shortest wavelength of the light wave spectrum of solar energy. Not only does this process not work, it is highly dangerous for the individuals performing this process, just as it is also dangerous to those consuming the irradiated foods.

In 1992, the FDA approved irradiation of poultry; and in 1997, it approved irradiation of red meats. There are many foods now that are being delivered to our supermarkets that have gone through this process. The food irradiation industry and the FDA claim that the food itself is not radioactive or contaminated. However, somewhat contradictorily, the FDA has also reported that irradiated food can increase the risks for developing tumors in laboratory animals; this report was made public in 1968.[7]

The FDA also reported that human cells appear to be very sensitive to gamma radiation and the altered byproducts in irradiated food. The major macro-nutrients, such as carbohydrates, fats, and proteins in irradiated foods have potentially serious and negative consequences, just as they also produce altered metabolic rates when they are ingested and digested by humans. For example, carbohydrates in irradiated food may impair cell division. Fats and fatty acids in irradiated foods are changed into peroxidases and other toxic metabolites, acting as free radicals and wreaking havoc on our cells and DNA. New compounds and potential contaminants are created during the irradiating procedures. These are called unique radiolytic products (URPs). No one really knows what these are capable of doing to the cells of human beings. Remember, we are not able to completely detoxify every toxic remnant in our body each day. As a matter of fact, some individuals' detoxification systems are so weak and damaged that they accumulate toxins rapidly. This bioaccumulation of "toxic stuff" is one of the reasons why so many Americans are sick and dying of cancers at accelerated rates today.

The one mineral that has been conclusively demonstrated to protect us from toxicity-induced cancers is the trace mineral selenium. It was discovered in the early 1960s at the Cleveland Clinic that cancer rates are always the lowest in those parts of the world where selenium levels are the highest, and vice versa. Ohio presently has the distinction of having the lowest amount of selenium in the soil, whereas North Dakota has the highest. We even know *why* this is the case—namely, because selenium is an essential cofactor in the highly protective antioxidant enzyme *glutathione peroxidase*. It takes four atoms of selenium to make one functional molecule of this life-saving enzyme. Indeed, several medical studies have conclusively demonstrated that a mere 200 micrograms of selenium per day can slash our overall risk of cancer anywhere from 40 percent to an astounding 82 percent. Other studies have shown that selenium is a more effective mood enhancer than all other mood enhancing drugs and nutrients, undoubtedly because of its profound detoxifying ability within the body. Selenium can even detoxify mercury, one of the most horrendously dangerous of the heavy metals. It simply latches on to the mercury atom and converts it into the relatively harmless compound mercury selenide, which is then safely excreted out of the body. However, it must be remembered that like most everything else in our diet, too much of a good thing can be dangerous, so try to limit your overall selenium intake to approximately 400 to 800 mcg per day.

There are many web sites available where you can find out more about the effects of various toxins in our food supply. Go to www.citizen.org/cmep/foodsafety/food_irrad.htm to find the local grocers that are accepting irradiated foods into their stores.

## GMOS

Where do GMOs (genetically modified, altered, and biotechnical designed foods) play into this picture? According to Nathan Batalion, between 1997 and 1999 gene-modified foods (GM) ingredients suddenly appeared in two-thirds of all U.S. processed foods.[8] Between the years of 1997 and 2004, these foods increased 47-fold across the globe. Although there seems to be a downward trend in biotech crop production and FDA approvals, it is still a significant concern. Most soy, cotton, and canola are genetically modified, in addition to half of the corn produced.

GMO seeds and crops do not focus on nutrition, and even if added to the seed, may not be delivered properly into our bodies. A very real health concern related to eating these foods is whether or not the genetic manipulation of the seed will lead to increased risk of diseases, such as cancer or even disabling deformities. Biotechnology is a vital issue that impacts us all, as poignantly stated by Nathan B. Batalion in his document *50 Harmful Effects of Genetically Modified Foods*. He states, "The central problem underlying all of this technology is not just its short-term benefits and long-term drawbacks, but the overall attempt to 'control living nature based on an erroneous mechanistic view.' "[9]

GMOs give us crops that are bigger, stronger, and produce greater yields, yet at what cost? We are not just what we eat—we are what we *ate*. If genetically altered food has the potential to genetically alter *us*, as well as our not-yet-conceived children, then we definitely need to take another look at this disturbing issue.

More and more Americans are demanding to know what foods contain GMOs. An ABC news poll found that 92 percent of Americans want mandatory GMO labeling on foods.[10] Many labels, especially in health food stores, are now making it a point to let us know that the foods we are purchasing have no genetically modified organisms in them.

## EASY SOLUTIONS TO SAFER FOODS

- Eat only whole, natural organic foods. Organic foods by definition must be free from all GM organisms and produced without artificial pesticides and fertilizers and from an animal reared without the routine use of antibiotics, growth promoters, or other drugs. There are local farmers markets and whole food co-ops in every area of the country. The Organic and Natural foods industry has exploded and made it much easier for people in busy populated cities to obtain clean whole foods that have not been processed (or perhaps just moderately processed). For rural folks the best bet is still to try to find the time to grow a garden, visit your local growers, eat fruit and vegetables in season and grown locally. In addition as mentioned previously, purchase your protein (i.e., meats, eggs, and dairy) from grain-free, grass-fed cattle growers (i.e., www.texasgrassfedbeef.com) or, if you have Internet access, do a Google search for local farmers in your area for items such as beef, chickens, eggs, turkey, goat, and raw dairy products.

▪ Never eat anything with "hydrogenated" or "partially hydrogenated" oils in it.

▪ Read labels—if a label lists ingredients such as corn flour and meal, dextrin, starch, soy sauce, margarine, and tofu, there is a good chance that it has come from GM corn or soy.[11]

▪ Look closely at produce stickers. These stickers on fruit and vegetables contain different PLU codes depending on how the item was grown. The PLU code for conventionally grown fruit consists of four numbers; organically grown fruit has five numbers, prefaced by the number 9; and GM fruit has five numbers prefaced by the number 8.

▪ Avoid all fortified or enriched foods. This is the equivalent of taking all the natural oil out of your hair and then adding conditioner.

▪ Avoid all processed foods. These are the foods most likely to have GM ingredients.

▪ Avoid eating food from airports and train stations, as the food in these locations has been irradiated.[12]

> **What is the best way to protect yourself? Create and support a strong immune system as your first line of defense.**

## Cosmetics and Fragrances

Up to 400 different toxic chemicals are used in a single perfume manufactured today, and today's fragrances are 97 percent synthetic chemicals. To get our shampoo to smell like watermelon or strawberry, chemists must manipulate our neurosensors, making us believe that we are detecting the smell of those fruits. No one is standing over a perfume bottle squeezing essence of watermelon into the bottle! Instead, combinations from among the 6,000 available chemicals are combined to create smells that range from "new car smell" to facsimiles of very expensive French perfumes.

Perfumes and colognes were once reserved for special occasions only. Today, man-made fragrance chemicals are used in everything from cleaning materials and toys to garbage bags and kitty litter. One study found that people wore or used an average of 21 synthetically scented products daily.[13] The fragrance industry is a self-regulated industry, and the unhappy truth is that 84 percent of these chemical ingredients have never been tested for human toxicology or have been tested only minimally.[14] An EPA study found the air in department stores contained more chemicals than that of car body shops. The most abundant chemical in both perfume departments and body shops was *toluene* (a component of gasoline), which is a *teratogen* (a chemical that can damage the developing fetus).[15] Below are some of the physiological effects of some of these chemicals:

- *Toluene*—An EPA study found that 100 percent of the perfumes examined in the study contained toluene, a known mutagen and sensitizer that can easily accumulate in the body. Toluene not only triggers asthma attacks, it is known to produce asthma in previously healthy people.[16] Repeated exposure to toluene can damage bone marrow, as well as the liver and kidneys, slow reflexes, and at the very least cause headaches and trouble concentrating.[17]

- *Negatively Affects the Brain and Nervous System*—Fragrance can impact the brain and nervous system along with the immune system. The olfactory pathways provide the most direct connection to the brain and also provide a path for toxic substances to reach the brain. Several research studies indicate that fragrances can affect emotion, feelings, and even have druglike effects, such as decreased alertness.[18] Chemically sensitive and toxic people exhibit anxiety, irritability, then immediate fatigue and even hypoglycemia when exposed to fragrances. The fight-or-flight response to the triggered immune system weakens the adrenal glands along with other hormonal communication. A series of studies by Dr. Tyler Lorig of Washington and Lee University on the use of commercial perfume products to supply odors concluded that the studies "provide clear evidence that undetected odors alter neurophysiology and behavior."[19]

- *Language and Learning Impairments*—The Asthma Society notes that "confusion, the inability to follow conversation, impaired word finding, and other language impairments have been associated with exposure to indoor air volatiles such as fragrance chemicals." See www.asthmasociety.com.
- *Allergies/Asthma*—Virtually every respiratory health organization lists fragrance as a trigger for asthma. According to the U.S. Food and Drug Administration, fragrances cause 30 percent of all allergic reactions, and 72 percent of asthmatics experience respiratory symptoms when exposed to fragrances.[20] It only takes one person entering a building wearing a scented product to affect the air quality. This is because scented products can drift throughout an entire area wherever the air takes them. Workers in the perfume industry are among those with the highest rates of asthma.[21] An epidemiological study of children living near perfume factories found a higher rate of asthma than the normal population.[22]
- *Hormone Irregularities*—Many fragrance materials are known to have estrogenic characteristics. For example, *citral*, a common ingredient in fragrances, causes prostate gland enlargement. Men working in a perfume and soap factory in Sweden were found to have high incidence of prostate cancer.[23] Diethyl phthalate (DEP), a plastic commonly found in tissues of childbearing-age women, is a hormone disruptor. An analysis of a popular perfume found DEP made up over 10 percent of the product.[24]

## HEALTHIER/SAFER BRANDS OF COSMETICS/FRAGRANCES/HAIR PRODUCTS

- Skin Deep Report (www.ewg.org/reports/skindeep/browse_products.php)— input the brand names of cosmetics and personal care items you use and get a toxicity report.
- *Elemis* (www.elemis.com)—offers skin care and aromatherapy products made from absolutes and essential oils.

- *Aubrey Organics* (www.aubrey-organics.com)—completely natural hair and skin products, with organic ingredients, and devoid of synthetics or petrochemicals.
- *Bee Alive* (www.beealive.com)—natural skin care products.
- *Burt's Bees* (www1.burtsbees.com)—natural personal care products, from cosmetics to hair care.
- *Evan's Garden* (www.evansgarden.com). These makeup and facial care formulations are derived from live plants, pure essential oils, trace minerals, and antioxidants. The skin care line contains all known nutrients in whole food form, complete trace mineral complex, and skin-rejuvenating antioxidants.
- *Naturtint*—a natural alternative to chemical hair dyes that are extremely toxic and particularly hard on the liver and neurological system. These toxic ingredients include ammonia, resorcinol, and p-phenylenediamine.

## WEB SITES THAT EDUCATE AND PROVIDE HEALTHY HOME OPTIONS

- www.safer-products.org—a great place to learn what is taking place in your own home due to the consumer products you choose to bring into it.
- www.safecosmetics.org—discover all the many chemicals that are allowed to go into the manufacturing of your favorite and most commonly used cosmetics, deodorants, shampoos, lotions, and nail polishes.
- www.janices.com
- www.healthyhome.com
- www.heartofvermont.com
- www.livingsource.com
- www.natural-lifestyle.com

## E. Coli

E. coli is a source of well-recognized food-borne bacterial infections. The specific strain of E. coli, known as "O157:H7," can release a powerful toxin that attacks the lining of the intestine. Children under the age of five, the elderly, and people with impaired immune systems are the most likely to suffer from illnesses caused by E. coli. It is now the leading cause of kidney failure among children in the United States.[25]

An extraordinarily resilient microbe that is easy to transmit, E. coli is also difficult to eradicate. It is resistant to acid, salt, and chlorine. It can last weeks in moist environments. It survives freezing and heat of up to 160°F. A small uncooked particle of hamburger can contain enough of the pathogen to kill you. According to Eric Schlosser, author of the bestseller *Fast Food Nation*, who researched the conditions in U.S. meat slaughtering houses, "Anyone who brings raw ground beef into his or her kitchen today must regard it as a potential biohazard, one that may carry an extremely dangerous microbe, infectious at an extremely low dose."[26] A recent USDA study found that during the winter about 1 percent of the cattle found at feedlots carry E. coli O157:H7 in their guts. This can rise to as much as 50 percent during the summer months.[27]

> **Ask the Lord to give you wisdom to make the right dietary and lifestyle changes. He will show you the way to health.**

Eating meat from cattle infected with E. coli is also responsible for urinary tract infections (UTIs), the most common infectious disease in women. One-third of women in the United States are diagnosed with at least one UTI that requires medical treatment before the age of 24. Many women are finding it difficult to manage this disease, as an increasing number of UTIs are resistant to sulpha drugs—medications used commonly to treat the infections. According to studies, these multi-drug-resistant UTIs may be linked to an unlikely source: cattle infected with a multi-drug-resistant strain of E. coli bacteria.[28]

Careful purchasing, handling, and preparation of foods are essential for combating the threats of persistent bacteria such as E. coli, along with many other toxins. Below are some tips that will help protect you and your family.

## COOKWARE, FOOD PREPARATION, AND FOOD STORAGE RECOMMENDATIONS

Quality cookware helps you maintain good health and, in some cases, even enhances flavor. It's also useful to know the foods that most quickly react to plastic storage containers and to aluminum and cast-iron cookware. A vitreous enamel cooking surface is completely hygienic and impervious to acids and other chemicals. Not only does it provide superior cooking functions, it is perfect for foods that require marinating or for storage (raw or cooked) in the refrigerator or freezer. Here are a few recommendations:

- Don't cook with aluminum pots and pans or aluminum foil.
- Surgical steel is an excellent option for skillets and frying pans. Look for Flavorite cookware (www.regalware.com).
- Use Le Creuset cookware. Le Creuset pans are handcrafted in France of cast iron, which absorbs heat slowly and provides even heat transfer. The cast iron is coated with porcelain enamel, is lead-free, requires no seasoning, and cleans easily. It is available at www.williamsonoma.com.
- Store food in pottery or glass, which is lead-free. (But avoid Mason Jars, as they are not.) See www.glashaus.com.
- Store meat in paper not plastic or aluminum foil.
- Refrigerate perishable foods promptly.
- Wash your hands thoroughly and often.
- Keep preparation area and utensils clean.
- Don't cross-contaminate (contamination happens when bacteria from raw foods are passed to cooked foods by hands or cooking utensils). All raw products can carry harmful bacteria.
- Keep hot foods hot (140°F or above).
- Keep cold foods cold (41°F or below).

To learn more, go to the Partnership for Food Safety Education web site: www.fightbac.org/main.cfm.

## Mold, Mycotoxins, Fungus, and Parasites

One in three people has had an allergic reaction to mold, which is a microscopic fungi that lives on plant and animal matter. Molds can be found in nearly every environment and can be detected year-round, both outdoors and indoors. Warm and humid conditions encourage mold growth. Over time, exposure to certain foods and fungi can toxify your body's systems with poisonous substances called *mycotoxins.* They are found primarily in grain and nut crops, but are known to also be on celery, grape juice, apples, and other produce. The most notorious mycotoxins are aflatoxins, which have been associated with various diseases, including cancer. Other health problems connected to mycotoxins include asthma and heart disease.[29]

When the immune system has been compromised in some way, through illness or diet, it opens the door for parasites and intestinal worms to set up house in your liver and pancreas. A healthy intestinal tract is a key to preventing attacks by these various pathogens. The stronger and healthier you are, the less likely you will be a host.

To learn more about this problem, go to www.yeastconnection.com, www.allergyreliefstores.com, or read *The Fungus Link* by Dr. David Holland and Doug Kaufmann.

## WHAT YOU CAN DO TO MINIMIZE MOLDS

- Avoid alcoholic beverages, corn, wheat, barley, sugar, sorghum, peanuts, rye, and cottonseed. With cheeses, it is generally not a good idea to eat mold, as sometimes the spores from the mold establish an infection. Generally, with hard cheeses, such as cheddar, mozzarella, and such, it is best to cut the moldy section off and use the remaining portion. The hyphae of the mold do not penetrate very deep into the cheese. The hyphae are the portion of the mold that grows into the cheese to gather nutrients. In hard cheeses, these penetrate only a millimeter or two, but with soft cheeses, such as cottage cheese, the hyphae are able to rapidly penetrate deep into the cheese. When these soft cheeses go moldy, do not eat them, because you cannot easily remove the moldy portion as you can with hard cheeses.

- Cleanliness is essential, as molds can build up in your refrigerator, dishcloths, and other cleaning utensils. Clean out the inside of the refrigerator every few months with one tablespoon of baking soda dissolved in a quart of water.
- Clean out mold from any parts of your house or drains and keep dishcloths, towels, sponges, and mops clean and fresh.
- Keep the humidity level in the house below 40 percent.
- Check your foods carefully before buying them. Examine the stems on fresh produce and avoid anything that looks bruised.
- When serving food, keep it covered to prevent exposure to mold spores in the air.
- Empty opened cans of perishable foods into clean storage containers and refrigerate them promptly.
- Use leftovers within three to four days so mold doesn't have an opportunity to grow.
- If you find a moldy food item, don't sniff it. Instead, wrap it carefully in covered trash where children and animals can't get to it. Clean around the area where the moldy food had been found and check any nearby items the moldy food might have touched.
- Install an air exchanger in your home.
- Consider a liver and gall bladder flush once or twice a year. I use a product from American Botanical Pharmacy (www.herbdoc.com/p34.asp) called L-GB. There are many brands available in your local health food store as well as digestive cleaning formulas and supplements from Renew Life, Inc. (www.renewlife.com). These are not recommended if you have stones in your liver, gall bladder, or kidneys. Most people do these types of cleanses on their own, but they really should be done under the supervision or guidance of an experienced health practitioner.

## WHAT YOU CAN DO TO MINIMIZE PARASITES

- Get in the habit of using garlic, oregano, and coconut, which are naturally antiparasitic and antimicrobal.

- Eat onions, figs, and pumpkin seeds to create an uninhabitable environment for worms.
- Eat a diet rich in protein and vitamins.
- As absorption in the intestines is impaired by infestations, the body requires large amounts of nutrients found in fresh organic vegetables, almonds, and blackberries.
- Take a daily high quality probiotics supplement (friendly bacteria, such as those found in fermented foods).
- Avoid diets high in meat and dairy, sugar, and acid-forming foods.
- Combine a diet high in fiber with regular exercise and hydration to help prevent constipation, which is a condition that allows parasites to flourish.

## Heavy Metals

In low traces, some heavy metals, such as copper and zinc, are essential to maintaining good health and metabolism within the human body. But in higher concentrations, even beneficial metals can be toxic and poisonous to us. What makes heavy metals particularly dangerous is their tendency to bioaccumulate, meaning we are unable to keep up with removing toxins, and chemicals increase in concentration in our body over time.

> Unfortunately, parasites will never go away, thus our defenses can never be let down.

Heavy metals enter our body through the food we eat, the air we breathe, the water we drink, and the products we use. Pesticides, soil depletion, radiation, mercury from dental amalgam fillings, cadmium from cigarettes and secondhand smoke, chemicals from the air, and lead from old mines, gasoline, tap water, and lead-based paints are just a few of the toxins we are exposed to on a daily basis. The primary heavy metal contaminants are lead, mercury, cadmium, aluminum, and arsenic.

The free-radical damage that results from heavy metal pollution has been linked to many diseases, including heart attacks, stroke, cancer, impotency, decreased intelligence in children, muscle weakness and aches, and nervous system disorders.

Perhaps the single most notorious heavy metal that most of us are exposed to on a daily basis is mercury—because it is found in the silver amalgam fillings in most of our mouths (where it comprises 50 percent of the overall mass of the filling). This is a controversial subject, to be sure, but the bottom line is that many developed countries have actually banned the use of amalgam fillings, yet many dentists and even the American Dental Association continue to defend their use. But why take the risk? Interestingly, most of the dentists I know do not put amalgam fillings in the teeth of their family members. Not everyone has the same level of sensitivity to amalgam fillings. They can result in a health crisis in one person and yet not present any noticeable health issues in others. If you currently have amalgam fillings, please don't rush to your dentist and have them removed. Unless you have a biologically trained and certified dentist, the removal process can be far more dangerous than leaving them in. This is exponentially more important if you are in poor health. To find a biologically trained dentist in your area, go to the web site of The International Academy of Oral Medicine and Toxicology, at www.iaomt.org.

## WHAT SHOULD WE DO?

- Testing is essential to determine personal toxicity. Find a practitioner who is trained in Biomedical Analysis and Clinical Nutrition. Go to www.acam.org or www.functionalmedicine.org or www.internalbalance.com. Personal lab testing is available at www.lef.org.
- It is also important to achieve proper, balanced nutrition by choosing fresh (organic when possible) fruits, vegetables, grains, and lean meat.
- Consider taking supplemental antioxidants, herbs, minerals, amino acids, phytoextracts, detoxifying agents, protective agents, and fiber as adjuncts to a healthy diet to enhance vital organ functioning and to aid in your body's natural detoxifying actions.

- Place thick doormats at each entry door and ask people to either remove or wipe their shoes thoroughly before entering.
- If possible, use area rugs rather than wall-to-wall carpeting.
- Clean your floors with a wet mop and wipe down all other surfaces (including walls) with a damp sponge.
- Take these recommended supplements: glutathione, lactoferrin, selenium, and zinc, cilantro, garlic, green tea, alpha lipoic acid, minerals, essential amino acids, cysteine and n-acetyl cysteine, glycine, alfalfa, chlorella, rutin, dietary fiber, SAMe (an antidepressant and liver-protective agent), and silibinin from the milk thistle plant (another liver-protective agent).

## Cell Phones and Damaging Electromagnetic Frequencies (EMFs)

Electromagnetic waves were discovered in 1888 by Heinrich Hertz and have found extensive application in today's society. Over the years, there has been an ever-increasing concern over environmental factors relating to the generation of these waves. *Electromagnetic Fields and the Life Environment* by Karel, Mahara, Jan Musil, and Hana Tuha of the Institute of Industrial Hygiene and Occupational Disease in Prague highlighted many of the unforeseen and invisible dangers through the use and distribution of these damaging frequencies. More recently, the research of Dr. George Carlo, chief scientist of the world's largest research effort into wireless safety, has brought to light the potential dangers and many unknowns of cellular phones and wireless technology.

Electromagnetic waves are transmitted by cell phones and other electrical devices (portable phones, microwaves) in a way that can damage our cells. When you talk on your cell phone, your voice is transmitted from the antenna as radio frequency radiation (RFR) between 800 MHz and 1,990MHz—a frequency within the range of microwave radiation. Depending on how close the cell phone antenna is to your head, between 20 and 60 percent of the radiation emitted is transferred to and penetrates your head. With or without a headset, every time you put your cell phone up to your head, you expose your brain to the danger of radiation. While there are numerous contradictory reports as to the overall effect of cell phones on our health, there is a growing body of evidence that cell phones affect multiple facets of your brain function, behavior, and health in general.

When our immune system is weak, we are more susceptible to the damage incurred by the waves. Most people do not think about what is happening when they plug in a household appliance or move into a home that is positioned close to a high output 50KV power line. Everyday technologies, such as cell phones and computers, all come with a cost to the human body. When our immune system is weakened, then EMF is even more damaging at the cellular level.

## RECOMMENDATIONS

- Avoid ear piece units unless you have a radiation blocker attached. The ear pieces have been shown to concentrate radiation into the soft tissue via the ear. The Biopro Cell Chip neutralizes EMF's on cell phones and is available at www.internalbalance.com.
- Use a speaker phone whenever possible (apologize for voice quality first).
- Take antioxidants and potassium iodine supplements before having any medical X-rays done.
- Take potassium iodine supplements.
- Stay well hydrated.
- Consider a home-based Harmonizer that harmonizes the electromagnetic waves in your home. Two other products to consider are the Biopro QLink Pendant and the Hands-Free Headset, which are available at www.internalbalance.com.
- Do not microwave foods. *Never microwave plastics.* Try to use your oven or stove top for all cooking purposes.
- Consider purchasing the Quantronic Resonance System. Used once or twice a day for eight minutes, the QRS is a medical appliance that is thought to assist the body's natural mechanisms to strengthen the immune system, make the respiratory system more efficient, dissolve plaque buildup on the walls of

blood vessels, reduce stress, regenerate body cells, increase the partial oxygen pressure to the vessels, increase oxygen and nutrient intake by cells, remove impurities from cells, and increase energy and the sense of well-being. Go to www.high-techhealth.net to find out more.

## CHECK OUT THESE WEB SITES

- www.bioprotechnology.com—offers a number of technologies for dealing with EMFs.
- www.electricalpollution.com—under "Solutions," you will find ways to mitigate your exposure to high frequencies from electrical pollution.
- www.stetzerelectric.com—manufactures electrical filters for high-frequency currents.
- www.phillipstein.com—offers high-end watches with EMF protection. This is a favorite of mine.
- www.teslar.com—offers lower-end watches with EMF protection. Prices are reasonable enough to buy for kids. They can also inexpensively insert a chip into your favorite watch.

To learn more, read *Cell Phones: Invisible Hazards in the Wireless Age* by Dr. George Louis Carlo and Martin Schram.

## Indoor Air Quality

Most people don't realize that the air in their homes can contribute to health problems, particularly during peak summer months when ozone pollution is at its highest. Indoor air pollutants, such as pollen, pet dander, dust mites, cockroaches, and tobacco and cooking smoke particles, can cause asthma attacks as well as itchy eyes, sneezing, and runny noses. Additionally, VOCs (volatile organic compounds), a major contributor to ozone, are also an air pollutant, two to five times more prevalent in indoor air than outdoor air because they are present in many household products, including our carpets, paints, deodorants, cleaning fluids, cosmetics, air fresheners, and more.[30]

We may not be able to do much about the air outside our homes, but we can definitely impact the air inside our homes. The EPA suggests three primary ways for improving indoor air quality:

- *Source Control.* This means eliminating individual sources of pollution or reducing emissions. Some sources, such as those that contain asbestos, can be sealed or enclosed; others, such as gas stoves, can be adjusted to decrease the amount of emissions.
- *Ventilation Improvement.* This involves increasing the amount of outdoor air that comes indoors. Opening windows and doors, operating window or attic fans, when the weather permits, or running a window air conditioner with the vent control open increases the outdoor ventilation rate. Local bathroom or kitchen fans that exhaust outdoors remove contaminants directly from the room where the fan is located and also increase the outdoor air ventilation rate.
- *Purchase an Air Cleaner.*[31]

## MORE AIR PURIFYING TIPS

- Put an air exchanger in your home to get rid of "out-gassing." For air filter and purifier products, go to www.homeenvironment.com (click on "air purifiers"), www.iqair.com, www.austinair.com, www.allerair.com, or www.healthyhome.com.
- Use house plants as a natural air purifier. According to NASA, the plants that are most effective in removing formaldehyde, benzene, and carbon monoxide from the air are: bamboo palm, Chinese evergreen, English ivy, gerbera daisy, Janet Craig, marginata, mass cane/corn plant, mother-in-law's tongue, pot mum, peace lily, and Warneckii.
- Try to avoid wall-to-wall carpeting, as this collects dust, lint, mold, and other environmental toxins brought from the outside by shoes. Area rugs, preferably organic, that can be easily laundered, are the best.
- Avoid the use of pesticides.

- Ensure regular maintenance of the furnace.
- Reduce moisture and mold in the home by repairing roof and foundation cracks.
- Grade soil to allow water to flow away from the house.
- Dehumidify the basement.
- Reduce the amount of stored materials in the house.
- Choose building and renovating materials with low levels of chemical emissions.
- Minimize the use of harsh chemical cleaners and deodorizers and use unscented cleaning compounds.

To learn more, go to: www.ext.colostate.edu/pubs/consumer/09938.html. This site has a variety of remedies for indoor air pollution. Also, go to www.healthyindoorair.org or www.epa.gov/iaq.

## Immunizations (Mercury and Viral Load)

The evidence is compelling that there are significant health issues associated with vaccines, and that the risk of vaccines far exceeds the diseases they are purported to prevent. Vaccine manufacturing companies first began producing vaccines in 1933. The first reported case of autism occurred after *thimerosal*, a preservative for immunizations, was added to vaccines. Since then, the incidence of autism has increased at an alarming rate. Thimerosal is not a necessary additive and is toxic to the human body, yet it has been used for years. And although thimerosal has been phased out of childhood vaccines, the vast majority of flu shots given to children and adults still contain it, and it is believed that many pediatricians are still using unexpired vials of thimerosal-containing vaccines.[32]

> Armed with the Seven Golden Keys and the grace of God, you are now powerful enough to defend yourself and your family from the many hazards around us.

In addition, just because a vaccine says "thimerosal-free" doesn't mean that it is mercury-free. Mercury is used in vaccines because it incorporates very well into the DNA of the virus. But is difficult to get rid of because it also incorporates itself into *our* DNA.

As consumers, we must be very judicious in our choice of whether to have vaccines or what vaccines are expedient. Extra immunizations do not necessarily mean better health. Because pharmaceutical companies are not liable for vaccines, injured parties must submit their claim to a Vaccine Compensation Fund.

## RECOMMENDATIONS

- Research the issue for yourself and determine what is best for your family. These web sites and publications will tell you more: *The Natural Medicine Guide to Autism* by Stephanie Marohn, www.909shot.com, www.vaccinfo.karoo.net, www.vaccineinformation.org, www.vaccination.inoz.com, defeatautistimyesterday.com, holisticmed.com/www/vaccine.html.

- Go to a vaccine information center to get requirements by individual states and to find a practitioner that will accept you as a patient.

- If you do choose to immunize, wait as long as possible to immunize your children (they should be at least two or three years of age), and choose only vaccines that are targeted toward lethal diseases.

- Carefully read the labels of every shot you take and those that will be administered to your children.

- Call in advance to make sure your pediatrician is using a thimerosal-free flu or immunization shot. Remember that thimerosal is only one of the many serious issues with immunizations. But another option is to request Flu-Mist, a nasal mist vaccine that does not contain thimerosal.[33]

- Don't have the same vaccines multiple times. More is not better in this case.

- Have tetanus shots only when needed.

Most states in the U.S. have religious and medical exemptions to immunization readily available.

## CRITICAL CONSIDERATIONS FOR PREGANCY AND CHILDBIRTH

Obviously, it is crucial for a pregnant woman to manage all Seven Golden Keys. However, other than doing her own research and coming up with her own immunization strategy, there are two critical steps an expectant mother can take regarding pregnancy and child-birth. First, both mother and child benefit in countless ways by taking high quality fish oil together with a full spectrum vitamin E throughout the pregnancy and beyond (see Healthy Fats). Second, in my opinion the most critical step is to delay the clamping and cutting of the umbilical cord until the umbilical cord completely stops pulsing (see www.cordclamping.com). This one- to four-minute delay can have enormous benefit to the baby's health.

Even if you are not interested in having a natural childbirth, for your own education I strongly recommend that you take the Bradley Method® of Natural Childbirth course (www.bradleybirth.com) or read the book, *The Bradley Method*. My wife and I have had all four of our children using this method, and we highly recommend it.

## Secondhand Smoke

A study in the United Kingdom followed the progress of more than 123,000 participants over the course of seven years. Some of the participants had never smoked, and others had stopped smoking, but all the participants had been exposed to secondhand smoke during their childhood. It was found that children who grow up with smokers in their homes are three times more likely to develop lung cancer in their later years than those who come from non-smoking homes.

The study results pointed to a definite link between lung cancer and passive smoking:

- 97 people developed lung cancer.
- 20 more had related cancers, such as cancer of the larynx.
- 14 died from chronic obstructive pulmonary disease.

- Ex-smokers faced up to twice the risk of respiratory diseases from passive smoke than those who had never smoked.[34]

Don't smoke! And if you are living with someone who does, insist that he or she smoke outside and away from children.

## Fish

As noted previously in both the Ten Myths About Health and Golden Key #2—Nutrition, we've polluted our life-giving oceans with mercury and petroleum byproducts to the point where virtually every species of fish is unsafe to eat, particularly by pregnant women. The EPA is currently warning pregnant women to greatly limit their fish intake, due to the mercury content of many types of fish, including farm-raised varieties. A recent report by the Research Institute of Public Health in Finland shows a significant increase in heart disease in men with elevated mercury levels.[35] Nearly all Americans are now known to harbor cancer-causing pesticides, PCBs (polychlorinated biphenyls), and dioxins, not to mention toxic heavy metals, such as cadmium, lead, and mercury, in their fat cells. PCBs, although banned in the U.S. for decades, are still found prevalently in our environment, particularly in farm-raised salmon.

To help navigate through this confusing issue, the Audubon Society ranks the levels of toxicity in fish and the oceans from where they originated (see www.audubon.org to learn more). The Alaskan Wild Caught Species seems to be the cleanest fish source currently available for human consumption. The company Vital Choice (www.vital-choice.com) is another good resource for these types of fish and information on contaminated species from other waters and oceans.

It is critical to take the right fish oil (see Golden Key #2—Nutrition/Healthy Fats).

## Trans Fatty Acids

Trans fatty acids and hydrogenated oils are prevalent in fast foods and processed foods. They wreak havoc with the critical cellular membranes of our brain cells, displacing the normal essential fatty acids in these neuronal membranes, where they in turn cause a profound disruption in our mental and neurological functioning.

To learn more about trans fats, see Golden Key #2—Nutrition/ Healthy Fats or www.goodfatsbadfats.com and the kinds of saturated and unsaturated fats that are healthy for you to eat.

## Adverse Drug Reactions

A serious hazard to be aware of is the potential reaction you may have to a prescription drug. The Lazarou study analyzed records for prescribed records for 33 million U.S. hospital admissions in 1994. It found 2.2 million serious injuries due to prescribed drugs: 2.1 percent of inpatients experienced a serious adverse drug reaction; 4.7 percent of all hospital admissions were due to a serious adverse drug reaction, and fatal adverse drug reactions occurred in .19 percent of inpatients and .13 percent of admissions. The authors of the study estimated that 106,000 deaths occur annually due to adverse drug reactions.[36]

In a study of drug trends among the elderly conducted in 2003 by Dr. Robert Epstein, chief medical officer of Medco Health Solutions Inc., it was found that seniors are going to multiple physicians, getting multiple prescriptions, and using multiple pharmacies. Among 6.3 million seniors who received more than 160 million prescriptions, a total of 7.9 million medication alerts were triggered: less than one-half that number, 3.4 million, were detected in 1999. About 2.2 million of those alerts indicated excessive dosages unsuitable for seniors, and about 2.4 million alerts indicated clinically inappropriate drugs for the elderly. Kasey Thompson, director of the Center on Patient Safety at the American Society of Health System Pharmacists, noted: "There are serious and systemic problems with poor continuity of care in the United States." He says this study represents only "the tip of the iceberg" of a massive national problem.[37]

## Antibacterial Soaps

Because of their potential to cause antibiotic resistance, the AMA (American Medical Association) and the FDA (Food and Drug Administration) have been concerned about the overuse of antibacterial soaps for several years. Now research published in *Environmental Science & Technology*, April 2005, has now shown that in normal dishwashing situations antibacterial soaps (with the ingredient *triclosan*) have been shown to react with the chlorine from typical tap water. The result of this reaction is chloroform and in some cases dioxins, which are suspected and known human carcinogens respectively.

Do not use antibacterial soaps. Avoid soaps and other products with the ingredient triclosan (i.e., toothpastes, lotions, and acne treatments).

## Pharmaceutical Personal Care Pollutants (PPCPs)

There is a new contaminant that we are creating in our environment from what we take into our bodies. Neither water treatment plants nor the EPA knows what to do with this massive problem. It is in our sewage treatment plants, our streams, creeks, rivers, and lakes. It's called PPCPs (Pharmaceutical Personal Care Pollutants).

The 2002 National Drinking Water Standards reported that 80 percent of streams sampled in the U.S. Geological Survey showed evidence of drugs, hormones, steroids, and PPCPs, such as soaps and fragrances. An investigation is to be launched into the environmental effects of pharmaceuticals amid new fears that scores of other toxic drugs are polluting rivers, threatening fish life, and getting into drinking water. Current drinking water standards *do not require testing* for any of the 70,000 PHARMA compounds being prescribed today. These are being metabolized by our bodies, urinated into our sewage and septic systems, and pumped right into the outfalls and streams. No treatment is in place for managing this growing problem.

A report written in the *Sunday Herald*, United Kingdom, March 5, 2005, points to well-substantiated evidence that these contaminants do indeed exist, and explains their potential impact. Pharmaceutical companies are being given until the end of the year to supply data on their drugs to the Environment Agency in the United Kingdom so their impact can be researched. Scientists in Europe have discovered that increasing numbers of complex drugs—including heart medication, antidepressants, anti-epileptics, anti-cancer chemicals, cholesterol-lowering medicines, sex hormones, antibiotics, hormone replacement, aspirin, vitamins, and ibuprofen—are surviving the human digestive system, passing through sewage works, and entering rivers and the sea.

Although much of this preliminary research on this topic has been done in the United Kingdom, it is just as relevant a concern for us in the United States. The U.S. Environmental Protection Agency's Office of Research and Development has been attempting to foster awareness and attention to this concerning topic and pollutant since 1999.[38]

PCPPs are a huge issue that we will be dealing with in the future. Industry and government are working hard to agree on PCPP testing standards and solutions for this issue. Hopefully the purification answer will come soon. In the meantime, avoid drinking open tap water and eating seafood (see Golden Key #1—Hydration and Golden Key #2—Nutrition). Issues such as this one make the next chapter even more important.

I strongly recommend you read Dr. Don Colbert's book, *Toxic Relief: Restore Health and Energy Through Fasting and Detoxification.* You'll want to implement a safe detoxification plan into your life, and Colbert's is excellent.

As I mentioned at the beginning of this chapter, many environmental hazards are out of our control, but numerous hazards are a result of the daily decisions we make. The bottom line is to eliminate the threats we have control over and to follow the Super Health principles to maximize our personal immunity for the threats we cannot control. I encourage you to get started today.

# Meditation
# and Prayer

**God created us with a destiny to fulfill, but
many of us live our lives disconnected from Him.**
*Many of the afflictions and symptoms of depression, alienation,
and many other disorders that we deal with are the result of
having lost our connection with God. Meditation and prayer
are by far the most important of the Seven Golden Keys, because
we were created to know and love God and to have fellowship
with Him in this life . . . and for eternity. Meditation prepares
our spirit, soul, and body to speak and listen to God, and prayer
is the act of speaking with God. Meditation and prayer reignite
the spiritual flame that burns inside of us. They promote physical and psychological health, allowing us to relax, to focus on
the positive, to think of others with forgiveness and compassion,
and to turn our pain and distress over to a compassionate and
attentive Father. Prayer actually brings about change.*

*But his delight is in the law of the LORD,
and in His law He meditates day and night.*

PSALM 1:2

SUPER
HEALTH

7 Golden
Keys to
Unlock
Lifelong
Vitality

# Meditation and Prayer

*Return to your rest, O my soul,*
*for the LORD has dealt*
*bountifully with you.*

PSALM 116:7

Are you weary from being continuously on the run? Stressed out from trying to keep up and never quite getting ahead? Always thinking about the next thing that needs to be done? In today's relentless world, there is never enough time, money, or breaks from pressures of everyday life. Between juggling a career, a family, hobbies, and public duties, a million demands scream for our attention and can cause overwhelming anxiety. If they reach our heart, they can destroy our peace, overwhelm our emotions and minds, and can easily escalate into health problems at every level.

But in the midst of all this commotion, God is speaking to us, "Be still, and know that I am God" (Psalm 46:10). Have we stopped to listen? Can we hear Him? "How?" you may ask. Through meditation and prayer, of course. The Lord is asking us to quiet our soul, to sit at His feet, and listen to Him. He wants to be our friend, and He wants to spend time with us.

Meditation and prayer are the two major elements that determine the ultimate quality of our life, and I will provide significant scientific evidence that verifies this. They are by far the most important of the Seven Golden Keys, because we were created to know and love God and to have fellowship with Him for this life . . . and for eternity. Living in a loving relationship with God as our Father, we receive the gracious blessings of the children of God. As we deepen our relationship with Him, and God becomes our best friend, the more profound of an impact He will naturally have on our life and health.

We have seen the importance of our physical and mental health in the first six Golden Keys, which dealt primarily with the body and soul. And now it is time to move on to the inner man, the human spirit, where meditation and prayer are the keys to our spiritual health. God created you as a three-dimensional person, that is, as a three-part being—you have a spirit (wisdom, consciousness, and commune), a soul (mind, will, and emotions), and a body (bone, blood, and flesh). It only makes sense that He wants you to optimize the health of all three of these parts.

## Meditation and Prayer

Meditation and prayer involve a two-part process of communicating with our Lord. Meditation prepares our spirit, soul, and body to speak and listen to God, and prayer is the act of speaking with Him. What happens within our spirit has a profound effect on our whole being.

> God counts the stars and call them all by name, yet He hears our prayers as our Father.

God the Father is real and personal. He created us to love Him and to enjoy His world. Since we were created in His image, we are here because He is here, and we can only make sense of our lives when we exist in a meaningful relationship to Him. We run into trouble the moment we lose touch with Him. Faith begins when we accept that He is God, our God, and that He waits lovingly for us to respond to Him with our love.

Through meditation and prayer, we take the time to get alone with Him, for only His presence will fulfill the desires of our spirit. He longs for us . . . waits for us to come to Him with all our heart. He knows that many of the life issues we are trying to deal with will vanish when we know Him as our heavenly Father. He wants to meet our deepest needs. The yearning within us, as St. Augustine once pointed out, will only be satisfied when we find God, and He cannot be found in the midst of noise and restlessness.

What a relief it is to discover that God has placed within us a desire to know Him and to find pleasure in Him, which is truly satisfied through a relationship with Him. Through our faith in Him, we receive an inner power and strength from God that brings confidence to our personality and joy and love to our inner man. It is this inner dynamic that empowers us to be who we really are. Faith enables us to move forward with courage when crossing mountains of adversity or taking new steps in our life.

## Spiritual Warfare

With the importance of our spiritual relationship to God, it is no surprise that this vital area of our life is a battle ground. The Bible warns us that the Christian life is an actual arena of spiritual warfare against Satan and spiritual hosts of wickedness in the heavenly places (Ephesians 6:10–20), and much of the battlefield is in our own mind. "For the weapons of our warfare are not carnal but mighty in God for pulling down strongholds, casting down arguments and every high thing that exalts itself against the knowledge of God, bringing every thought into captivity to the obedience of Christ" (2 Corinthians 10:4–5).

The African Bishop Tudor Bismark explains this powerful spiritual principle in this way: our thoughts, whether right or wrong, turn to words, and our words create an atmosphere or attitude that surrounds our life; a prolonged atmosphere creates a climate; a prolonged climate creates a stronghold, and a prolonged stronghold creates a culture. By allowing the wrong thoughts in our minds, and speaking the wrong words, we create negative attitudes and strongholds in our lives. However, if we capture the wrong thoughts before they become words and replace them with positive thoughts and the truths of God's Word, it becomes a blessing instead! This is why the Bible tells us to take every evil thought captive to the Lord Jesus Christ.

That is what meditation and prayer can do: they change the atmosphere, climate, and culture of our lives. When we deliberately change this atmosphere with our prayers, we can immediately sense the difference. We have a supernatural arsenal at our disposal that is mighty through God, because God is in us. Prayer is a legitimate power in the world, and apart from it we will never experience the fullness of God's will for our lives.

To be healthy spiritually and to be strong in spiritual battle, we must meditate on the truths and promises of the Word of God and pray to God in faith and confidence. It begins by establishing a genuine prayer life where we commune with our Father in heaven, Who is the source of spiritual power. It is strengthened by daily feedings on the Word of God, the sword of the Spirit. The truth and holiness that are at work in our lives naturally overthrow and destroy the enemy's work. If we allow the Gospel to come into our daily life with the power of the Holy Spirit, we will be armed for the fight and victorious in the battle.

## When We Lose Touch

The Bible tells us that faith without doubt can move mountains (Mark 11:23)—that's power. It tells us that the prayer of faith can heal the sick—"And the prayer of faith will save the sick, and the Lord will raise him up. And if he has committed sins, he will be forgiven" (James 5:15). That's life-changing, my friends. And Jesus said that believers will do the same things He did and even greater things—"Most assuredly, I say to you, he who believes in Me, the works that I do he will do also; and greater works than these he will do, because I go to My Father" (John 14:12). That's almost unfathomable!

> If you do not allow the enemy a foothold in your life, he cannot establish a stronghold.

God created us with a destiny to fulfill, but many of us live our lives disconnected from Him. Although our spiritual selves are more important than our minds and our bodies, they often appear to atrophy through a lack of use. We are spiritually out of shape and suffer the consequences of our neglect. Many of the afflictions and symptoms of depression, alienation, and many other disorders that we deal with are the result of having lost our spiritual center in God. We have allowed ourselves to be out of touch with God, our Creator, so it isn't surprising that we are out of touch with His transforming purpose for our lives.

If we fail to walk in the center of the will and purpose of God, it will affect our entire life. It's even possible that our career may not be what He has in mind for our life, and if that's the case, think of the impact that is having on our life and health. If you are new to the faith or confused about the will of God for your life, I highly recommend the *New York Times* best-selling book, tapes, and journal called *A Purpose Driven Life* by Rick Warren. This is the book through which Ashley Smith was finding renewed meaning in her own difficult life when she was taken hostage on March 12, 2005. Forced at gunpoint to provide sanctuary for an accused rapist who had broken out of an Atlanta courtroom and killed a judge and three others, Ashley was empowered by God to question her captor's motivation for his life, and he in turn became receptive to the message.

Meditation and prayer are extremely powerful tools to reignite the spiritual flame that burns inside us. They promote physical and psychological health through spiritual methods that allow us to relax, to focus on the positive, to think of others with for- giveness and compassion, and to turn our pain and distress over to a compassionate and attentive Father.

> **Prayer enlarges the heart until it is capable of containing God's gift of Himself.**
> MOTHER TERESA

God's manifold blessings, of which His presence with us is easily the greatest, come to us as we abide in our relationship with Jesus. Indeed, Jesus made it clear that apart from Him, we can do nothing (John 15:5). To "live in Me" means to be vitally one with Jesus, to enjoy all that it means to be in Christ. Prayer is a natural expression of a heart that is abiding in Christ. To live in His presence, to be in communion with Christ, is to know joy unspeakable and full of glory! We won't receive the fullness of God's blessings if we don't spend time with God.

## The Scientific Case for Meditation and Prayer

Although our ancestors knew the connection between spirituality and health, over the past fifty years medicine has essentially disregarded this fact. More and more clinical evidence of the power of faith, prayer, and meditation continues to surface in major medical journals. Once again science, which is a system that attempts to explain created things, is discovering the Creator. Additionally, patients are demanding that a higher value be placed on spirituality. More than 30 U.S. medical schools now offer courses on religion, spirituality, and health, and 77 percent of hospitalized patients want physicians to consider their spiritual needs in their treatment.[1]

The wonderful thing about meditation and prayer is that they are sacred, internal, and deeply personal activities—nothing else can touch them. Meditation and prayer do not depend upon our surroundings or the circumstances in which we find ourselves. They are enacted within our minds and hearts, free from the constraints or influences of other humans. Recall the biblical story of Joseph, who remained intimately connected to God even after he was betrayed by his brothers, left for dead, sold into slavery, and imprisoned among strangers in a land far from his home (Genesis 37—41). There are countless stories of people who were able to endure torture, imprisonment, and unbearable psychological cruelty through a vital connection to their faith and to their God. Prayer and contemplation became their lifeline—not just for strength and solace but for their very survival.

> **Turn your cares instantly into prayers and leave them in God's presence.**

There has been much research conducted recently in the area of alternative therapies, and spirituality and religious belief are among the more fascinating to receive scientific scrutiny. In fact, an entirely new branch of science has emerged called "neurotheology," which is the study of the neurobiology of religion and spirituality. Such studies have unearthed data that suggests we may be "hard-wired" for spirituality, and that the brain's spirituality circuits could explain why religious rituals have the power to move believers and nonbelievers alike.[2] There has always existed within man a subconscious awareness of God.

The impact that faith, prayer, and meditation have on physical and mental healing is compelling. Below are some recent scientific studies that have conclusively demonstrated the extremely potent effect of prayer and meditation in our lives. Many of the following studies refer to religion, but keep in mind that religion is man-made. Spirituality is a more accurate term when referring to a personal relationship with God the Father, Son, and Holy Spirit.

- *Increases Longevity*—Regular attendance at religious functions may be related to longevity. Researchers combined the results of 29 studies that included information about the religious habits of nearly 126,000 people. They found that people who had more religious involvement had lower mortality and increased survival rates compared with those who did not.[3]

- *Enhances Recuperation*—Research has shown that adults 50 years old or older who had strong spiritual beliefs tend to recuperate better when hospitalized with an illness. Such individuals tended to receive better social support and showed better mental and physical health than those without spiritual beliefs.[4] In addition, prayer may reduce the number of complications experienced by hospitalized heart patients. Heart patients who were prayed for by others, but were not aware of being the object of prayers, had an 11 percent reduction in medical complications or the need for surgery or medication while in the hospital.[5]

- *Lowers Blood Pressure*—Researchers who examined the health and religious habits of nearly 4,000 North Carolina residents over the age of 65 for a six-year period found that older people who attended religious services weekly and who engaged in daily prayer or Bible study tended to have lower blood pressure than those who were less religiously active.[6]

- *Alleviates Depression*—Older people often experience periods of depression related to changes in their physical health and living circumstances. A strong religious faith helps expedite recovery from this depression and allows them to better cope with changes.[7]

- *Benefits Former Addicts*—In a study of 235 recovering alcoholics and drug addicts, it was found that higher levels of religious faith and spirituality among recovering substance abusers were associated with higher resilience to stress, greater optimism, greater social support, and less anxiety.[8]

## The Faith Factor

In his book, *The Faith Factor*, Dr. Dale Matthews, Associate Professor of Medicine at Georgetown University School of Medicine and a practicing physician, draws upon cutting-edge scientific research and moving anecdotes of his patients. He demonstrates that religious involvement helps people prevent illness, recover from illness, and live longer. Dr. Matthews sees a vital connection between the healing that patients experience and their reliance on faith, as well as their use of components of spirituality, such as prayer, Bible study, and community support.

Here are a few of the benefits of faith that Dr. Matthews documents:

- Helps us stay healthy and avoid life-threatening and disabling diseases, such as cancer and heart disease.
- Helps us recover faster and with fewer complications if a serious illness develops.
- Helps us live longer.
- Helps us avoid and reduce life-threatening encounters and unanticipated terminal illnesses with greater peacefulness and less pain.
- Helps us cope more effectively with stress and avoid mental illnesses, such as depression and anxiety.
- Helps us avoid problems associated with alcohol, drugs, and tobacco.
- Helps us enjoy a happier marriage, as prayer brings intimacy between husband and wife and family life.
- Helps us find a greater sense of meaning and purpose in our lives.[9]

Much research has pointed to a single variable that has the most pronounced impact on patient health—*worship service attendance*. Dr. Matthews believes that there are a number of reasons why this one religious variable makes such a difference in our health and well-being:

- We overcome the wear and tear of life. (Equanimity)
- We honor our body as a temple of the Spirit. (Temperance)
- We appreciate art and nature. (Beauty)
- We worship with our whole being. (Adoration)
- We confess our sins and start over. (Renewal)
- We bear one another's burdens. (Community)
- We gain strength through shared beliefs. (Unity)
- We take comfort in familiar activities. (Ritual)
- We find a purpose in life. (Meaning)
- We let go and "Let God." (Trust)
- We connect with ultimate hope. (Transcendence)
- We care and are cared for. (Love)[10]

Medicine has made great strides in embracing the "whole-person" model that recognizes the patient's physical, psychological, mental, and social status as part of the health assessment. But faith remains the "final frontier." It is critical that physicians begin to recognize the influence of spirituality and religious commitment in patients' lives, and the important role that prayer and meditation play in health and healing.

> It's not mind over matter. That means if you don't mind, it doesn't matter. This is faith over circumstances.

## Christian Meditation / Eastern Meditation

The word *meditation* is a red flag to many Christians because of its prominent role in the New Age Movement (which is a rehash of Eastern mysticism, including Buddhism and Hinduism). Meditation and prayer were designed by God for our fellowship with Him and are practiced all over the world by people of all faiths and walks of life. Christianity, Judaism, and many other religions have extolled the virtues and benefits of sitting quietly and nurturing an attitude of stillness, concentration, and mindfulness. According to the Centers for Disease Control and

Prevention, 8 percent of adults in the United States now practice meditation, in a variety of forms and styles. An additional 12 percent utilize deep breathing exercises, and 5 percent practice yoga.[11]

Meditation is simply the art of concentrating and focusing on several words or a single sentence on a persistent and intense basis. It incorporates and utilizes all the sensory processes, especially visualization, for an extended period of time. During the study, we allow our mind to consider all the possible thoughts and meanings that can be derived from whatever we are meditating on. The ultimate purpose is to develop a deeper understanding of it.

> The knowledge of God is absolutely necessary for our spiritual life— it is life eternal.
>
> JOHN 17:3

It is important to understand the difference between physiological and psychological meditation and true meditation, which includes the spirit.

Meditation provides many wonderful and clinically proven benefits, both mentally and physically, but unless we are communing with God's Spirit, we are only getting that two-part benefit. Meditation is meant to lead us into communion with God and all the spiritual benefits that He works in our lives. That relationship with God takes place in our spirit, and its influence affects the soul and body. Many people who meditate believe they are having a spiritual experience, when, in fact, they are having a deep experience of the soul (the mind, will, and emotions).

Christian meditation differs from Eastern meditation in these ways. Eastern meditation focuses on emptying the mind, withdrawing from reality, and results in a loss of personal identity; Christian meditation focuses on filling the mind with an awareness of God's presence, knowing God in reality, and results in gaining our true identity in Jesus Christ. Eastern meditation recognizes no objective truth and is dependent upon the person's ability to meditate; Christian meditation recognizes the Word of God as the only standard for truth and a dependency on the Holy Spirit to accomplish God's purposes in us. Eastern meditation has no goal outside of the experience itself, whereas the goal of Christian meditation is a greater love for God and others.

## What Happens When We Meditate

During meditation, the brain's activity, as mapped by an EEG (electroencephalograph), alters significantly. EEG tests show that electrical waves produced during meditation are different from those brain wave patterns we produce at other times, whether asleep or awake. They are slower, more even waves. With regular sustained practice, this evenness and regularity in brain wave patterns continue after meditation.

The most well-known brain waves evident during many kinds of meditation are called *alpha* waves. When the brain moves into an alpha wave state, many physiological changes occur. One of these is that the parasympathetic nervous system (which calms the body) is activated, lowering blood pressure, decreasing heart rate and metabolism, and reducing stress hormones. As meditation deepens, brain activity decreases further. The EEG then registers an even smoother, slower pattern of activity that is called *theta* waves. These alpha and theta waves are normal waves that are demonstrated during a normal or routine EEG while the patient is resting in a chair or a bed. They have not been instructed to pray or meditate, but they have every reason to remain in a quiet mode. Studies on meditators have shown decreased perspiration and a slower rate of respiration accompanied by a decrease of metabolic wastes in the bloodstream. In turn, meditation lowers blood pressure and enhances the immune system.[12]

For many years it has been a commonly held belief that connections among brain nerve cells were fixed early in life and did not change in adulthood. This assumption is now being disproved by some fascinating research into the ways meditative practices and mental discipline are literally changing the workings of the brain. An article in a recent issue of the *Proceedings of the National Academy of Sciences* reported on a study of the neurological states of eight highly experienced meditators compared with 10 student volunteers. The meditators were studied when their brains were in a neutral state and when they were meditating on generating a state of "unconditional lovingkindness and compassion." Researchers found that when the experienced meditators generated a strong feeling of compassion, there was a strong increase in the *gamma* frequency in the left side of the prefrontal cortex, and also that the movement of the waves through the brain was better organized and coordinated than in the student volunteers.

Thought to be the signature of neuronal activity that knits together far-flung brain circuits, gamma waves underlie higher mental activity, such as consciousness. The novice meditators showed a slight increase in gamma activity, but the experienced meditators showed extremely large increases, suggesting that mental training can bring the brain to a greater level of consciousness. These findings give new credence to the notion that the mind can be trained, and that genuine altruism, loving-kindness, empathy, and openness are crucial factors to happiness that can all be cultivated through meditation.[13]

## Other General Benefits of Meditation

Meditation can help us cope with the physical and emotional affects of stress. A recent study at West Virginia University in Morgantown assessed 62 "stressed out" subjects and the effects of meditation on their psychological distress levels. Thirty-five of the subjects entered an intensive program involving 28 hours of group learning, including 2.5 hour classes once a week and one eight-hour retreat. They learned four methods of meditation, general yoga postures, and techniques for coping with stress. The 35 subjects who underwent this "mindfulness training" experienced an average 54 percent reduction in psychological distress from the beginning of the program to three months later. The 27 control subjects, by contrast, had no significant reduction in this measure.[14]

Here are just a few of the documented benefits of meditation:

- Better sleep.
- Reduced substance abuse.
- Decreases in incidences of headaches and backaches.
- Help and alleviation in the treatment of conditions such as cancer, fibromyalgia, and psoriasis.

- Improved self-esteem.
- Strengthened immune system.
- Improved circulation.
- Reduction in stress.
- Improved cognitive function (a more alert yet calm mind).
- A more caring and compassionate spirit.
- Increased energy levels.
- A decrease in muscle tension.

## Breathing Techniques and Self-Awareness

A vital aspect in effective meditation is mastering the art of breathing. At a first glance, this might seem like a silly statement. After all, we breathe unconsciously all day. However, most of us breathe incorrectly, which can contribute to a wide variety of illnesses, from chronic fatigue to muscle spasms. One of the risks of stress is to develop periodic increased respirations on an unconscious basis. This can cause hyperventilation if maintained for over fifteen or twenty minutes, which is manifested as tingling, numbness, lightheadedness, and crying. This occurs because blowing off carbon dioxide creates a condition referred to as respiratory alkalosis. This can be resolved by pinching the nose with the fingers as a reminder to stop rapid breathing.

As the air we breathe becomes more and more congested with foreign toxins, and as our workplaces continue to confine us in unnatural and tedious positions, the need for proper and healthy breathing becomes critical not only to our meditation practice but also to our overall health.

What *should* happen when we breathe? We must—

- Learn to relax the abdominal and pelvic floor muscles so that the diaphragm can descend down into the belly.
- Release the intercostal muscles through movement so they can effectively pull the ribs up and away from the hips during inhalation.
- Learn to intervene in the tension of muscles that are constraining the breathing process.

■ Become aware of the tide of air entering and leaving the body, so that we can slow it down, and encourage the return of a full flow of saliva into the mouth.[15]

Conscious breathing gives us a direct route to the unconscious tensions that we all hold. As we begin to examine the areas of the body that are housing our tension, we begin to observe the stress-holding patterns our body adopts, and the places where trauma has affected specific muscles. You need to be in charge of you. This muscular "armoring" in turn inhibits and compromises breathing. We see then how breathing becomes much more than lungs moving in and out, but involves the whole body—contracting, expanding, and resting in equilibrium.

> **God is the friend of silence.**
>
> MOTHER TERESA

Oftentimes, high-stress individuals need some help in achieving an effective meditative state. This can be accomplished by the use of a fairly inexpensive biofeedback machine. A biofeedback machine uses electrodes attached to the body to bring about an audible rendition of one's overall state of relaxation, or lack thereof. The higher the audio pitch that one hears, the tenser one becomes. However, by consciously focusing on the pitch of the audible tone itself, one can consciously lower the pitch over time, thereby inducing a profound state of calm throughout the mind and body. This calm can help in the reduction of bodily stress and anxiety, mitigate the effects of depression, and promote better sleep patterns.

## Concentrative Meditation

Concentrative meditation, or focused meditation, involves limiting our field of vision in order to still the mind and allow greater clarity and enlightenment to occur. During this type of meditation, some people focus on their breath, on an image (such as a candle flame), or on a sound (such as a musical tone). Here are some focus points that I find helpful:

- *A single spiritual principle*, such as compassion or gratitude. Focus on these and repeat them over and over, either out loud or silently. Consider the fruit of the Spirit: Love, Joy, Peace, Patience, Kindness, Gentleness, Faithfulness, Goodness, and Self-Control (Galatians 5:22–23).

- *Affirmations.* With affirmations we utilize self-talk for a positive result. These positive declarations, repeated over and over, are often of a personal nature, such as "This is the day the Lord has made. I will rejoice and be glad in it" or "I am a child of God." One of my all-time favorite affirmations is from one of my favorite books, Dr. Norman Vincent Peale's *The Power of Positive Thinking*: "I believe I am divinely guided; I believe I will always make the right turn in the road; I believe God will always make a way where there is no way!" Affirmations such as these become "self-fulfilling prophecies," in that we tend to materialize in our own lives .the various thoughts and beliefs that we truly possess deep inside. The Bible says, "As he [a man] thinks in his heart, so is he" (Proverbs 23:7). This is an extremely powerful principle that we can use to help generate positive outcomes in our lives.

- *Creative Visualization.* With creative visualization, we turn from language to mental pictures. Drawing, painting, and writing are all forms of meditation. Here we imagine or visualize ourselves in certain positive contexts. For example, we might mentally envision ourselves delivering a speech or passing a test. We might also conjure up an image of Jesus Christ as the Good Shepherd to whom we go when we are distressed or frightened.

- *Anytime, anyplace.* Meditation doesn't have to occur exclusively in formalized settings, such as a church service. A contemplative spirit can be accessed anytime—while waiting for the bus, washing the dishes, or mowing the lawn. Always contemplate and nurture an attitude of thankfulness throughout the day.

- *Guided Meditation.* This usually involves a recording facilitator or narrator who leads us on a journey that has a specific purpose. For example, a minister might guide a person or group through a series of steps that allow the person to achieve relaxation and deeper intimacy with God. I highly recommend the CD, *Come to the Waters—Ancient Paths, Volume 1* (www.worshipmusic.com), for setting the atmosphere for meditation and prayer.
- *Music Meditation.* Listening to music, humming, and singing are all types of therapeutic meditation. Studies have shown that music can help improve the mobility of stroke or Parkinson's disease patients. Some researchers believe that singing benefits a stroke victim because music is an original language and involves a different area of the brain that wasn't injured. It lifts depression and anxiety and can even lessen the amount of anesthesia needed by women in childbirth.[16] Many doctors stress the importance of exposing the fetus in the womb to music during gestation. There are units made for pregnant women to strap around their belly with music coming from the speakers.

    Don Campbell, a recognized authority on the transformative power of music, wrote a fascinating book about the power of music to heal the body entitled *The Mozart Effect.* In it he documents how music can slow down and equalize brain waves; affect respiration, heartbeat, pulse rate, and blood pressure; reduce muscle tension and improve body movement and coordination; increase endorphin levels; regulate stress hormones; boost the immune function; enhance creativity; help in the treatment and rehabilitation of many illnesses; and much more. Campbell shows how many types of music meditation, from Gregorian chants and Mozart concertos to indigenous music and drumming, can bring healing.[17]

    You can tune into worship music with your favorite melodies. If you are not familiar with the tremendous amount of worship music available today, go to a Christian bookstore and sample some of the collections. The only way to know if the music helps you to establish an atmosphere for meditation is to experience it. Music that will relax you should have a frequency of approximately sixty beats per minute. This can be measured by a metronome. Such music will have the deepest penetration into your subconscious mind. This calming effect will be lost if you use music that goes well beyond sixty beats per minute.

## Mindfulness Meditation

Mindfulness meditation focuses on the mental and physical self and being fully present and available to what is happening in the moment. In mindfulness meditation, we are aware of our body, our breathing, and directing our thoughts. We apply the same mindfulness to spiritual meditation, or prayerful meditation, that allows us to tap into the power of God. It enables us to draw on inner guidance that comes from a relationship with God, and it involves receptivity to God's will and directives.

**Make prayer a deep source of strength and pleasure.**

## Movement Meditation

Movement meditation uses a physical technique, such as slow dance movements, Qi Gong, walking meditation, or tai chi to compose and quiet the mind by coordinating our breath and bodies through gentle and repetitious movements.

You may be concerned about the Eastern mysticism often associated with movement meditation and the martial arts. My wife and I had similar concerns for us and our children and discovered an organization called Karate for Christ International (www.karateforchrist.com) and Grace Martial Arts Fellowship (www.gmaf.org), through which we were introduced to a Christian martial arts system called Yon Ch'uan, which includes tai chi. Tai chi began to gain popularity in the United States in the 1960s. It enhances balance, flexibility, gait, and posture, but also contributes to physical and mental well-being. Many older people have turned to tai chi, as it can help them manage chronic medical disorders, such as Parkinson's, Alzheimer's, and multiple sclerosis. *Yang* tai chi, in particular, is increasingly popular with the elderly, as its movements are slow and continuous. Because it is a body-mind activity, it seems to be a better exercise for people with neurological disorders than more aerobic activities. The theory behind this is that tai chi engages the brain through concentrated breathing and that this kind of breathing begins to shift primary neurological functions to other brain regions.[18]

## Meditation and Prayer Tips

- *Set the mood with music, nature sounds, or Christ-centered guided meditation recordings.* Again, I highly recommend the CD, *Come to the Waters—Ancient Paths, Volume 1* (www.worship-music.com). It will blow you away.

- *Find a Quiet, Solitary Place*—Set aside a special place for meditation and prayer. Silence and freedom from distraction are essential when meditating. Creating this special area in your home reinforces for yourself and others the priority of your spiritual life.

- *Relax.* Sit quietly in a comfortable position. Close your eyes. Deeply relax all your muscles. Breathe slowly and naturally, and as you do, repeat your focus word, phrase, or prayer silently to yourself as you exhale.

- *Internal Chatter*—Meditation beginners often become frustrated by the mental clutter and chatter that interrupts the flow of meditation. Don't fret about it. Let the intrusive thoughts come and go. Acknowledge them, and then get back to it. Think of meditation as an opportunity to relax rather than as another task you need to master. The more pressure you put on yourself, the more difficult it will be.

- *Cleanliness*—For many people, meditation is a deeply sacred time when they come before God with an open heart and mind. For this reason, they believe both their outward and inward selves should be clean. Bathing before meditation also relaxes the body and prepares the mind for receptivity.

   Conversely, a clean body is of little consequence if we have been consumed with matters that sully, defile, and dampen our spirits. Have we been wasting our time, energy, and emotions on meaningless activities, violent television shows, or overwork? Have we been compromising our bodies with excessive self-indulgence—too much alcohol, sugar, caffeine, etc.? Have we been dwelling on negative thoughts, complaints, or grievances? These are all choices that can impact our spiritual consciousness and lead us down destructive rather than constructive paths.

- *Comfort*—Try not to think of meditation and prayer as a rigid ascetic discipline involving discomfort and sacrifice. If you are uncomfortable, you will be easily distracted. Wear clothing that's loose and soft. If you can sit comfortably in a cross-legged position, do so. If not, then sit with your back against a wall or in a chair that has a back and with your feet flat on the ground. You might spread your palms outward and open in a position of receptiveness. It's generally better not to lie flat on your back or stomach, as you might fall asleep in this position.

- *Regularity and Consistency*—It's best to meditate and pray regularly and at a consistent time of day. Many people prefer early morning, as this is often the most solitary and uncomplicated time of day. Because our bodies and minds naturally gravitate toward rituals, you will be able to move into meditation with greater ease if you are habitual in your practice.

> **Learn to praise, pray, and sing. It will change you.**

## Powerful Meditation Affirmations— the 12 Revelatory Names of God[19]

1. ELOHIM: God, My Creator
"In the beginning God created the heavens and the earth." Genesis 1:1

2. JEHOVAH: My Father, Covenant
"And the LORD God formed man of the dust of the ground, and breathed into his nostrils the breath of life; and man became a living being." Genesis 2:7

3. JEHOVAH EL-SHADDAI: My Supply

"As for Me, behold, My covenant is with you, and you shall be a father of many nations." Genesis 17:4

4. ADONAI: My Lord and Master

"My Lord, if I have now found favor in Your sight, do not pass on by Your servant." Genesis 18:3

5. JEHOVAH JIREH: My Provider

"And Abraham said, 'My son, God will provide for Himself the lamb for a burnt offering.' " Genesis 22:8

6. JEHOVAH ROPHE: My Healer

"If you diligently heed the voice of the LORD your God and do what is right in His sight, give ear to His commandments and keep all His statutes, I will put none of the diseases on you which I have brought on the Egyptians. For I am the LORD who heals you." Exodus 15:26

7. JEHOVAH NISSI: My Victory

"And Moses built an altar and called its name, The-LORD-Is-My-Banner." Exodus 17:15

8. JEHOVAH M'KADDESH: My Sanctifier

"Consecrate yourselves therefore, and be holy, for I am the LORD your God. And you shall keep My statutes, and perform them: I am the LORD who sanctifies you." Leviticus 20:7–8

9. JEHOVAH SHALOM: My Peace

"So Gideon built an altar there to the LORD, and called it The-LORD-Is-Peace." Judges 6:24

10. JEHOVAH TSIDKENOU: My Righteousness

"Behold, the days are coming," says the LORD, "that I will raise to David a Branch of righteousness; a King shall reign and prosper, and execute judgment and righteousness in the earth. In His days Judah will be saved, and Israel will dwell safely; now this is His name by which He will be called: THE LORD OUR RIGHTEOUSNESS." Jeremiah 23:5–6

11. JEHOVAH ROHI: My Shepherd

"The LORD is my shepherd; I shall not want. He makes me to

lie down in green pastures; He leads me beside the still waters. He restores my soul; He leads me in the paths of righteousness for His name's sake. Yea, though I walk through the valley of the shadow of death, I will fear no evil; for You are with me; Your rod and Your staff, they comfort me. You prepare a table before me in the presence of my enemies; You anoint my head with oil; my cup runs over. Surely goodness and mercy shall follow me all the days of my life; and I will dwell in the house of the LORD. Forever." Psalm 23

12. JEHOVAH SHAMMAH: The Lord Is There
"All the way around shall be eighteen thousand cubits; and the name of the city from that day shall be: THE LORD IS THERE." Ezekiel 48:35

## Prayer

For Christians, the real purpose of meditation aims at bringing us to a state of loving attention to God. In his famous book, *New Seeds of Contemplation*, Thomas Merton wrote: "The real purpose of meditation is this: to teach a man how to work himself free of created things and temporal concerns, in which he finds only confusion and sorrow, and enter into a conscious and loving contact with God in which he is disposed to receive from God the help he knows he needs so badly, and to pay to God the praise and honor and thanksgiving and love which it becomes his joy to give. The success of your meditation will not be measured by the brilliant ideas you get or the great resolutions you make or the feelings and emotions that are produced in your exterior senses. You have only meditated well when you have come, to some extent, to realize God."[20]

According to a poll commissioned by *Newsweek* in 1996, 54 percent of Americans pray daily, and 29 percent report that they pray more than once a day.[21] An estimated one-third of adults use prayer, in addition to conventional medical care and complementary and alternative therapies, for health concerns, according to a national survey conducted by Anne M. McCaffrey, M.D. and her colleagues at Harvard Medical School. Between October 1997 and February 1998,

2,055 people (age 18 or older) were studied as to the prevalence and patterns of the use of prayer for health concerns. The study found that:

- 35 percent of the people surveyed used prayer for health concerns.
- 75 percent used prayer as a way to seek recovery from a health condition.
- 22 percent directed their prayer for specific medical conditions.
- 69 percent of those praying for specific medical conditions claimed they greatly benefited from the use of prayer.[22]

It is easy to become part of these statistics by giving prayer an opportunity to become part of your activities of daily living.

## Jesus' Prayer Life

"And when He had sent the multitudes away, He went up on the mountain by Himself to pray. Now when evening came, he was alone"

> **To know God in the personal experience of His presence and love is life indeed.**

(Matthew 14:23). If Jesus Christ made it a regular priority to be alone in prayer, do we really think we can do without it? His life demonstrated the tremendous value of prayer. On the solitary mountain, He came before His Father in heaven to commune face-to-face. By His example we know that our spiritual life must be renewed daily. We must have our times of being alone with our Father if we would have our heart filled with peace and our mind opened to the daily revelation that God gives to those who love Him. Make it a pattern for your life as well.

Get alone and quiet your spirit and soul. Learn to love the silence, for it is in solitude with God where you learn to depend on Him alone. Reflect upon God and His wondrous personality. Give Him the opportunity to show Himself to you and to do all that He says He'll do for you. To *hope* in God, to *rest* in the Lord, to *wait* on Him, to *know* Him—these express the purpose and joy of prayer.

You can talk with God, telling Him of your joys and hopes and desires, and receive back His answers to your own heart. In prayer God comes to us and calms our fears, gives us His perspective on our lives, and grants us understanding of the things that please Him. To know God in the personal experience of His presence and love is life indeed.

In those quiet times He comforts us in His loving arms and touches us with His grace. He brings light to our darkness. He cleanses us from sin through the blood of Jesus. He brings healing through His wounds. He brings joy and peace through His presence. He brings eternal life through His Spirit. By His grace He makes certain that nothing in heaven or hell shall separate us from His love.

Jesus was alone on the mountain, teaching us to pray—how to pray, where to pray, and when to pray. We must have our times of withdrawing from society if we would get a strong hold of life and be master of its worrisome details. Time with God makes us more than conquerors in the day of battle. Solitude, meditation, and prayer fill our heart with heavenly peace and open the mind to the daily revelation that God gives to those who love Him.

## Seven Prayer Principles

1. *Give Worship, Thanks, and Praise to God.* Open the eyes of your soul to the person and majesty of God as your Father. Hope in God and open your heart to praise Him today!
2. *Read the Bible.* Leave behind whatever you may have been trusting in and come to Christ as your only source of hope. Open His timeless Book and hear His gentle voice speaking to you. Study to show yourself approved by God.
3. *Meditate on the Word of God.* His Word will breathe life into you with power, His truths will be inscribed on your heart, and you will find His secrets to living a fulfilled life.
4. *Ask Forgiveness for Your Sins and Forgive Others Who Have Sinned Against You.* Fix your trust in Jesus Christ as the One who gave His life to save you from your sins, who rose from the dead as the Lord of life, and who calls you to love and follow

Him. Unforgiveness of others will block the fullness of God's will for your life. It is like drinking a cup of poison and expecting it to hurt someone else.

5. *Pray for Others.* Keep a list of the prayer needs of others and offer them to God. In the Old Testament, Hannah would not let go of God as she wrestled in prayer until her petition for a son was granted (1 Samuel 1). Pray with Hannah's intensity. Pour out your soul to the Lord in prayer for others.

6. *Pray for Yourself.* In the Psalms, David talked to God about how he was feeling, and so should you. His prayer life dealt with the real issues he was facing, and so should yours. Keep a list of your needs and the desires of your heart and ask God to meet them. You have not because you ask not or you ask amiss. Periodic fasting can take you to new levels of prayer. An excellent resource is *Seven Basic Steps to Fasting and Prayer* by the late Bill Bright.

7. *Meditate and Listen for the Still Small Voice of God.* Peace is the potting soil of revelation.

## Pray the Word of God in Your Prayers

Whenever possible pray the Word of God in your prayers. There is tremendous power when you offer up God's living Word to Him. The Bible tells us that God is faithful and just to perform His Word. An excellent resource is Beth Moore's *Praying God's Word.*

Here are two samples of prayers that you'll find are very effective:

### THE LORD'S PRAYER

"Our Father in heaven, hallowed be Your name. Your kingdom come. Your will be done on earth as it is in heaven. Give us this day our daily bread. And forgive us our debts, as we forgive our debtors. And do not lead us into temptation, but deliver us from the evil one. For Yours is the kingdom and the power and the glory forever. Amen." Matthew 6:9–14

## A PERSONAL FAITH CONFESSION

This prayer is directly quoting and praying scripture from the Bible.

"My faith is the substance of things I hope for, the evidence of the things I do not see. By faith I understand that the worlds were formed together by the Word of God, so that what I see was not made out of things that are visible. My faith pleases God. I believe that He exists and that He is my Rewarder, for I earnestly and diligently seek Him. I trust in the Lord with all my heart and lean not on my own understanding. In all my ways I acknowledge Him, and He directs my paths. I walk by faith and not by sight or appearance, because I know that things that are visible are temporal and things that are invisible are eternal. When I walk by faith, I am being empowered by faith. I am fully persuaded that what God promises, He will do. God dealt to me a measure of faith. Because I am born of God, I have overcome the world by faith. My faith comes by hearing, and hearing by the Word of God. The Word profits me because I mix it with faith and do not doubt; therefore, all things are possible to me. My faith doesn't waver. I set my eyes on Jesus. Whatever I ask for in prayer, having faith and truly believing, I will receive. Because I cast my cares on Him, I stand firm in faith against the wiles of the devil. I am strong in the Lord and in the power of His might. My faith works by love. My heart is being purified, sanctified, and justified by faith, and I have peace with God through the Lord Jesus. Amen."

(Hebrews 11:1, 3, 6; 2 Corinthians 5:7; 4:18; Romans 4:21; 12:3; 1 John 2:14; Romans 10:17; Mark 9:28; Matthew 11:24; 1 Peter 5:7; Ephesians 6:10; Galatians 5:6; Romans 5:1)

## A Personal Word for You

If you died today, are you certain you would wake up in heaven? Life is uncertain, and only the Lord knows the number of our days. The Bible tells us that Jesus is the only way to heaven (John 14:6). Salvation is God's gift of grace to us, and it has nothing to do with how good you are. If you do not personally know Jesus Christ, God says "that if you confess with your mouth the Lord Jesus and believe in your heart that God raised Him from the dead, you will be saved" (Romans 10:9). You may have believed and received Jesus into your heart, but are currently not following His Word. If you want to make certain that heaven is your final destination, or if you just want to get your life back on track, please pray the following words out loud:

"Jesus, I turn away from my sins and ask You to be my Lord and Savior and to forgive me for my sins. Lord, search my heart and know me and remove anything in me that is not pleasing to You. Create in me a clean heart and renew a right spirit in me. I believe You are the Son of God and that You died for my sins. Lord, I ask you to fill me with power from on high. Please fill me to overflowing with Your Holy Spirit and baptize me. I want to know You, and I want everything You have for me. I want to walk in Your power. I want my life to make a difference for You. Please lead me and guide me in all my thoughts and all my ways. Amen."

I pray that God grant you Super Health and abundant life with every spiritual, mental, and physical blessing. I leave you with the high priestly blessing: "The LORD bless you and keep you; the LORD make His face shine upon you, and be gracious to you. The LORD lift up His countenance upon you, and give you peace" (Numbers 6:24–26).

## Spiritual Resources

www.paulawhite.org
www.withoutwalls.org
www.joycemeyer.org
www.cbn.org
www.bethmoore.org
www.billygraham.org
www.bennyhinn.org
www.purposedrivenlife.com
www.tudarbizmark.org

www.superhealth7.com

INDEX A

# Comprehensive Panels to Evaluate Health Status

I recommend that the following panel of blood tests be taken to give you a comprehensive evaluation of your health. For a variety of reasons, your doctor may not order these during "blood work." Costs vary. If your insurance company will not pay for all the tests, discuss the relative importance of each one with your doctor. You may have to consider paying for a test or two. If you only can afford one test, even if it is only a finger stick, make it fasting glucose. Why? Because by itself it is a reliable predictor of both diabetes and heart disease.

The following comprehensive panels are from the Life Extension Foundation. Go to lef.org for more information.

## Male Panel

This comprehensive panel is used to evaluate male health status. The following tests are included in this panel: Chemistry Panel, CBC, Free Testosterone, Total Testosterone, DHEA-s, PSA, Estradiol, Homocysteine, and Cardiac CRP. *Please Note:* This panel requires a fasting blood level; therefore, a 12-hour fast is required before the collection of a blood sample.

- Chemistry Panel/CBC
  This panel is a comprehensive blood evaluation consisting of 35 tests.

- Free Testosterone
  This test is used to evaluate function in clinical states where the testosterone binding proteins may be altered (obesity, cirrhosis, thyroid disorders).
- Testosterone, Total
  This test is used to evaluate gonadal and adrenal function. It is also helpful in diagnosing hypogonadism, hypopituitarism, Klinefelter's syndrome, and impotence.
- Dehydroepiandrosterone (DHEA) Sulfate
  This test is used to identify the source of excessive androgen (hirsutism and/or virilization) and in the identification of adrenocortical disease, including congenital adrenal hyperplasia and adrenal tumors.
- Prostate-Specific Antigen (PSA)
  PSA is produced by normal, hyperplastic, and cancerous prostatic tissue. Serum PSA has been found to be the most sensitive marker for monitoring individuals with prostate cancer and to enhance efficacy in monitoring progression of disease and response to therapy.
- Estradiol
  This test is used to assess hypothalamic and pituitary functions. In males it is helpful in the assessment of gynecomastia or feminization syndromes.
- Homocysteine
  Homocysteine has been shown to be an independent risk factor for the premature development of coronary artery disease and thrombosis. This test is intended for use in screening individuals who may be at risk for heart disease and stroke. Studies have shown that even moderate levels of homocysteine pose an increased risk for arteriosclerosis compared with the lowest 20th percentile (<7.2 mcmol/L) of population controls.
- C-reactive protein (Cardiac) (High sensitivity)
  This test is used to assess risk of cardiovascular and peripheral vascular disease.

## Female Panel

This comprehensive panel is used to evaluate female health status. The following tests are included in this panel: Chemistry panel, CBC, Free testosterone, Total testosterone DHEA-s, Estradiol, Progesterone, Homocysteine, and Cardiac CRP. *Please Note:* This panel requires a fasting blood level; therefore, a 12-hour fast is required before the collection of a blood sample.

- Chemistry Panel/CBC
  This panel is a comprehensive blood evaluation consisting of 35 tests.
- Free Testosterone
  This test is used to evaluate hirsutism and masculinization in women and to evaluate function in clinical states where the testosterone binding proteins may be altered (obesity, cirrhosis, thyroid disorders).
- Testosterone, Total
  This test is used to evaluate gonadal and adrenal function.
- Dehydroepiandrosterone (DHEA) Sulfate
  This test is used to determine female infertility, amenorrhea, or hirsutism and to aid in the evaluation of excess androgen/ adrenocortical disease, including congenital adrenal hyperplasia and adrenal tumors.
- Estradiol
  This test is used to assess hypothalamic and pituitary functions, menopausal status, and sexual maturity.
- Progesterone
  This test is used to establish the presence of a functional corpeus luteum or luteal cell function, confirm body temperature for occurrence of ovulation, obtain indication of day of ovulation, evaluate the functional state of corpeus luteum in experiencing infertility, assess placental function during pregnancy, and evaluate ovarian function.

- Homocysteine
  Homocysteine has been shown to be an independent risk factor for the premature development of coronary artery disease and thrombosis. This test is intended for use in screening individuals who may be at risk for heart disease and stroke. *Please Note:* Studies have shown that even moderate levels of homocysteine pose an increased risk for arteriosclerosis compared with the lowest 20th percentile (<7.2 pmol/L) of population controls.
- C-Reactive Protein (Cardiac)(High Sensitivity)
  This test is used to assess risk of cardiovascular and peripheral vascular disease.

## Summary CHD Risk Factors

| RISK FACTOR | OPTIMUM | RISK | SERIOUS RISK |
|---|---|---|---|
| C-REACTIVE PROTEIN | <1 | >2 | >3 |
| FASTING GLUCOSE | 87 | >100 | >110 |
| FIBRINOGEN | <235 | >235 | >350 |
| HOMOCYSTEINE | <8 | >8 | >12 |
| LIPOPROTEIN(A) | <20 | >25 | 30 |
| LDL CHOLESTEROL | - | >240 | - |
| TOTAL CHOLESTEROL | - | >350 | - |
| HDL (MEN) | >60 | <60 | <40 |
| HDL (WOMEN) | >70 | <70 | <50 |
| TRIGLYCERIDES (TG) | <100 | >100 | >150 |
| TG/HDL RATIO | 1:1 | 2:1 | 4:1 |

# Notes

## INTRODUCTION

1.  "A Potential Decline in Life Expectancy in the United States in the 21st Century," *The New England Journal of Medicine*, Volume 352: 1138–1145, March 17, 2005, Number 1.

## SUPER HEALTH GOLDEN KEY #1

1.  Michael A. Corey, *The God Hypothesis* (Lanham, MD: Rowman and Littlefield, 2002), pp. 90, 120–122.
2.  Ibid., pp. 120–121.
3.  Marq de Villiers, *Water: The Fate of Our Most Precious Resource* (New York: Jacobus Communications Corporation, 2000).
4.  "Water Arithmetic Doesn't Add Up," BBC News, March 13, 2000.
5.  "100 New Commitments Pour in as Water Forum Closes," Environment News Service, March 24, 2003.
6.  Douglas Jehl, "In Race to Tap the Euphrates, the Upper Hand Is Upstream," *The New York Times*, August 25, 2002.
7.  Mark D. Uehling, "Free Drugs From Your Faucet," *Salon*, October 25, 2001.
8.  "Americans Relate Water to Well-Being, but Most Don't Get Their Fill; Survey Shows 33 Percent of What Americans Drink Can Cause Dehydration," The Rockefeller University, New York, for the International Bottled Water Association, New York, May 30, PRNewswire.
9.  Jane E. Brody, "Must I Have Another Glass of Water? Maybe Not, a New Report," *The New York Times*, February 17, 2004, Section F; Column 1; Health & Fitness.
10. F. Batmanghelidj, M.D., *Water for Health, for Healing, for Life* (New York: Time Warner Group, 2003), pp. 32–35.
11. F. Batmanghelidj, M.D., *Your Body's Many Cries for Water* (Vienna, VA: Global Health Solutions, Inc., 1995).
12. See www.watercure.com.
13. Yoshitaka Ohno, M.D., Ph.D. and Howard Reminick, Ph.D., "Healing Powers of Water: How the Condition of Your Body's Water Affects Bacteria and Its Lifelong Influence on Health and Aging," *Explore*, Volume 10, Number 3, 2001.

14. F. Batmanghelidj, M.D., *Water for Health, for Healing, for Life.*
15. Ibid.
16. *Epidemiology*, 1997; 8: 615–620.
17. *Epidemiology*, 1998; 9 (1): 21–28, 29–35.
18. An excerpt from the testimony by Professor Marc Edwards, Department of Civil Engineering at Virginia Tech University, to the Committee on Government Reform Hearing on Lead in D.C. WASA Water on March 5, 2004. Please refer to www.dcwatch.com/wasa/040305h.htm.
19. J Bone Miner Res, 2001, May; 16(5): 932–9.
20. *Community Dentistry and Oral Epidemiology*, October 2000; 28: 382–9 and the Canadian Dental Association Board of Governors, March 2000.
21. "Fluoridation Increases Lead Absorption in Children," by New York State Coalition Opposed to Fluoridation, *The Journal of the LEAD* (Lead Education and Abatement Design) Group Inc., Volume 7, No 4.
22. Katharine Q. Seelye, "13 Million in U.S. at Increased Cancer Risk Due to Arsenic in Water," abstracted from *The New York Times*, September 11, 2001.
23. *American Journal of Epidemiology*, 2000; 152: 59–66.
24. Vincent Standley, "Picking Plastics? The Green Guide Cracks the Codes," The Green Guide Institute (www.thegreenguide.com), January 27, 2005.
25. "Bottled Water: Pure Drink or Pure Hype?" www.nrdc.org/water/drinking/bw/bwinx.asp
26. Ibid.
27. Ibid.
28. Steve Meyerowitz, *Juice Fasting and Detoxification* (Great Barrington, MA: Sproutman Publications, 2002).
29. Zoltan P. Rona, M.D., "Early Death Comes from Drinking Distilled Water," http://chetday.com/distilledwater.htm.
30. Gina Kolata, "New Advice to Runners: Don't Drink the Water," *The New York Times*, May 6, 2003, Section F, Col. 1, Health & Fitness, page 5.

## SUPER HEALTH GOLDEN KEY #2

1. Kenneth R. Weiss, "Fish Farms Become Feedlots of the Sea," *L.A. Times*, December 9, 2002.
2. Dr. Kaayla T. Daniel, *The Whole Soy Story* (Washington, D.C.: NewTrends Publishing, 2005).
3. *JAMA (The Journal of the American Medical Association)*, September 12, 2001; 286: 1195–1200.
4. *Science*, Vol. 307, January 21, 2005, p. 373.
5. Roy Walford, *Beyond the 120 Year Diet* (New York: Four Walls Eight Windows, 2000), pp. 45–59.
6. *Science*, Vol. 307, p. 374.
7. Ibid., p. 376.

8. Walford, *Beyond the 120 Year Diet*, pp. 45–90.
9. Roy Walford and Lisa Walford, *The Anti-Aging Plan* (New York: Four Walls Eight Windows, 1994), pp. 45–71.
10. "Nutrition: Nutrients Shrink as Veggies Grow," *Miami Herald*, March 7, 2005.
11. "Glycemic Index and Obesity," *American Journal of Clinical Nutrition*, July 2002; 76(1): 281S–5S.
12. Stephen Holt, M.D., *Combat Syndrome X, Y and Z* (Newark: Wellness Publishing, 2002), p. 32.
13. Stephen Holt, M.D., Lecture, "Combating Syndrome X and Enhancing Low Carb Diets" (Washington, D.C.: Natural Products Expo East/Organic Products Expo—BioFach America, October 15, 2004).
14. Ibid.
15. Cheryle Hart, M.D. and Mary Kay Grossman, *The Insulin-Resistance Diet* (Sylmar, CA: NTC Publishing Group, 2001), pp. 67–81.
16. Deborah S. Romaine and Jennifer B. Marks, *Syndrome X: Managing Insulin Resistance* (New York: Harpertorch, 2000), pp. 157–181.
17. *Diabetes Care*, February 2002; 25: pp. 364–369.
18. Lester Packer and Carol Colman, *The Antioxidant Miracle* (New York: John Wiley & Sons, Inc., 1999), p. 24.
19. Ibid., p. 118.
20. Diana Schwarzbein and Nancy Deville, *The Schwarzbein Principle: The Truth About Losing Weight, Being Healthy, and Feeling Younger* (Florida: HCI Publications, 1999), pp.1–38.
21. Andrew L. Stoll, *The Omega-3 Connection* (New York: Simon & Schuster, 2002), p. 46.
22. Ibid., p. 39.
23. Ibid., p. 116.
24. *Journal Nutrition*, October 2001; 131(10): pp. 2753–60.
25. "Combination of Fish Oil and GLA," *American Journal of Clinical Nutrition*, January 2003; 77: pp. 37–42.
26. *National Resources Defense Council Report*, March 1999.
27. *JAMA (The Journal of the American Medical Association)*, April 20, 1999; 281: pp. 1387–1394.
28. www.mercola.com/2002/nov/13/eggs.htm.
29. *JAMA (The Journal of the American Medical Association)*, August 26, 1998; 280: pp. 701–707, 737–738.
30. Al Watson, *21 Days to a Healthy Heart* (Minneapolis: Bronze Bow Publishing, 2004), p. 173.
31. Jennie Brand, Editor, *The Glucose Revolution* (Newport, Rhode Island: Marlowe and Company, 1999).
32. Robert Uhlig, May 18, 2002 Telegraph.Co.Uk.
33. Walford, *Beyond the 120 Year Diet*.

34. *The Lancet,* 2001; 357: pp. 505–508.
35. *Pediatrics,* May 2001; 107(5): pp. 1210–13.
36. *Scientific American,* July 2000, p. 16.
37. *Diabetes Care,* February 2002; 25: pp. 364–369.
38. *Addiction,* 1998; 93: pp. 183–203.
39. *Journal of the American Dietetic Association,* October 1999; 99(10): pp. 1228–33.
40. Third International Symposium on the Role of Soy in Preventing and Treating Chronic Disease, November 3, 1999. Sponsored by the American Oil Chemists' Society in Washington, D.C.
41. Center for Science in the Public Interest, June 17, 2002.
42. Center for Science in the Public Interest, June 25, 2002.
43. *Archives of Ophthalmology,* August 2001; 119: pp. 1191–1199.
44. Annual Experimental Biology 2002 Conference, New Orleans, Louisiana, April 22, 2002.
45. *Archives of Ophthalmology,* pp. 1191–1199.

## SUPER HEALTH GOLDEN KEY #3

1. Chris Crowley and Henry S. Lodge, M.D., "Young at Heart," *Reader's Digest,* February 2005, pp. 88–90.
2. Annual Meeting of Society for Neuroscience Conference in San Diego, California, November 2001.
3. *British Journal of Sports Medicine,* April 2001; 35: 114–117.
4. *Journal of Sports Medicine and Physical Fitness,* December 2001; 41: 539–545.
5. *Archives of Neurology,* March 2001; 58: 498–504.
6. Rob Stein, "Study: Activity, Weight Affect Length of Life," *The Washington Post,* December 23, 2004.
7. *The Washington Post,* August 9, 2001.
8. *American Journal of Preventative Medicine,* January 2005; 28(1): 9–18.
9. *JAMA (The Journal of the American Medical Association),* March 21, 2001; 285: 1447–1454.
10. *Arteriosclerosis, Thrombosis, and Vascular Biology,* July 2001; 21: 1226–1232, 1097–1098.
11. *Obstetrics and Gynecology,* October 2000; 96: 609–14.
12. *British Medical Journal,* December 9, 2000; 321: 1424–1425.
13. *American Journal of Clinical Nutrition,* 2001; 73: 240–245.
14. *Urology,* August 2000; 56: 302–306.
15. John Peterson, *Pushing Yourself to Power* (Minneapolis: Bronze Bow Publishing, 2003), pp. 67–68.
16. Annual Meeting of the North American Association for the Study of Obesity at Charleston, South Carolina, November 1999.
17. *Medicine & Science in Sports & Exercise,* September 2002; 34: 1468–1474.
18. John Peterson and Wendie Pett, *The Miracle Seven* (Minneapolis: Bronze Bow Publishing, 2004), p. 31.

## SUPER HEALTH GOLDEN KEY #4

1. "UCSF-Led Study Suggests Link Between Psychological Stress and Cell Aging," *Proceedings of the National Academy of Sciences,* University of California, San Francisco, November 29, 2004.
2. Hans Selye, *The Stress of Life,* Revised Edition (New York: McGraw-Hill, 1956, 1976).
3. T. H. Holmes and R. H. Rahe, "The Social Readjustment Rating Scale," *Journal of Psychomatic Research,* 1967; 11: 213–17.
4. "Anxiety Disorders Research at the National Institute of Mental Health: NIMH," National Institute of Mental Health, NIH Publication No. 99-4504, printed 1999.
5. Ron Ball, "Workplace Stress Sucks $300 Billion Annually from Corporate Profits," September 3, 2004, Broadcast Interview Source, Inc. Yearbook of Experts (R) News Release Wire.
6. Arline Kaplan, "Implications of Stress, Psychosocial Factors on the Immune System," *Psychiatric Times,* October 1999, Vol. XVI, Issue 10.
7. Brain, Behavior, and Immunity online 2001; 10.1006.
8. *Psychosomatic Medicine,* March 1999; 61: 175–180.
9. *Fertility and Sterility,* October 2001; 76: 675–687.
10. *Proceedings of the National Academy of Sciences,* USA, September 26, 2000; 97: 11032–11037.
11. Jeff Elder, "What Stress Does to Your Brain," *The Charlotte Observer* (North Carolina), November 15, 2004, Page 1E.
12. R. J. Wurtman and J. J. Wurtman, "Brain Serotonin, Carbohydrate-Craving, Obesity, and Depression," *Obesity Research,* 3, 477S–480S, 1995.
13. Recommended natural health remedies from Life Extension found at: health-marketplace.com; www.health-marketplace.com/depression.htm.
14. *The Journal of the American Medical Association,* April 14, 1999; 281: 1304–1309, 1328–1329.
15. Dr. Gregg D. Jacobs, "The Power of Stress-Reducing, Sleep-Enhancing Attitudes and Beliefs," www.talkaboutsleep.com/sleepdisorders/insomnia_drjacobs_positive_attitudes.htm.
16. Herbert Benson, Ph.D., *Timeless Healing* (New York: Fireside, 1996).

## SUPER HEALTH GOLDEN KEY #5

1. *The Lancet,* October 23, 1999; 354: 1435–1439.
2. Phyllis A. Balch, CNC and James F. Balch, M.D., *Prescription for Nutritional Healing, Third Edition* (New York: Avery, 2000), p. 476.
3. Dr. Gayle Olinekova, *Power Aging* (New York: Thunder's Mouth Press, 1998), p. 54.
4. Julie B. Freeman Clark, Sherry F. Queener, and Virginia Burke-Karb, *Pharmacologic Basis of Nursing Practice* (St. Louis: Mosby, 1993).

5. Olinekova, *Power Aging*, p. 56.
6. Amanda Dunn, *Sydney Morning Herald*, June 12, 2004.
7. Balch and Balch, *Prescription for Nutritional Healing, Third Edition*, p. 473.
8. Ibid.
9. *JAMA (The Journal of the American Medical Association)*, August 16, 2000; 284: 861–868, 880–881.
10. *Journal of Clinical Endocrinology & Metabolism*, August 2001; 86: 3787–3794.
11. Olinekova, *Power Aging*, p. 58.
12. "Melatonin Slows Breast Cancer," *LifeExtension* magazine, December 2003.
13. *Pediatrics*, May 2003; 111: e628–e635.

## SUPER HEALTH GOLDEN KEY #6

1. Dr. Joseph Mercola, "How to Avoid the Top 10 Most Common Toxins," February 19, 2005; www.mercola.com/2005/feb/19/common_toxins.htm.
2. Fritjof Capra, *The Turning Point* (New York: Simon & Schuster, 1982), pp. 253, 256.
3. "Trade Secrets: A Moyers Report," March 2004; www.pbs.org/tradesecrets.
4. "What's in your water bottle besides water?" The Green Guide, February 8, 2005, www.greenguide.com.
5. Dr. Joseph Mercola, "How to Avoid the Top 10 Most Common Toxins."
6. Ibid.
7. Nathan B. Batalion, *50 Harmful Effects of Genetically Modified Foods* (published by Americans for Safe Foods in 2000).
8. Ibid.
9. Ibid.
10. W. K. Hallman, W. C. Hebden, H. L. Aquino, C. L. Cuite, and J. T. Lang, *Public Perceptions of Genetically Modified Foods* (Publication number RR-1003-004). New Brunswick, New Jersey; Food Policy Institute, Cook College, Rutgers—The State University of New Jersey, 2003.
11. Dr. Joseph Mercola, www.mercola.com/2005/feb19/biotech_foods.htm.
12. Paul Chek, *You Are What You Eat* (A C.H.E.K Institute Production, 2002).
13. S. A. Rogers, *Tired or Toxic* (Syracuse: Prestige Publications, 1990).
14. Nicholas A. Ashford and Claudia S. Miller, *Chemical Exposures: Low Levels and High Stakes* (Hoboken, New Jersey: John Wiley and Sons, 1998).
15. Betty Bridges, "Fragrance: Emerging Health and Environmental Concerns," *Flavour and Fragrance Journal*, Volume 17, Issue 5, 2002, pp. 361–371.
16. "Making Sense of Scents," Citizens for a Toxic-Free Marin, P.O. Box 2785, San Rafael, CA. 94912-2785, 1996.
17. Betty Bridges, op. cit.
18. Ibid.
19. Ibid.
20. Healthy School Handbook, published by the U.S. National Education Association.

21. D. J. Ross, H. L. Keynes, and J. C. McDonald, "Surveillance of Work-Related and Occupational Respiratory Disease in the U.K.," *Occupational Medicine* (London), November 1998; 48(8): 481-S.1998.

22. B. A. Revich, "Air Pollution and the Prevalence of Bronchial Asthma Among the Pediatric Population of Moscow," *Med Tr Prom Ekol.* 1995; (5): 15-9. Russian.

23. Betty Bridges, op. cit.

24. FDA Petition #99P-1340, 1999.

25. Eric Schlosser, *Fast Food Nation* (New York: Houghton-Mifflin Company, 2002), p. 200.

26. Ibid., p. 221.

27. Ibid., p. 203.

28. Christen Brownlee, "The Beef About UTIs," *Science News Online,* January 22, 2005, www.sciencenews.org/articles/20050122/food.asp.

29. Costantini, The Garden of Eden Longevity Diet. Fungalbionics Series, 1998. www.ansci.cornell.edu/plants/toxicagents/aflatoxin/aflatoxin.html.

30. "Sources of Indoor Air Pollution—Organic Gases (Volatile Organic Compounds—VOCs); www.epa.gov/iaq/voc.html.

31. "Indoor Air Quality," United States Environmental Protection Agency and the United States Consumer Product Safety Commission Office of Radiation and Indoor Air (6604J) EPA Document #402-K-93-007, April 1995; www.epa.gov/iaq/is-imprv.html.

32. "Controversial Study Reignites Debate Over Autism and Childhood Vaccines," *Wall Street Journal,* September 7, 2004, Page D1.

33. Ibid.

34. BBC News, http://news.bbc.co.uk/1/hi/health/4214369.stm.

35. "Mercury, Fish Oils, Risk of Acute Coronary Events, and Cardiovascular Disease and All-Cause Mortality in Men in Eastern Finland," *Arteriosclerosis, Thrombosis, and Vascular Disease,* 205; 25: 228–233.

36. J. Lazarou, B. Pomeranz, and P. Corey, "Incidence of Adverse Drug Reactions in Hospitalized Patients," *JAMA (The Journal of the American Medical Association),* April 15, 1998; 279: 1200–1205.

37. "Overmedication of U.S. Seniors," *Reuters Health,* May 21, 2003.

38. Published in an article written in *NORCAL SETAC News 2003, (14)1: (5-15) March 2003.* Many additional articles can be located at www.epa.gov/nerlesdl/chemistry/pharma/index.htm.

## SUPER HEALTH GOLDEN KEY #7

1. *The New England Journal of Medicine,* June 22, 2000, Volume 342, No. 25.

2. Sharon Begley, "Religion and the Brain," *Newsweek,* May 7, 2001, p. 50.

3. "The Religiously Active Live Longer," *Health Psychology,* 2000: 19.

4. Ibid.

5. *Archives of Internal Medicine,* October 25, 1999; 159: 2273.

6.  *International Journal of Psychiatry in Medicine*, 1998; 28: 189–213.

7.  *American Journal of Psychiatry*, 1998; 155: 536–542.

8.  American Psychological Association Convention, August 2000; Washington, D.C.

9.  Dale A. Matthews, *The Faith Factor: Proof of the Healing Power of Prayer* (New York: Penguin Group, 1998), p. 16.

10. Ibid., pp. 186–191.

11. Patricia Barnes, M.S., Eva Powell-Griner, Ph.D., Kim McFann, Ph.D., and Richard Nahin, Ph.D., "Complementary and Alternative Medicine Use Among Adults: United States, 2002," *Advance Data*, May 27, 2004, Number 343.

12. Mara Carrico, "Let's Meditate," *Yoga Basics*, Yoga Journal Online, www.yoga-journal.com/meditation.

13. Marc Kaufman, "Meditation Gives Brain a Charge, Study Finds," *Washington Post*, Monday, January 3, 2005; and Stephen Pincock, "Uplifting Thoughts," *The Financial Times*, Science Matters, p. 13, London, England, January 15, 2005.

14. Kimberly A. Williams, "Meditation May Cut Stress, Improving Mental and Physical Health," Center for the Advancement of Health, July 6, 2001.

15. Ambikananda Saraswati, *Breathwork* (London: Thorsons First Directions, 2001), p. 17.

16. Dale A. Matthews, *The Faith Factor*, p. 45.

17. Don Campbell, *The Mozart Effect* (New York: HarperCollins Publishers, Inc., 2001, 1997).

18. Mark Derr, "Experts Assess the Merits of Meditation in Motion," by *Miami Beach*, April 12, 2005.

19. Benny Hinn, *The Names and Nature of God CD*, www.bennyhinn.org.

20. Thomas Merton, *New Seeds of Contemplation* (The Abbey of Gethsemani, Inc., 1961), pp. 217–218.

21. Kenneth L. Woodward, "Is God Listening?" *Newsweek*, March 31, 1997, pp. 56–57.

22. *Archives of Internal Medicine*, April 26, 2004; 164: 858–862.

## SUPER-FOOD MEAL REPLACEMENT

*LIVING FUEL Rx™ Super Greens and Super Berry™*

Living Fuel Rx™ contains organic super foods and proven supplements, giving you full, balanced coverage of all your nutritional needs—all in one product. Nutrient-dense, low calorie, low glycemic, and high in antioxidants, Super Greens and Super Berry™ are used by people from every walk of life, from the health challenged to elite athletes.

**Super Berry**—each serving contains over 120 g of whole organic berries, including blueberries, strawberries, raspberries, and cranberries. It is a taste you're sure to love, and the nutrition you come to expect.

**Super Greens**—each serving is jam-packed with organic spirulina, spinach, kale, broccoli, carrots, and more.

# HEALTHY FATS AND OILS

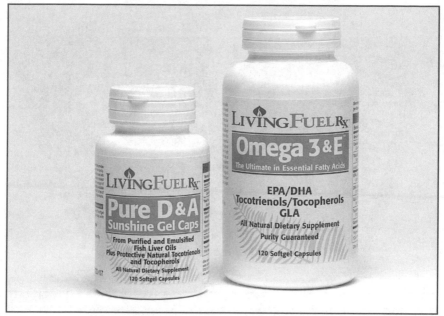

### *LIVING FUEL Rx*™ *Omega 3&E*™

OMEGA 3&E™, antioxidant-protected fish oil caplets. OMEGA 3&E™ is a powerful combination of omega-3 essential fatty acids EPA and DHA combined with therapeutic doses of full-spectrum Vitamin E (including of tocotrienols and tocopherols) to provide antioxidant protection inside the body. Kept in its natural form throughout the production process and rigorously tested to ensure it is free from impurities, OMEGA 3&E™ is one of the safest and healthiest products of its kind.

### *LIVING FUEL Rx*™ *Pure D&A*™ *Sunshine Gel Caps*

Pure D&A™ Sunshine Gel Caps is a safe and optimum source of Vitamin D for everyone in the family. An all-natural dietary supplement made from purified and emulsified fish oil livers, each softgel capsule contains the same amount of Vitamin D and Vitamin A found in one teaspoon of commercially available Cod Liver Oil. And Living Fuel Pure D&A™ is not factory made—it is all-natural, derived from mercury-safe fish.

# HEALTHY SNACK LINE

*LIVING FUEL Rx™ CocoChia™ Bars*

The CocoChia™ Bars are high energy, healthy fats products comprised of clean, organic fats, such as Coconut, Chia Seeds, Almonds, and more. In a convenient and tasty bar form, the CocoChia™ bars are filling, delicious, low glycemic, and excellent for you. Ideal for diabetics, dieters, school lunches, and travel. Now available in 4 healthy varieties— Original, Super Sea Greens™, Super Berry™, and Double Chocolate™.

# HEALTHY SNACK LINE

*LIVING FUEL Rx™ CocoChia™*

CocoChia™ is a blend of two powerful super foods—organic Coconut and Chia Seeds. CocoChia™ is lightly sweetened with Therasweet®, Living Fuel's proprietary sweetener. Unlike other shredded coconut products, our coconut is **THE** product, not a byproduct of the coconut oil industry. We retain the coconut oil, which is where the true nutritional value lies, resulting in a higher quality and better tasting coconut product! Chia seeds are one of nature's perfect foods, containing essential fatty acids, protein, soluble fiber, protective antioxidants, minerals, and vitamins. CocoChia™ is the ultimate snack fuel—nutritious, low glycemic, anti-microbial and energy boosting.

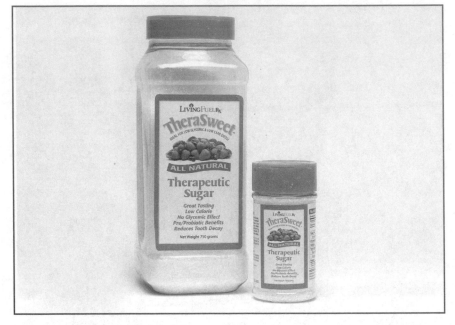

*LIVING FUEL Rx*™ *TheraSweet*™

TheraSweet™ is a safe and healthy alternative to the artificial sweeteners on the market today. Derived from organic and all-natural ingredients, it is an ideal sugar substitute for diabetics, those desiring weight loss, or anyone pursuing optimal health. With a sugar-like taste and texture, TheraSweet™ is a versatile sweetener that dissolves quickly and is heat stable for cooking and baking. TheraSweet™ is low calorie and has virtually no glycemic index.